"Shelette Stewart is not only a respected business leader, she is a committed Christian with a servant's heart for helping others succeed. Her book, *Revelations in Business*, is a great and powerful tool for progressive leaders who desire to bring insightful, empowering content to their teams to increase employee engagement, productivity, and overall profitability."

—Dan T. Cathy, President and Chief Operating Officer, Chick-fil-A, Inc.

"*Revelations in Business* will help you find personal significance through purpose and process."

—Jerry S. Wilson, Senior Vice President, The Coca-Cola Company, and coauthor of Managing Brand You.

"*Revelations in Business* is about not only excelling in business, but, more importantly, achieving your purpose and enjoying the journey in the process!"

—Auntie Anne Beiler, Founder of Auntie Anne's Pretzels

"At Georgetown College, we encourage students, faculty, and staff to identify and pursue their individual purpose and personal calling. *Revelations in Business* is an exceptional book that offers powerful insights for accomplishing this. I highly recommend this book for students and educators who desire to become more purpose-driven and mission-centric."

—Dr. William H. Crouch, Jr., president, Georgetown College

"Shelette's *Revelations in Business* is a spiritual marriage of business fundamentals to biblical principles! She successfully pulls from her deep understanding of scripture and Corporate America practice to reveal God's planning process. She elevates conventional business planning with a robust process to reveal what you and your business stand for from a biblical perspective. I have no doubt that paging through this well-written planning guide will lead you to recognize your superior brand value and set you on a path to live up to your highest self!"

—James Sila, Christian and Talent Leader in
Human Capital, The Coca-Cola Company

"*Revelations is Business* has one pursuit in mind: conducting business to honor God. Dr. Stewart gives us a road map on this exciting journey!"

—Chaplain Henry J. Rogers,
Interstate Battery System of America, Inc.

"Dr. K. Shelette Stewart is one of those rare individuals whose business acumen addresses a broad range of venues. Because her insights are captured in the form of principles and strategies, they can be customized to many challenging scenarios experienced by organizational leaders. The kernel of wisdom remains intact, but implementation adapts to the resources of organizations. Moreover, Dr. Stewart herself delivers these concepts with clarity, enthusiasm, and theological accuracy. Thus, she motivates as she equips. No dry scholarship from Dr. Stewart. On the contrary, lively interaction, stimulation to innovate and "let's get it done" mentality pervade the style and atmosphere of her persona and this is truly exemplified in *Revelations in Business*."

—Dr. Linden D. McLaughlin, Chairman and Professor of
Christian Education, Dallas Theological Seminary

"There is no higher plan for our life than God's plan, and that should apply to our business plan. Shelette Stewart provides dynamic yet practical guidance to business and professional people to find the real purpose for their life's work. If you are looking to define true success for your life as God would have it or even move beyond success to significance, you can find the answers with Shelette's clear biblical approach. We recommend *Revelations in Business* to anyone desiring to effectively represent Christ in their marketplace, and live for Him as they do, achieving the highest purpose for their life!"

—Curtis Hail, president & CEO,
e3 Partners & iamsecond.com

"Rick Warren encouraged us all to pursue our purpose in *The Purpose-Driven Life*. Now, Shelette Stewart picks up the torch with *Revelations in Business*, which is truly *The Purpose Driven Life* for business leaders! Each chapter of this effective book provides real-life examples and practical recommendations for applying the Word of God to your business regardless of your industry and business model. I recommend this book for business academicians and practitioners."

—Dr. JoyLynn Hailey Reed, Senior Lecturer
School of Management, University of Texas at Dallas

"*Revelations in Business* is one of the best books I have ever read for giving valuable insights to people who want their business and professional careers to be fulfilling and to be able to achieve the best they can for themselves and their enterprises. The emphasis on biblical values, superior quality services, and integrity is precisely what is needed in today's business place in order to succeed. *Revelations in Business* is a must-read for all who aspire to experience true success."

—Ray J. Berryman, Entrepreneur,
Philanthropist, and Servant for Jesus Christ

"In her book *Revelations in Business*, Dr. Shelette Stewart gives fresh, creative, and biblically based insights regarding a Christian's approach to business principles. I recommend *Revelations in Business* as required reading for anyone who wants to live out their Christian call in business, and especially for students attending Christian colleges and universities."

—H.K. Kingkade, Director for Religious
Life, Georgetown College

"*Revelations in Business* teaches you how to succeed in your career by applying the Word of God."

—Darryl Lesure, Manager, Purchasing,
Supply Chain, Chick-fil-A, Inc.

"Shelette validates once again that the only requirement to a successful business is to know what to do as well as what to stop doing. My advice for any would-be entrepreneur is to hop on board and take full advantage of her rich wisdom and wise counsel."

—Dr. Dennis Kimbro,
Author of *What Makes the Great Great*

"At Betenbough Homes, we believe that ordinary people can live each and every day with Kingdom passion and God-directed purpose. *Revelations in Business* offers an innovative and insightful guide for accomplishing this in the workplace and marketplace."

—Jon Jackson,
Chief Financial Officer, Betenbough Homes

REVELATIONS IN BUSINESS®

REVELATIONS IN BUSINESS®

Connecting Your Business Plan with
God's Purpose and Plan for Your Life

• •

DR. K. SHELETTE STEWART

TATE PUBLISHING
AND ENTERPRISES, LLC

Published by Tate Publishing & Enterprises, LLC
127 E. Trade Center Terrace | Mustang, Oklahoma 73064 USA
1.888.361.9473 | www.tatepublishing.com

Tate Publishing is committed to excellence in the publishing industry. The company reflects the philosophy established by the founders, based on Psalm 68:11,
"The Lord gave the word and great was the company of those who published it."

Book design copyright © 2012 by Tate Publishing, LLC. All rights reserved.
Cover design by Kristen Verser
Interior design by Joel Uber

Published in the United States of America

ISBN: 978-1-61777-924-4
1. Business & Economics: Strategic Planning
2. Business & Economics: Motivational
Library of Congress Control Number: 2012934435
12.05.02

Dedication

This book is dedicated back to God, from Whom it originated.

I am grateful for the wonderful family and friends God has placed in my life and for the many teachers who have generously and graciously shared their wisdom to guide and inspire me along my journey. I thank God for them. And I thank God for the honor and privilege of serving Him by serving you.

May the content of this book serve as a blessing to you as you seek God's divine revelation and ordained purpose and plan for your life (Proverbs 29:18).

Table of Contents

Introduction

Where there is no revelation, the people perish.

—Proverbs 29:18 (AMP)

"For I know the plans I have for you," declares the Lord, "plans to prosper you and not to harm you, plans to give you hope and a future."

—Jeremiah 29:11 (NIV)

Business people don't plan to fail; they simply fail to follow God's plan.

There are many books that teach us how to succeed in business. And there are many books that teach us how to apply the Word of God to our lives. What if there was a book that combined the two? *Revelations in Business: Connecting Your Business Plan with God's Purpose and Plan for Your Life* is that book.

My Testimony

It is one thing to know God's plan and yet another to submit to it. The Bible tells us that to everything there is a season or a time and purpose (Ecclesiastes 3:1) and that it is not sufficient for us to simply hear the Word of God. We must commit to being doers of His Word in order to be blessed (James 1:22-25; John 13:17; Luke 11:28). And herein lies my story. My testimony of how I had to face my fears, step out on faith, and commit to being not only a hearer but also a doer of God's Word by connecting my business plans with God's purpose and plan for my life.

Being a Hearer of His Word

Being born and raised in Dayton, Ohio, I grew up in the church, spending many of my formative years as a member of a Baptist church pastored by my uncle. I was first baptized at the age of ten and then rededicated my life to God again at the age of twenty-four. I've always been deeply spiritual and have felt a strong calling of God on my life. I have a younger brother, and our parents always expressed the importance of not only keeping God first place in our lives but also pursuing higher education. So my plan was the proverbial mantra of "going to school so I could get a good job" with "good job" equating to a leadership role in corporate America. And so I set out to accomplish my plan.

I attended the University of California at Berkeley and majored in psychology. After graduating, I accepted a sales position with BellSouth Corporation in Atlanta, Georgia, where I was responsible for selling voice and data products and services to small business customers. I quickly rose through the ranks and was promoted to national account sales, marketing, and strategic planning roles.

While BellSouth was a wonderful organization, and I enjoyed and excelled in most of my assignments, after about three years, I found myself beginning to feel disenchanted and bored. I wasn't being intellectually challenged. I felt as if I were not growing and as if I was somehow living below my potential. So *my plan* to address this was to challenge myself with higher education by going to graduate school at Clark Atlanta University and earning a master's degree in international affairs and development while working full time. My master's thesis was on strategic planning and growth in international firms. After six productive and enjoyable years with BellSouth, *my plan* was to join another company that I had always dreamed of working for: The Coca-Cola Company.

I interviewed with The Coca-Cola Company and was blessed to be one of twenty-seven individuals selected from a national pool of candidates to attend the company's bench-strength program, which was a fast-track, six-month intensive, accelerated executive development program. After completing the program, I was relocated to Los Angeles, California, as a business development manager and was later promoted to various assignments in national account sales, marketing, and strategic planning within both the retail and foodservice divisions of Coca-Cola North America. It was actually during this season, when I was living in LA, that the Lord revealed to me, in my spirit, that I was to write a book. *A book? About what?* Sure, I love to read, but I couldn't imagine writing four hundred pages about *any* topic. I don't even talk that much! But being the Type A person that I am, I immediately started attending writer's workshops for fiction writers. But the fictional writing didn't feel natural and the ideas never really flowed.

After living in Los Angeles for two years, I was relocated back to the company's world headquarters in Atlanta, Georgia, for a promotional opportunity managing the company's strategic, national partnerships with several nonprofit organizations. Shortly after moving back to Atlanta, those old feelings crept back into my life and slowly began to haunt me. Once again, even with all of the exciting projects I was working on—including the company's high-profile sponsorship of the 2002 Salt Lake City Winter Olympic Games—I began to once again feel disenchanted, discontented, and as if I were living below my potential.

By this time in my career, I had been in corporate America for about ten years. I was employed by a remarkable company with a rich heritage, iconic brands, and exceptional leadership. I was blessed to learn and grow personally and professionally by working with many talented individuals on a myriad of exciting projects and groundbreaking initiatives. And in turn, I shared my knowledge, skills, experience, talents, and gifts to make positive contributions to the company. So why was I still so disenchanted? With every job promotion and new assignment, why did I still find myself bored?

I have to admit that, as a Christian, I was becoming increasingly frustrated and disillusioned with some of the general business ideologies and corporate practices in place. They are not company-specific but rather culture-specific. They are simply indicative of business planning, politics, and practices in the Western world. But I still found them to be extremely contradictory to my personal values and belief systems. Here are a few examples:

- Arrogant leaders who didn't seem to realize that their leadership position comes from God and that they are ultimately accountable to Him.

- Coworkers stooping to corporate pretense, politics, and posturing for promotions out of a place of insecurity instead of being secure in God's sovereign power to control their destiny.

- Unmotivated and unfulfilled colleagues—including me—who were living below their potential and settling for less than their true calling.

- Business planning initiatives that focused disproportionately on achieving tactical, short-term, financial objectives—as opposed to strategic, long-term, sustainable, performance-driving, legacy-building goals—because of constant pressure from Wall Street.

Can you guess what *my plan* was, this time, for dealing with my disenchantment? You guessed it. I went back to school and earned a doctorate in business with a concentration in marketing and a dissertation on strategic planning and small business development at Nova Southeastern University in Fort Lauderdale, Florida.

By now, you're probably thinking that I am either a glutton for punishment or perhaps simply missed my true calling as a lifelong, full-time student. Seriously, I do enjoy the rigor of academia, learning, and challenging myself intellectually. But I must admit that after working full time in a demanding corporate role while completing my doctoral classes, empirical research, publication requirements, dissertation, comprehensive exam, and finally graduating, I was mentally and physically drained. Beat to the core. *My plan* was to mentally vegetate, after graduation, for a few months and perhaps watch mindless reruns of Tom and Jerry cartoons on the weekends. But God had other plans.

Exactly three months after I graduated with my doctorate and had accepted a new and challenging position managing The Coca-Cola Company's partnership with Burger King Corporation, God decided to reveal all of the details of *His plan* to me. I was incredulous! I had just graduated! *My brain is still fried from the dissertation, and You want me to write a book? Do I not get a few months just to relax?* My ranting was ignored by Him and soon forgotten by me once God began to unveil His marvelous plans. For what He revealed would forever change my life.

Being a Doer of His Word

After whispering a brief hint into my spirit about my writing a book and then remaining virtually silent on the topic for three years, God finally began to pour out the details of His will for the book that He desired for me to write. Over a matter of days, He revealed specific details on the entire platform, including how I was to approach the project, study and compile scriptures, organize the content, and arrange the chapters.

The Lord's directives to me were not audible. They took the form of an *innate knowing* and an *inner drive* in my spirit that I could not deny even if I tried. It was a strong compulsion and calling to follow the lead of the Holy Spirit. The Lord made it clear that I was to write a book that would resonate with business leaders and help them connect their business plans with His purpose and plan for their lives. He reinforced that this is the only way for us to truly maximize our personal fulfillment and professional success and significance.

I must admit I had my reservations about being able to accomplish what He was calling me to do. After all, I am not a theologian. I have not attended divinity school. But the Lord made it perfectly clear to me that *I* was not the one writing the book. *He was.* I simply needed to be obedient in serving as a vessel for Him. Enough said. And so I obeyed.

At the time, I had been working for The Coca-Cola Company for about five years and was traveling frequently across the country managing customer partnerships. The only time I had to devote to writing the book was on the weekends. I would write at home or take my laptop to a local café and work on the book there. And it was pure joy! My level of interest, passion, and excitement for this endeavor was higher than I'd ever experienced in all of my previous professional assignments combined! Finally, a mission that leveraged all of my innate talents, natural gifts, skill sets, and interests. A challenging and stimulating undertaking that was for a greater good. I was utterly enchanted!

After working on the manuscript for about four years while working full-time for The Coca-Cola Company, I came to a point where the next logical role for me, to expand my knowledge of the business holistically, would have been an international assignment, which I was open to considering. But here was the epiphany: I was so passionate about the calling God had placed on me that I actually considered pursuing an international assignment because I believed that it just might give me more time to work on my book! Clearly, my heart was with my book. My calling. And as wonderful as The Coca-Cola Company is, I knew it was time for me to move on. To stay would not be fair to me or to the organization.

I had finally come to the point where I could no longer address my disenchantment with corporate America by getting another degree, job, or even changing companies. I realized that the core of my disenchantment was not corporate America. *It was me.* Corporate America had always been the same. *I had changed.* I had outgrown the environment. I was hanging on to a past season. I now had a genuine sense of purpose and calling. It was now time to fully embrace and step into my new season. And I could hear the clarion call. He was calling me to trust Him and step out on faith. He was calling me to make some fundamental changes in my profession and honor what He had placed in my heart. And He was calling me to align my business plan with His purpose and plan for my life.

Pressing on in Obedience and Purpose

I am grateful to all of my employers for the wonderful opportunities and experiences they have afforded me. I've traveled all over the world and have even built five houses as an unmarried woman. Yes, I have been truly blessed. For the most part, I have lived a charmed lifestyle. I have always said that if the Lord decided to stop blessing me today, I will have already received more than my share of abundant blessings.

As God ushered me into my new season, I was both excited and scared—excited about the opportunity to pursue my passion and what I believed to be an integral part of my purpose but scared about how I would maintain my current "charmed" lifestyle if I resigned to work full-time on the book. Yet, I knew that God does not give us the spirit of fear (2 Timothy 1:7). It wasn't easy, but I trusted Him to work it all out. And I knew that if He gave me the *vision* for this venture, then He would surely make the necessary *provision* for it. *And He did.*

So after ten years of working for an extraordinary company, I resigned from The Coca-Cola Company to take a two-year sabbatical to finish my manuscript, get an agent, and pursue *His plan*. I finished the manuscript in the fall of 2008, which was probably the worst time in the history of mankind to try to sell a book. As I watched the stock market reach new lows every week, I prayed for God's guidance, and another door was opened for me in corporate America.

By the favor of God, Hostess Brands created a leadership role for me at their new headquarters in Dallas, Texas, a city I had hoped to relocate to since many of my family members, including my mother, had already migrated there. *Divine provision.* I was also blessed to sell my house in Atlanta, at a profit, and build another house in North Dallas. *Divine provision.*

Hostess Brands offered a tremendous team of insightful and accomplished professionals along with exciting projects and initiatives. But once again, as I began to settle into my new assignment, those old feelings began to slowly creep back into my psyche. Disenchanted. Stifled. Suffocated. Still living below my potential. I was shocked because I knew that God had opened the door for me to join this organization. They had created a position for me. Surely God didn't want me to resign this soon. *My plan* was to stay with the company at least a couple of years. But every day He made it clear to me that it was not about *my plan.* It was all about *His plan,* and I needed to get with it.

Once again, He was calling me to trust Him and to leverage the platform He had given me by starting a business with the same mission as the book. And so, once again, I obeyed and said, *Yes, Lord. Let's do this. Bad economy or good economy, we're doing this. Publisher for my book or no publisher, we're doing this.* Sure, I had brief moments of panic, questioning myself as to whether or not I was doing the right thing and if I was really hearing from God. And every time, He sent the Holy Spirit to give me a sense of peace and joy with the decision, confirming that I was exactly where He wanted me to be.

When I put my fear aside and stepped out on faith once again, this time in a new city without a strong, established, professional network for myself, here's what happened within three short months:

- Four publishing contracts appeared for my book.

- The true, divinely ordained publisher for my book appeared.

- All of the talented mentors and consultants I needed to help me get the business operational appeared.

- Business and church leaders, who didn't even know me, appeared through divine connections to help me begin building my clientele.

- Clients appeared before the business cards, corporate brochure, and website for my business were even completed.

That, my friend, is the power of God literally at work! He will show up and show out in your life in ways you could never imagine if you simply move over and allow Him to get behind the steering wheel. When you let Him drive, life becomes more joyful, purpose-filled, and enchanted! And this, my friend, is what I want for you! If you are already allowing Him to steer your career, then read on and you will be blessed with more insights and tools to take your success to an even Higher level of significance. If you haven't been allowing Him to steer your professional endeavors, then read on and you will be blessed with a life-enriching approach that will show you how to excel.

In retrospect, I can see so many magnificent aspects of *His plan* such as my three constant parallel paths of life themes (i.e., Christianity, business, and academia); how He used my career in corporate America as a marvelous venue and vehicle for developing the skill sets and expertise I needed as preparation for my calling; and, how He used my feelings of disenchantment as a springboard for catapulting me into my new season.

I have been, and will always be, transparent in sharing how God continues to manifest His divine favor, mercy, wisdom, and guidance in my life because I want my journey to serve as an inspiration for you to walk in your divine calling. I know that all of my experiences have led me to become a living testament for the importance of connecting your business plans with God's purpose and plan for your life.

The result to date: I am blessed to serve as the Associate Director for Executive Education for the Cox School of Business at Southern Methodist University, a prestigious, dynamic, world-renown institution. I am also blessed to serve as the founder and principal of Stewart Consulting, LLC, which is a leadership development and business consulting firm based in North Dallas, Texas, serving both corporate and nonprofit clients. Our corporate mission is to help business leaders connect their business plans with their purpose so that they maximize their personal fulfillment and professional success and drive performance, productivity, and bottom-line profitability for their organizations. The corporate vision is to ultimately help business leaders achieve their spiritual goals and individual purpose in cadence with their professional objectives and business imperatives.

We facilitate this by offering the innovative *Revelations in Business* program in the forms of keynote presentations, seminars, workshops, general consulting, and coaching sessions that are informative, insightful, and empowering in motivating teams to take their business to the Highest level of success and significance. Our firstborn publishing project is *Revelations in Business: Connecting Your Business Plan with God's Purpose and Plan for Your*

Life. It is an honor and a privilege to serve as a vessel for God. All glory and honor belong to Him.

"Do business till I come."
Luke 19:13 (NKJV).

We are instructed to be about our Father's business (Luke 2:49) and to do business until He returns (Luke 19:13). But "doing business" is becoming increasingly difficult every day for a myriad of reasons, including:

- Weak economic systems.

- Declining corporate revenue.

- Unemployment and underemployment.

- Corporate corruption.

- Job and career dissatisfaction. Example: In a recent survey of U.S. workers conducted by the Society for Human Resource Management (SHRM) and the *Wall Street Journal*, 65 percent of executives polled said they were actively looking for new employment, and 78 percent of workers currently employed said they were likely to start or accelerate a job search as the economy improves.

- Employee disengagement and absenteeism.

- Constant corporate downsizing and reorganization. Example: A recent study by The Conference Board, a leading research organization for the business community, reports that one of the main reasons that companies continue to reorganize is due to the lack of employee engagement.

- Global competition, spurred by technology offering instantaneous worldwide communication, requiring more businesses to operate globally in order to survive.

- High small business failure rates. Example: The U.S. Small Business Administration (SBA) continues to report that small firms account for more than 99 percent of all companies with employees; they employ 50 percent of all private sector workers, and they provide nearly 45 percent of the nation's payroll. Yet, over half of all small businesses fail within the first five years of operation.

- Decreasing customer satisfaction indices.

- Increasing sense of living doubles lives, i.e., our faith and work in silos.

- Need for a deeper connection between our spiritual calling and career.

- Lack of resources (e.g., books and seminars) to help us connect our profession with our purpose.

- Ongoing concerns of terrorist threats, particularly against institutions and infrastructure including commercial businesses, communication networks, and transportation systems.

These are just a few examples of some of the escalating challenges in today's business arena. As a means of coping with these issues, many of us are seeking a greater understanding of our purpose as individuals and a deeper connection between our work lives and spiritual lives.

The Importance of Connecting Your Business Plan with God's Purpose and Plan for Your Life

God desires to be intimately involved in every aspect of our lives, including our careers and commercial ventures. God ordained for us to have productive lives, and He makes it clear in 2 Thessalonians 3:10 that if we don't work, we don't eat. When you connect your business plan with God's purpose and plan for your life, your profession and your purpose, as an individual, become inextricably linked and ordained by God so that what you do in business, you are anointed to do, you are passionate about it, and you are positioned to excel. Only then will you truly begin to maximize your personal fulfillment and professional success. Only then will you become one of the elite groups of individuals who feel as if they are being compensated for a hobby. The prosperous people who make a living at what they would do for leisure. This is a blessing that many of us never experience.

In the *Harvard Business School Bulletin* titled "Spirit at Work: The Search for Deeper Meaning in the Workplace,"[1] the entire issue is devoted to discussing the fact that business people are beginning to realize that if they're going to spend the majority of their lives in the office, they would like for that time to be spiritually as well as materially rewarding.

In *Church on Sunday, Work on Monday: The Challenge of Fusing Christian Values with Business Life*[2], the authors, Laura Nash, senior research fellow for *Harvard Business School*, and Scotty McLennan, dean for religious life for Stanford University, explore the issue of why people of faith are not taught to apply their faith to their business endeavors.

The authors not only discovered a critical disconnect between the church and the business community, but they also found that business leaders have a sense of living in two worlds that never touch each other: *the spiritual* and *the commercial.* They are living double lives with their faith in one silo and their profession in the other. The authors concluded that *business professionals are looking for a greater degree of integration of faith and work,* and they want their professions to offer meaning and fulfillment beyond just a paycheck.

The Twofold Failure and Vicious Cycle

The profound disconnect between our faith and our professions along with constant economic, political, and social pressures, compounded by intense competition, have led to what I deem to be a twofold failure among many business professionals:

1. Intrinsic Failure: The failure to maximize our inner, personal, and spiritual fulfillment by achieving our purpose in life.

2. Extrinsic Failure: The failure to maximize our professional success and external significance in the workplace and marketplace.

So what are we to do when faced with mounting pressures in society and little or no connection between our faith and work? Herein lies the beginning of the vicious cycle, and it usually proceeds as follows:

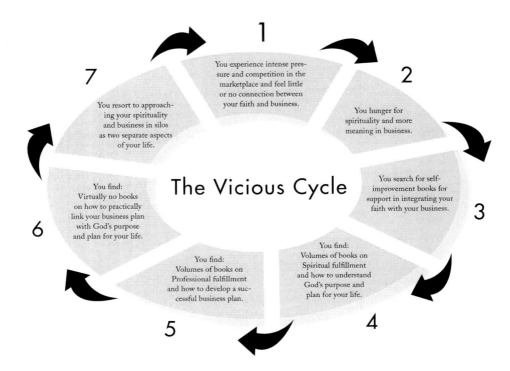

If you've found yourself on this vicious cycle like I have, then you know there's a gap. There's a lack of resources to help us understand how to align our spiritual beliefs and purpose as individuals with our professional business initiatives in practical ways. *Revelations in Business: Connecting Your Business Plan with God's Purpose and Plan for Your Life* was created to help fill this gap.

The Revelation of How to Maximize Your Personal Fulfillment and Professional Success in Business

Revelations in Business is for anyone who desires to excel personally and professionally. The focus of this book is on how we as Christian business leaders can maximize our personal fulfillment and professional success. We must transcend from a focus that centers on information to one that also includes revelation and transformation—the revelation of God's Word, combined with practical application of His principles to our professional endeavors, lead to genuine transformation in the workplace and marketplace. Transforming business to a Higher level. The Highest level. This book is about the redemptive revelation of God, the Father, through His Son, Jesus Christ, and how the only way for us to truly excel in the commercial arena is by knowing and applying God's principles, as revealed through His Word and Spirit (1 Corinthians 2:9-10; Ephesians 1:17; Galatians 1:12; Revelation 1:1; 2 Peter 1:3).

The Revelation that We Must First Seek the Will of God

Revelations in Business is about the revelation that God cannot be made to fit into our plans—including our strategic business plans. But we must align our business plans with His divine purpose and plan for our lives. We find ourselves struggling in the workplace and marketplace because we want God to help us with our will for our businesses as opposed to first seeking His will for our lives and businesses (Psalm 143:10; Matthew 6:10; Luke 11:2).

Western philosophy and conventional business teachings lead us to believe that we should first look *outside* ourselves to the needs of the marketplace and then subsequently create a business to try to fill a market niche. This is a worldly, or secular, approach and is out of God's order.

"It is better to trust in the Lord than to put confidence in man" (Psalm 118:8, NKJV). Our approach as Christian business leaders must be to first seek God and look spiritually *within* ourselves to understand our unique *purpose* as individuals and then align our professional goals and business plans against it. If God has indeed called you to be one of His ambassadors in the business arena, He will give you divine insights and instructions to enable you to succeed, and many of them are outlined in this book.

The Revelation of the Value of Having a Spiritual Foundation for Your Commercial Endeavors

Revelations in Business is about the fact that when our business plans originate from God, they are destined to succeed (1 John 5:4). As Christian business leaders, we must first discern God's will for our lives and businesses in the spiritual realm before we can bring them to fruition in the material realm. Once we spiritually discern God's will, we become positioned to excel because we have a spiritual foundation or grounding from almighty God for all of our professional and commercial endeavors.

As part of my graduate business studies, I surveyed over two hundred small business owners about their strategic plans and business growth to determine if there was a correlation between strategic planning and growth. My findings included a statistically significant positive correlation between strategic planning and growth. So I concluded that the development and execution of a strategic business plan are critical for achieving long-term business growth and commercial success.

Among the business owners I surveyed, there was a general consensus that business plans were important in supporting and guiding their commercial ventures. For instance, most of the respondents described a business plan as being the main "blueprint" or "roadmap" for a company.

As I continued my research, the Lord revealed to me, in my spirit, that He has actually ordained specific guidelines and principles that correlate with every element of a traditional business plan (e.g., executive summary, mission and vision, situation analysis, marketing, operations, management and organization, financial plan, and exit strategy). But most of us are not applying them. He also made me keenly aware of the fact that I had not come across any business plans that even remotely acknowledged God or incorporated spiritual principles. *Intriguing.*

Investigating the issue further, I decided to search for Christian-oriented, business management books on the topic of connecting your business plan with your purpose. I found very few. And virtually none of the books clearly outlined the process of how to apply God's Word to the major elements of a strategic business plan in practical, pragmatic ways that resonate with business leaders. I found myself wondering: How strong of a foundation do our businesses really have if our plans aren't firmly rooted in godly principles? Shouldn't our spiritual beliefs inform our commercial plans and practices? And we wonder why it's so difficult to excel personally and professionally in marketplace! Clearly, divine revelation is needed.

The Revelation that "a Man's Heart Plans His Way, but the Lord Directs His Steps" (Proverbs 16:9, NKJV)

Connecting Your Business Plan with God's Purpose and Plan for Your Life

Revelations in Business is the intersection between the spiritual and the commercial; it's the merger between Christianity and capitalism. This book will empower you to begin to completely reorient and recontextualize your perspective on business and elevate it to a Higher level, which is a godly level or one that conforms to God's principles and commandments (Colossians 3:1-2).

Revelations in Business seeks to tear down the silos between spirituality and commercial business by offering practical suggestions and pragmatic tools to help you apply your spiritual values to your business plans and integrate them into your operations. This book uses the elements of a traditional business plan as a framework for incorporating the Word of God into the context of conventional business planning and management. This new, unique, and spiritually rich approach to business planning found in *Revelations in Business* is called Divine Business Planning.

Why Merge Christianity and Capitalism?

Some people will be perplexed as to why I would integrate spirituality with commercial business, or Christianity with capitalism, particularly in Western society where doing so is often considered taboo. My response is that I am not trying to merge Christianity with capitalism. The two are already intrinsically connected.

In His omnipotent (*all-powerful*), omniscient (*all-knowing*), and omnipresent (*all-pervasive*) way, almighty God created the universe and everything in it including commercial business (Genesis 1:1; Deuteronomy 10:14; Acts 17:25; Psalm 146:6; Romans 11:36; Revelation 4:11; Isaiah 45:18-25). So as the late Jesuit priest Pierre Teilhard de Chardin eloquently stated, "We are not human beings having a spiritual experience, but spiritual beings having a human experience."

We've been operating in the realm of the spirit since the beginning of time. Everything is spiritual. Businesses consist of people, and people are comprised of the Spirit of God (Numbers 27:16; Job 33:4; Ezekiel 36:27; John 6:63; 1 Corinthians 3:16). As one business leader points out in *Church on Sunday, Work on Monday*[3]:

> Christianity is about this world. You look at business and you will find every aspect of human experience there. So any meaningful faith has to speak to the business world… life is not the monastery.

Christianity and capitalism are already fused. The spiritual and the commercial are already intertwined. Whether or not we choose to acknowledge this is an entirely separate issue. What are we going to incorporate into our professional ventures if not our faith? What is more vital to our success than our faith?

Your work matters to God. He cares about your profession. In the Western world, we spend most of our time at work. Our careers consume over half of our lives. And God ordained for each of us to lead productive lives (John 5:17; Exodus 34:21). When God created Adam, He also created a job for him, which was cultivating and managing the garden of Eden (Genesis 2:15). My goal in writing this book is to reinforce the fact that our profession is a vital part of our purpose as individuals. And the achievement of individual purpose and commercial leadership—as well as social, economic, and political dominion—all stem from faith and divine anointing. And both come only from God.

The Ultimate Business Planning Guide

So how do we ensure that our faith and values are incorporated into business planning, management, and execution? The answer has to do with structure, order, and guidelines.

One of God's first actions was to create structure, order, and guidelines (Genesis 1:1-5; 1 Corinthians 14:40). By creating the structures of heaven and earth and the order of day and night, He established guidelines for what denotes an actual day in time. Likewise, we also need divine structure, order, and guidelines for our professional endeavors. We need a God-ordained manual that serves as a guide, roadmap, or blueprint for our business ventures. Most of us already have this manual. We simply fail to apply it to our commercial ventures.

"In the beginning was the Word, and the Word was with God, and the Word was God" (John 1:1, NKJV). "For the Word of God is living and powerful" (Hebrews 4:12, NKJV) and "every Word of God proves true" (Proverbs 30:5, ESV). God has preserved His teachings over thousands of years and many generations through the continued existence of the Holy Bible.

God is the Author of the Bible. The prophecy of its scriptures did not come *from* men and women but *through* holy men and women when they spoke *as they were moved* by the Holy Spirit (2 Peter 1: 19-21). The Word of God never changes, and it is eternal truth (Matthew 24:35; John 17:17). There is no stronger foundation for our lives than that which is derived from the sovereign Word of God through the power of Jesus Christ (1 Corinthians 3:11). Jesus declares, "It is written, 'Man shall not live by bread alone, but by every word that proceeds from the mouth of God'" (Matthew 4:4, NKJV). He also tells us: "For it is written, you shall worship the Lord your God, and Him only you shall serve" (Luke 4:8, NKJV).

The Bible contains thorough instruction which, when followed, leads to salvation, righteousness, fulfillment, and remarkable success in all aspects of life—including our professional endeavors. The Word of God is a lamp to guide us and a light for our path and our plans. God's Word should serve as the final authority and solid rock (Psalm 119:105; Matthew 7:24-27) for the foundation, starting point, or baseline for all of our commercial ventures. If your business is not built on the foundation of godly principles, then your labor is truly in vain (Psalm 127:1).

We must surrender our professional goals and commercial plans to God because "the Lord's plans stand firm forever; His intentions can never be shaken" (Psalm 33:11, NLT). In order for us to build, reap, or harvest blessings in our businesses, we must first plant and sow godly principles into them. This is the reason *revelation*, *contemplation*, and *application* of the Word of God are so critical when it comes to our strategic plans. If your business plan is the blueprint, roadmap, or guide for your business, then the Bible should be the blueprint, roadmap, or guide for your business plan.

The Bible is the ultimate business-planning guide. It includes God's opinion, advice, and direction regarding how we should plan, manage, and execute our business initiatives because "all Scripture is given by inspiration of God, and is profitable for doctrine, for reproof, for correction, for instruction in righteousness, that the man of God may be complete, thoroughly equipped for every good work" (2 Timothy 3:15-17, NKJV).

Blessings in Business

When we diligently seek God and make His principles the foundation for our business plans, He promises to give us the wisdom and guidance we need to succeed (Proverbs 3:5-6; Psalm 37:4-5; 23; Hebrews 11:6). The Bible tells us that:

> This Book of the Law shall not depart from your mouth, but you shall meditate in it day and night, that you may observe to do according to all that is written in it. For then you will make your way prosperous, and then *you will have good success.*

> Joshua 1:8 (NKJV)

God is the sovereign Creator, the Lord of all. We are simply stewards over *His businesses.* And He holds us accountable for everything we do (Ecclesiastes 11:9), including how we plan, manage, and operate in the marketplace. God is not committed to sustaining or flourishing businesses that do not reflect His principles and teachings as outlined in the Bible.

When we obey God's commandments, principles, and plans in business, He will lead us to unlimited prosperity, success, longevity, and legacies of generational blessings. "The Lord will command the blessing on you in your storehouses and in all to which you set your hand, and He will bless you in the land which the Lord your God is giving you" (Deuteronomy 28:8). On the contrary, when we ignore God's directives in business, the results are often tragic. Scripture tells us, "He who despises the word will be destroyed, but he who fears the commandment *will be rewarded*" (Proverbs 13:13, NKJV). Furthermore, "'Woe to the obstinate children,' declares the Lord, 'to those who *carry out plans that are not mine*, forming an alliance, but not by my Spirit, heaping sin upon sin; who go down to Egypt without consulting me...'" (Isaiah 30:1-2, NIV). "The house of the wicked will be destroyed, but the tent of the godly will flourish. There is a path before each person that seems right, but it ends in death" (Proverbs 14:11-12, NLT). So "whether we like it or not, we will obey the Lord our God... for if we obey him, everything will turn out well for us" (Jeremiah 42:6, NLT).

Serving as an Ambassador for God in the Business Arena

An ambassador is generally defined as a diplomatic official of the highest rank. As Christian business leaders, we are all ambassadors for Christ and ministers of God in the workplace and marketplace (2 Corinthians 5:20; 6:4; Ephesians 3:7). God authorizes us to represent Him. Our professional success is to be used for His glory. He wants our commercial achievements to be shining examples for others to witness His divine work in our lives. By maximizing your potential and achieving your purpose as an individual, you become a powerful living testimony, bringing others closer to God. The ethical and operational standards of the business world must be transformed to a Higher level of excellence. And it's up to us as God's ambassadors to lead the effort. How are you using your influence in the business world?

It's important that I point out that I am *not* recommending we become radical preachers in the workplace and marketplace. The intent is not to alienate, interrogate, or bombard our colleagues with our religious beliefs and contemptuously impose our spiritual values on them. I am, however, advocating that we take a more thoughtful and holistic approach to business planning and execution by strategically incorporating spirituality and godly principles into the equation.

Our spiritual values influence the ways in which we manage and operate our businesses. Certainly, we must appreciate the legalities of religious discrimination in the workplace, particularly in corporate America. But here's a key point to remember: Christian values actually teach *acceptance* of the myriad of differences among us, not rejection and discrimination (Acts 10:34). And ultimately, the efficacy of these values, when applied to the business arena, will be measured not so much by what we *say* but by what we *do*.

Overview of This Book

Revelations in Business is for those who desire to excel personally and professionally. Regardless of whether you are a seasoned leader or just beginning your career, this book is for you. Whether you are an entrepreneur, corporate executive, manager, administrator, minister, church leader, educator, or student, this book provides powerful real-life examples from business leaders, spiritual principles, practical tools, and pragmatic suggestions for maximizing your personal fulfillment and professional success. Revelations in Business is for leaders of all types of organizations: corporate, nonprofit enterprises, churches, educational institutions, and professional business associations.

The goal of this book is to transform our mind-set and *reorient*, *reconceptualize*, and *recontextualize* the concept of business and take it to the Highest level of excellence by incorporating godly principles. This requires that we elevate our collective consciousness about commercialism and capitalism. One of the reasons I wrote this book was because of the lack of personal and spiritual fulfillment in my own previous career in corporate

America. Unfortunately, many of us are extremely dissatisfied with our jobs and careers. This continues to be substantiated by numerous empirical studies that consistently report declining job satisfaction among workers, particularly in the United States. This is a widespread issue and one that is not just endemic to Christians.

It's important to note that because I am a Christian, this book is written from a Christian perspective. Now, you may be wondering: *Does this mean I have to be a Christian to understand and apply the principles laid out in this book?* Absolutely not. Regardless of your religious beliefs and values, you'll find that *Revelations in Business* offers spiritual principles, practical tools, and real-life examples to help position you for success in business so that your job or career is much more meaningful and rewarding.

Revelations in Business offers a unique approach to strategic planning that allows you to achieve your spiritual goals and individual purpose in cadence with your professional objectives and business imperatives because we don't have a *personal life* and a *professional life*. We have *one life* during our short time on earth. Let's make it count! This book combines both sacred and secular insights to guide you through the process of developing a solid business plan that will position you to excel.

Revelations in Business leverages the commonly accepted framework and proven methodology of a conventional business plan to take you through a practical and pragmatic eight-step Divine Business Planning process that is grounded in the Word of God. Biblical principles are incorporated into each step of the process along with solid strategies and practical applications from successful leaders that you can begin applying immediately.

So if you don't have a business plan, then *Revelations in Business* will give you the key elements of one and, more importantly, one that exemplifies business planning God's way so that you will be positioned to excel. If you already have a business plan, then *Revelations in Business* will give you spiritual insights and practical tools to enhance your plan and take your business to the Highest level of success and significance. Every chapter contains real-world examples and applications that will minister to you regardless of your professional position and occupation.

With chapters arranged in order of a traditional commercial business plan, *Revelations in Business* incorporates comprehensive *Divine Business Planning* elements including:

1. *Divine executive summary*, where you connect the executive summary, or *purpose*, for your business with God's executive summary, or *purpose*, for your life.

2. *Divine mission and vision*, where you learn how to connect the mission and vision for your business with your personal mission and vision as an individual.

3. *Divine situation analysis*, where you discover how to spiritually discern industry trends and uncover the most powerful *threefold feature* of an effective competitive intelligence network and response system.

4. *Divine marketing plan*, where you uncover your superior brand attributes, discover the fifth *P* of marketing, and learn how some of the most successful companies glorify God in their marketing initiatives.

5. *Divine operations plan*, where you learn ways to take inventory of your thoughts, use quality control measures for your environment, and operate *in* the business world without being *of* the business world.

6. *Divine management and organization plan*, where you remember *Who* you work for, consider the importance of

servant leadership and management, and learn how to discern your divine assignment within an organization.

7. *Divine financial plan*, where you consider the importance of pursuing *prosperity* over *profitability*, the dangers of having an *in-the-red* mind-set, and how to follow God's spiritual economics for financial dominion.

8. *Divine exit plan*, where you discover why your *donation* is more important than your *duration* and why your *history* is ultimately *His Story*.

Each chapter in *Revelations in Business* includes:

- An overview of the specific business plan element.

- Three Planning Proverbs, which provide insights on what the Bible says about the particular business plan element.

- Real-life examples from business leaders sharing their experiences and testimonies.

- Directives for execution, which offer practical tips and pragmatic suggestions for how to apply the principles and insights to your life and how to execute them in your profession (i.e., what this all means for you and your business).

A Few Points of Clarification

Before we go deeper into the ways in which Revelations in Business will help you grow in your purpose and excel in business, it's important that I clarify a few key terms. First, the phrase "Revelations in Business" refers to the revealing, or unveiling, of God in our professional endeavors. It pertains to what God reveals to us about commercial business through His Word. This is critical because without the redemptive revelation of God, not only will our businesses fail, but we will also perish (Proverbs 29:18). As Jesus tells us:

> For there is nothing hidden which will not be revealed…if anyone has ears to hear, let him hear…take heed to what you hear. With the same measure you use, it will be measured to you; and to you who hear, more will be given.
>
> Mark 4:22-24 (NKJV)

Secondly, when I mention the term *business* I am referring to your profession, trade, or occupation in the broadest sense, with particular emphasis on commercial enterprises. *Business* refers to any organization, company, or ministry with which you might be employed or affiliated. I also use the term *business* to include commercial ventures, church and ministry outreach efforts, and nonprofit initiatives as well as academic programs and educational pursuits.

The phrases "business leader" and "business professional" will be used interchangeably. You will notice that I use the phrase "business leader" liberally. The reason I refer to us as business leaders has nothing to do with *position* and everything to do with *perspective*—your perspective of who you are in God. If you are a believer, then you are a leader. You don't have to be in a formal position of running a company or managing an organization to be considered a leader. You are a leader as long as you possess a kingdom-centric mind-set and attitude, realizing that you are an ambassador for God and a steward over His business for kingdom-building purposes.

The fact that you are reading this book suggests that you have a genuine interest in God and in learning how to align your plans with His purpose. You have a desire to excel as one of God's chosen ambassadors in the business world. You are a business leader.

The individuals and companies serving as real-life examples in this book have been highlighted because certain aspects of either their business philosophy or practices are reflective of godly principles and commandments. Not all of the companies highlighted are Christian. But most of them exemplify excellence, and we serve an excellent God (Philippians 1:10-11; Psalm 8:1; Romans 2:18). My intent in including them is to share a few publicly reported, best-in-class examples with you. My intent *is not* to ascribe any particular spiritual values and religious beliefs to these individuals personally or to their organizations collectively beyond what they have shared publicly.

Although most of the business cases included in *Revelations in Business* are modern-day examples, I've also included a few biblical illustrations of how some of the principles outlined in this book have applied to individuals who lived thousands of years ago. You may be thinking, *Well, Shelette, those Bible miracles were for people back then, but things are different now. Times have changed.*

Here's my response: *Certainly, times have changed. But God has not changed* (Hebrews 13:8). The promises of God as outlined in the Bible apply to you and your business today just as they did for people who lived ages ago. His Word is still true today.

Lastly, when I mention the terms *spirituality* and *spiritual*, I am referring to our moral character and personal relationship with God as individuals in general and specifically to the Holy Spirit that we receive through our acceptance of God through our confession of Jesus Christ as our Savior. The focus is not on a particular religion or denomination. The focus is on God.

Surrender Your Business to the Lord and It Will Succeed

"Commit to the Lord whatever you do, and your plans will succeed" (Proverbs 16:3, NIV; 2 Chronicles 20:20). This includes your business plans. God reminds us that He is "the Alpha and the Omega, the Beginning and the End" (Revelation 1:8, NKJV; 21:6) and that He rewards those of us who diligently seek and obey Him (Hebrews 11:6; Deuteronomy 4:29; 8:1-20; 27:10). We as Christian business leaders must surrender our businesses to Him. Every step of our business planning and execution process should begin and end with Him, and we must proactively seek His divine wisdom, knowledge, insights, and guidance at every stage (1 Corinthians 1:30; Isaiah 11:2).

When we connect our business plans with God's purpose and plan for our lives, our professional lives become significantly less stressful and so much more enjoyable, fulfilling, and rewarding. Regardless of whether you are a seasoned professional or an intern just starting your career, it is *never* too late, nor too early, to begin learning how to fulfill God's sovereign plan for your life and business.

Nothing can stop the purpose and plan of God (Job 42:2; Proverbs 19:21). The Bible says that King David succeeded in everything he did because the Lord was with him (1 Samuel 18:14). When we consult with God first about His plan for us, He will guide us into levels of success that are Higher than we could ever imagine (Psalm 92:13).

My Promise to You

My promise to you is that after you read this book, you will never think about business the same way again. Your perspective will be at a much Higher level, a godly level. Every chapter is full of information and insights that will minister to you and bless you.

I pray that *Revelations in Business* will inspire you to bring more of a *spiritual perspective* and *foundation* to your *commercial endeavors*. I pray that this book will offer a unique viewpoint and rich ideology that will help reframe and enhance your business plans and practices. I hope that you will experience a renewed appreciation and reverence for the fact that commercial enterprise was created by God and belongs to Him. You are simply a steward over *His business*.

I pray that this book will offer a new perspective on business and an inspiring way of thinking about capitalism. I hope *Revelations in Business* provides a sense of transcendent meaning to the concept of commercialism that will establish a new paradigm and a Higher standard for how we operate in the workplace and marketplace. And I hope and pray that this new standard will inspire insightful thinking, progressive dialogue, and positive action that will enlighten and bless generations to come.

Scripture says that if we keep God's commandments, He will bless us (Deuteronomy 30:16). But in order to for us to keep His commandments, follow His guidelines, and apply them to our businesses, we must first have *knowledge* and *understanding* of them (Proverbs 4:7; Hosea 4:6).

So are you ready to gain the knowledge that will allow you to maximize your personal fulfillment and professional success? If so, then, as Jesus implored, let's be about our Father's business (Luke 2:49). We'll begin our journey by gaining a deeper understanding of our purpose as individuals in the next chapter on the divine executive summary.

The Divine Executive Summary

Before I formed you in the womb I knew you before you were born I set you apart; I appointed you as a prophet to the nations.

—Jeremiah 1:5 (NIV)

There are many plans in a man's heart; nevertheless the Lord's counsel will stand.

—Proverbs 19:21(NKJV)

What is God's purpose for your life? How does your profession relate to your purpose as an individual? Most of us in the business arena would agree that the executive summary is one of the most important parts of a comprehensive business plan. As the first section of the plan, the executive summary introduces your commercial venture by offering a clear and concise explanation of its *purpose* and viability. This section provides an overview of the business concept and model and includes vital information such as the company name, location, corporate statement of purpose, management, market niche, competitive advantages, and preliminary financial projections.

The executive summary may be targeted to external investors and venture capitalists as well as to internal teams and departments within an organization such as a major corporation, small business, church, or educational institution. The executive summary serves as the initial platform for convincing others that you have a well-conceived and potentially successful venture by:

- Introducing and describing the *purpose* of your business

- Serving as a brief snapshot of the total picture of your business plan.

Now, let's consider these two points within the context of your life: What is your executive summary, or purpose, as an individual? What is the brief snapshot of the total picture of your life that God has revealed to you? How does your purpose relate to your business? We'll explore the answers to these questions and more in this chapter.

Three Planning Proverbs for the Divine Executive Summary

Following are the three Planning Proverbs for this chapter:

1. God is The Chief Executive Officer (CEO) and Master Strategist for your life and your business.

2. Align the executive summary for your business with God's executive summary for your life.

3. Always remember: It's not about you.

Now let's proceed with the first Planning Proverb:

God Is The Chief Executive Officer (CEO) and Master Strategist for Your Life and Your Business.

· · · · · · · · · · · · · · · · · · · ·

CEO and Master Strategist of All

In case we have any doubts about who He is, God makes it perfectly clear for us in Isaiah 44:6 (NKJV): "'I am the First and I am the Last; besides Me there is no God.'"

> The Lord *is* the true God; He *is* the living God and the everlasting King (Jeremiah 10:10, NKJV; John 17:3). *There is* one body and one Spirit...one Lord, one faith, one baptism; one God and Father of all, who *is* above all, and through all, and in you all (Ephesians 4:4-6, NKJV).

"The Lord has made the heavens his throne; from there he rules over everything" (Psalm 103:19, ESV). God created the universe and everything in it including the world's social, political, and economic systems (Genesis 1:1; Deuteronomy 10:14; Psalm 24:1; 50:12; Romans 11:36; Matthew 6:13; 1 Corinthians 11:12; 1 Chronicles 29:16).

> All things were made through Him...in Him was life, and the life was the light of men. (John 1:3-4, NKJV)

> For by Him all things were created that are in heaven and that are on earth, visible and invisible, whether thrones or dominions or principalities or powers. All things were created through Him and for Him (Colossians 1:16-20, NKJV; Psalm 104:24; Isaiah 43:10-13).

All that is good in life comes from God (James 1:17), including commercial business success. The Bible tells us that as stewards "we have been approved by God to be entrusted with the gospel, even so we speak, not as pleasing men, but God who tests our hearts" (1 Thessalonians 2:4, NKJV).

God calls us as believers to preach the gospel of His kingdom throughout the world (Matthew 24:14; Luke 9:60). "For the kingdom of God *is* not in word, but in power" (1 Corinthians 4:20, NKJV). As stewards over His businesses, we are to be faithful servants of Christ and stewards of the mysteries of God (1 Corinthians 4:1-2). God has entrusted us to preside over His commercial enterprises and to manage them according to His principles and guidelines for advancing His kingdom.

Predestined Business Leaders

God chose us before the foundations of the world (Ephesians 1:4). "*It is* He who made us, and not we ourselves" (Psalm 100:3, NKJV). Not only did God know us before He formed us in the womb, but He also knew the plans that He has for each one of us and the purpose of our lives as individuals (Jeremiah 1:5). Because we were founded in God, we must make Him priority and the foundation for every aspect of our lives.

In order to understand who God created us to be and what He desires for us to accomplish in life and in business, we must seek His wisdom daily through His teachings. For instance, if you believe in Jesus Christ and follow His teachings, take a few moments to contemplate the following questions and identify the one that more strongly resonates with you today:

1. Are you a business professional who just happens to be a Christian?

2. Are you a Christian who just happens to be a business professional?

The Bible tells us "there is neither Jew nor Greek, there is neither slave nor free, there is neither male nor female; for you are all one in Christ Jesus" (Galatians 3:28, NKJV; Romans 10:12). We "are all sons of God through faith in Christ Jesus" (Galatians 3:26, NKJV). So the appropriate answer would be no to the former question and yes to the latter. Who we are in God should always be foremost in how we see and define ourselves regardless of our professional titles, credentials, and possessions. Your self-worth is not defined by your net worth. So the correct answer would be that you are a Christian who just happens to be a business professional.

Before we were even born, God *predestined* us to carry out His will and purpose (Ephesians 1:11). Now, you might be wondering, *What is meant by the term predestined?* We commonly speak in terms of *destiny* or fate, which are often used synonymously and generally defined as something that will happen or is believed to be determined beforehand in spite of later efforts to change or prevent it. But the Bible introduces us to a Higher form of the concept of destiny, which is *predestiny.*

God speaks and operates in the spiritual realm of *predestiny,* which consists of what was preordained, prepared beforehand, or planned before the beginning of time. The concept of predestiny was created by God before He created mankind. God knew us before we were even born, as He explains in Jeremiah 1:5 (NKJV):

> Before I formed you in the womb I knew you; Before you were born I sanctified you; I ordained you a prophet to the nations.

God created the executive summary, or purpose, for your life before you were even born. The Bible says that Jesus Christ was chosen and predestined before the foundation of the world but was manifested in the last days for our sake (1 Peter 1:20). Scripture goes on to explain:

> For whom He foreknew, He also predestined to be conformed to the image of His Son, that He might be the firstborn among many brethren. Moreover, whom He predestined, these He also called; whom He called, these He also justified; and whom He justified, these He also glorified.
>
> Romans 8:29-30 (NKJV)

God first predestined Jesus and then He predestined us in the likeness of Jesus. God adopted us as His children and "chose us in Him before the foundation of the world, that we should be holy and without blame before Him in love, having predestined us to adoption as sons by Jesus Christ to Himself, according to the good pleasure of His will" (Ephesians 1:4-5, NKJV).

We are God's workmanship created in the image of Jesus Christ to do good works, which God predestined that we should walk in or manifest in our lifestyle (Ephesians 4:1; 2:10). In these ways, God foreordained, predetermined, preselected, and prepared His purpose for all of us even before He created the world.

God predestined His business leaders. Your interest in reading this book and understanding how to align your business plan with God's purpose and plan for your life is a good indication that you are one of His chosen ambassadors in the commercial sector. In order to succeed, you only need to pursue what He has already predestined for you. Walk in your predestiny. Even the executive summary, or purpose, for the life of Jesus had to line up with God's predestined plan:

> I do not seek My own will but the will of the Father who sent Me.
>
> John 5:30 (NKJV)
>
> For I have come down from heaven not to do My own will and purpose but to do the will and purpose of Him Who sent Me.
>
> John 6:38 (NKJV)
>
> My food is to do the will of Him who sent Me, and to finish His work.
>
> John 4:34 (NKJV)

Jesus continues to educate us about His purpose, saying, "I have come that they may have life, and that they may have it more abundantly" (John 10:10, NKJV). He tells us, "I am the light of the world. He who follows Me shall not walk in darkness, but have the light of life" (John 8:12, NKJV).

He explains:

> For God so loved the world that He gave His only begotten Son, that whoever believes in Him should not per-

ish but have everlasting life. For God did not send the Son into the world to judge the world, but that the world might be saved through Him.

John 3:16-18 (NKJV); Acts 16:31; 1 Thessalonians 5:10

And He makes it perfectly clear when He says,

You did not choose Me, but I chose you and appointed you that you should go and bear fruit, and that your fruit should remain, that whatever you ask the Father in My name He may give you.

John 15:16 (NKJV)

In this case, the term fruit generally refers to godly conduct and results.

At this point, you may be wondering, *Does this concept of pre-destination mean that we, as individuals, have no power or influence whatsoever when it comes to achieving our purpose in life? Do we have to acquiesce to God's plan for our lives and businesses?*

God gives us free will to make our own choices. However, because of God's supreme sovereign power, there are aspects of our lives that are unchangeable. But we have a responsibility to pray and seek His guidance to determine what He has predes-tined for us. And when He reveals it, we are to be obedient in pursuing it. Obedience to all of God's commandments is of utmost importance. Jesus said, "If you love Me, keep My com-mandments" (John 14:15, NKJV). This process can be as easy or as difficult as we want to make it. We'll go into more details about God's will for us and how much control we have as individuals in fulfilling it when we get to our second Planning Proverb later in this chapter.

Choosing Him as CEO and Master Strategist of Your Life and Business

In order to excel in the business arena, you and I must first make God the CEO and Master Strategist of our life and business. God has set before us life and death, blessings and curses, and we are instructed to choose life so that we and our descendents may live (Deuteronomy 30:19). But it's up to us as to whether or not we choose to follow His instructions. As an individual, you must choose this day whom you will serve (Joshua 24:15). The choice is yours.

The Bible is full of fascinating accounts of the lives of individuals, like ourselves, who experienced a myriad of challenges and opportunities that ultimately helped them mature and accomplish God's purpose and plan for their lives. But God loved us so much that He knew we would need a supreme role model, mentor, coach, and confidant to help us through the process of living abundant, purpose-filled lives. So He sent His Son, Jesus Christ, to serve in this capacity for us.

Believing and Receiving Salvation

When we decide to surrender our lives and businesses to God, it's vital that we not only *believe* in God but that we also *receive* Him into our lives. Scripture says that "as many as *received* Him, to them He gave the right to become children of God, to those who *believe* in His name" (John 1:12, NKJV). This distinction between believing and receiving is critical because anyone can believe in God without receiving Him. Case in point: Satan believes in God and has even presented himself before God (Job 2:1-2). But Satan never received God as his Savior.

Belief in God through Jesus Christ is the only way to be redeemed of our sins and achieve salvation and everlasting life

(Colossians 1:14; 3:24; 1 Peter 2:24; 1 John 2:2; Acts 4:12). The Bible says "the Father has sent the Son *as* Savior of the world" and "whoever confesses that Jesus is the Son of God, God abides in him, and he in God" (1 John 4:14-16). "For *there* is one God and one Mediator between God and men, *the* Man Christ Jesus Who gave Himself a ransom for all" (1 Timothy 2:5-6, NKJV).

Jesus tells us, "I am the way, the truth, and the life. No one comes to the Father except through Me" (John 14:6, 3:16). Jesus died for our sins and was raised from the dead to make us right with God (Romans 4:25; 5:9; 1 Peter 3:18; Hebrews 7:25; 9:26). If you "confess with your mouth the Lord Jesus and believe in your heart that God raised Him from the dead, you will be saved, for with the heart one believes unto righteousness, and with the mouth confession is made unto salvation" (Romans 10:9-10, NKJV; 3:22-26; 1 Corinthians 15:3-4). "Everyone who believes that Jesus is the Christ has become a child of God. And everyone who loves the Father loves His children too" (1 John 5:1, NLT).

When it comes to salvation, God does not force compliance. The decision is ultimately ours. While no one has absolute free will, God gives us just enough free will to either choose to believe in Him or not. The Bible provides us with God's instructions for living as well as the implications and ramifications of *not* following them. Scripture makes it clear: "For the wages of sin *is* death, but the gift of God is eternal life in Christ Jesus our Lord" (Romans 6:23, NKJV). The Apostle John reinforces this when he states:

> Whoever has the Son has life; whoever does not have God's Son does not have life. I have written this to you who believe in the name of the Son of God, so that you may know you have eternal life.
>
> 1 John 5: 12-13 (NLT)

"We all have sinned and fall short of the glory of God" (Romans 3:23, NLT; Isaiah 53:6). But the Bible says that we are made righteous, or right with God, when we believe that Jesus sacrificed His life and shed His blood for our sins (Romans 3:24-26). "If we confess our sins, He is faithful and just to forgive us our sins and to cleanse us from all unrighteousness" (1 John 1:9, NKJV; Isaiah 1:18). So we must repent of our sins and turn to God so that our sins may be wiped away (Acts 3:19). "For whoever calls on the name of the Lord shall be saved" (Romans 10:13, NKJV; Acts 2:21).

The Blessing of the Holy Spirit

Once we accept Jesus as our personal savior, we receive the blessing of the Holy Spirit and "by this we know that we abide in Him and He in us, because He has given us of His Spirit" (1 John 4:13, NKJV; Acts 2:38). The Holy Spirit, which is the Spirit of God, allows us as Christians to receive power through Jesus Christ and brings us into fellowship with God. The power of the Holy Spirit lives within us as believers (2 Timothy 1:14). As Jesus tells us: "God is Spirit, and those who worship Him must worship in spirit and truth" (John 4:24, NKJV).

The Bible refers to the Holy Spirit as a person. In Romans 8:26, the Holy Spirit is described as the "Spirit *Himself*" and is the third person in the holy Trinity: God, Jesus Christ, and the Holy Spirit (Matthew 28:19). Jesus tells us that we receive power when the Holy Spirit comes upon us (Acts 1:8), and He refers to the Holy Spirit as a "Helper" that He has sent to us (John 16:7). The Holy Spirit:

- Helps us when we are weak or in distress (Romans 8:26).

- Prays and makes intercessions for us according to the will of God (Romans 8:26-27).

- Allocates our spiritual gifts (1 Corinthians 12:11).

- Teaches and reminds us of everything God tells us (John 14:26).

- Guides us into all truth and shows us things to come (John 16:13).

- Becomes grieved when we're disobedient (Ephesians 4:30).

As a Christian business leader, you'll find that the Holy Spirit is a phenomenal resource for guiding you toward what God has called you to accomplish in the commercial arena. But you have to first invite the Holy Spirit to work in your life and stay open and flexible to God's promptings through the Holy Spirit.

Once you have made the commitment to follow God and accept Jesus as Lord and Savior over your life and receive the blessing of the Holy Spirit, *rejoice*! You now have the sovereign power of the only true and living God working through you! You have opened yourself up to a never-ending source of love, divine wisdom, guidance, strength, and protection. "Be strong in the Lord and in His mighty power" (Ephesians 6:10, NLT). With almighty God as the head of your life and business, you can't help but to excel (2 Chronicles 13:12)!

Business Is a Form of Ministry

For us as Christian business leaders, church auxiliaries are not the only valid ministries within our society. Business is also a form of

God's ministry and should be governed as such. You don't have to be a preacher to have a pulpit. Everyone has a pulpit. You don't have to be an ordained minister to have a ministry. Everyone has a ministry. The Bible tells us that "there are differences in ministries, but the same Lord" (1 Corinthians 12:5, NKJV).

Your business is a part of your ministry, and it can be a powerful vehicle for glorifying God, blessing others, and bringing them closer to Him. So contrary to conventional business philosophy, our commercial ventures shouldn't just start with a start with a good idea. They should start with a divinely inspired idea. A God-ordained idea. A blessed idea.

The free enterprise system is not just a means for achieving our professional and financial goals. It's also a platform for missionary work and advancing God's kingdom agenda. We are all missionaries for God. When conducting business, we are given numerous opportunities daily to minister the Word of God to others in words and deeds, such as sharing encouraging comments and modeling integrity and excellence in our business practices.

Christians must be represented among the highest echelons of the international business arena in order to help facilitate God's kingdom agenda. This is the reason that, wherever you are, "you must let your light shine before men, that they may see your good works and glorify your Father in heaven" (Matthew 5:16, NKJV). Our presence in corporate boardrooms, in departmental meetings, at conferences, and on the proverbial golf course is necessary if we are to be witnesses for God with our constituents, including associates, colleagues, customers, clients, suppliers, investors, and competitors.

You and I must be shining examples of how God desires for business to be conducted. We are to "walk worthy of God who calls us into His own kingdom and glory" (1 Thessalonians 2:12, NKJV). The key point here is that:

This perspective of your business being a critical part of manifesting God's kingdom agenda on earth, as opposed to it just facilitating your own personal agenda, is the fundamental difference between your business philosophy and that of an unbeliever.

Real-Life Examples: What Happens When We Don't Make God The CEO and Master Strategist of Our Life and Business?

Dissatisfaction with Our Jobs and Careers in Business

> So I decided there is nothing better than to enjoy food and drink and to find satisfaction in work. Then I realized that these pleasures are from the hand of God. For who can eat or enjoy anything apart from him? God gives wisdom, knowledge, and joy to those who please Him. But if a sinner becomes wealthy, God takes the wealth away and gives it to those who please Him.
>
> Ecclesiastes 2:24-26 (NLT)

The only way for us to find satisfaction in work is to recognize that our work is a form of ministry for God and to allow Him to be our Ultimate CEO and Master Strategist.

Oftentimes, we make the profound mistake of placing God in a silo by separating Him from our professional lives. We become so busy with our schedules that we find it difficult to fit God into them. How ironic given the fact that we wouldn't even *have* a schedule if it were not for Him. The Word of God says:

> Do not love the world or anything in the world. If anyone loves the world, the love of the Father is not in him For everything in the world—the cravings of sinful man, the lust of his eyes and the boasting of what he has and does—comes not from the Father, but from the world.
>
> 1 John 2:15-16 (NLT)

In Western society, most of us spend a great deal of time pursuing the world. When I mention "the world," I'm referring to the secular world system. It's common for us collectively to formally pursue God twice a week—on Sunday mornings and during a designated weeknight Bible study. But we formally pursue the world seven days a week.

We spend the majority of our week, and thus the majority of our lives, pursuing the world. By this, I mean we spend an inordinate amount of time pursuing:

- The world of fortune.

- The world of entertainment.

- The world of fame.

- The world of Wall Street.

- The world of Madison Avenue.

You get the picture. God doesn't want us to seek Him only on Sundays or only within the confines of a church or synagogue. He doesn't desire for us to pursue Him only during our personal time alone or with our families. He doesn't want us to acknowledge Him only during our prayers at bedtime or over meals. And He doesn't wish to be sought only during times of emergency and crisis.

God desires for us to constantly and fervently seek Him and His divine wisdom and guidance in every aspect of our lives, during every day of the week. God is *not* to be separated from any aspect of our lives, including our commercial business endeavors. But sadly, we as Christian business professionals often experience a sense of living our professional and spiritual lives in silos.

I recently came across this interesting excerpt titled "Tom Says Good-bye to Jesus," which appears in the book *Workplace Spirituality: A Complete Guide for Business Leaders* by Nancy R. Smith:

> Tom would talk with Jesus as he drove to work every day. Then, when he parked the car, he would say, "Well, bye Jesus; see you at five o'clock," and leave Him in the car during the workday. Expressing his personal faith at work would be unthinkable.

Can you relate to Tom? Sadly, this illustration of an employee checking his spirituality at the door of his job is particularly common in the U.S.

In American society, for generations we've been discouraged from sharing spirituality and discussing religion in the workplace. As a result, many of us feel that we are leaving our faith at home or in the car whenever we go to work. In doing so, we leave God out of a substantial number of hours of each day. This, consequently, causes dissatisfaction in our professional lives because they are not strongly connected with our faith.

In the book *Executive Influence: Impacting Your Workplace for Christ*, the founder of Auntie Anne's Pretzels, Anne Beiler, comments:

> I don't understand how a Christian can be in business and not have God at the core. I know some people try to separate their business and their personal lives, but I think you're one in the same. If you are a Christian, God is with you. How can you not take Him to work?

In *Church on Sunday, Work on Monday*, the authors, Nash and McLennan, found that business leaders experienced a profound disconnect between Sunday and Monday in that they were not embracing their spiritual values and faith at work to the same extent as they were in church or at home. Their research includes insights from several corporate executives such as the former chairman of the $3 billion ServiceMaster Company, which owns such well-known brands as ServiceMaster Clean, Merry Maids, TruGreen, and Terminix. C. William Pollard, mentions:

> The line between the sacred and the secular often separates the thinking and understanding among Christian leaders and leaders in business who are also Christian... the essence of faith requires integration in all areas of life, so why isn't there more common ground?[4]

J. McDonald Williams, the retired chairman of Trammel Crow Company, a leading real estate development corporation, echoes this sentiment with his observation that "more business people are seeking deeper spiritual understanding..."[5]

Laura Nash expounds on this dilemma as she describes the perspective of many of the CEOs who were interviewed in her empirical research studies:

> Just across the board, interviewees would be saying, "This is a life as a business leader that is very lonely. It requires many masks and many responsibilities that aren't from the same person I am at home and in my church on Sunday, and I don't know how to navigate that transition."[6]

But not all of the executives shared this sentiment as one CEO points out: "There is no secular aspect to my world. God is in everything."[7]

National Catastrophes

What is truly regrettable is that while we're engrossed in our occupations, we fail to realize that the *individual* choices we make to de-prioritize God can produce disastrous consequences at a *national* level. Example: In the United States, we acknowledge God in many aspects of our culture from the reference to God in the Declaration of Independence to the adage "In God We Trust" inscribed on our currency. Yet, many of our citizens have unfortunately fallen into the preposterous, satanic trap of trying to keep God out of certain aspects of society by trying to separate:

- Religion from politics.

- Prayer from schools.

- References to God from the Pledge of Allegiance.

- References to God from the national currency.

- References to Christ from the greeting "Merry Christmas."

- And the ridiculous list goes on…

As a result of sowing efforts to try to segregate God from fractions of our society, we are reaping some disastrous consequences in the forms of colossal national debt, wars, corporate scandals, social immorality, high business failure rates, and rampant diseases.

National Progress toward Making Him CEO and Master Strategist

Clearly, there is a need to bridge the Sunday-Monday disconnect that so many of us experience. And fortunately, in recent years the United States has experienced a growing faith movement that has permeated virtually all aspects of society, including business and politics in general and the motion picture and publishing industries in particular.

This faith-based movement has spawned phenomenally successful projects, including Rick Warren's best-selling prolific book, *The Purpose Driven Life*, which has sold over 30 million copies, and Mel Gibson's epic film, *The Passion of the Christ*, with its record-breaking box office receipts that have grossed over $600 million worldwide.

In the business arena, major corporations are beginning to not only acknowledge but also support their employees' desire to honor their faith at work and in their professional endeavors. Example: During his tenure as CEO of AES Corporation, a $12 billion company and one of the world's largest providers of electricity, Dennis Bakke explains:

> At AES, we want our people to bring their faith—whatever it is—to work with them. Instead of saying, "This is business and it has its own set of rules," we want them to be the same people here they are in their homes and in their places of worship...there shouldn't be two sets of rules for life. This is what we mean by integrity.[8]

A number of leading companies are beginning to offer spiritual support services, such as on-site facilities for prayer groups and Bible studies as well as chaplains who are available for employee counseling and support.

In order to maximize your personal fulfillment and professional success in business, your faith and spiritual values must be seamlessly interconnected, intertwined, and interwoven into your business plans and initiatives. Your spiritual values should inform your business plans and practices.

A good example of this approach is described in the *Business Week* cover story, "Religion in the Workplace: The Growing Presence of Spirituality in Corporate America."[9] In this issue, the president and CEO of Timberland, Jeffrey B. Swartz, reportedly uses his religious beliefs to guide business decisions and, in some cases, company policy, often consulting his rabbi about ideas and work challenges.

Once you have made God the CEO and Master Strategist for your life and business, the next step is to discern God's executive summary, or purpose, for your life and understand if and how it connects to your business. Our next Planning Proverb will guide us in accomplishing this.

Align the Executive Summary for Your Business with God's Executive Summary for Your Life

When we commit our lives to God, it's critical that we align every aspect of our lives with His principles and guidelines. We know that the executive summary of a business plan describes the purpose of the business and serves as a brief snapshot of the total picture of the business plan. Likewise, we as Christian business leaders must align the executive summary, or purpose, for our businesses with God's executive summary, or purpose, for our lives. If your goal is to gain both personal fulfillment and professional success, then this step is imperative. It is nonnegotiable. You must align the purpose of your business with God's purpose for your life. And the process begins with understanding the will of God.

Understanding the Will of God

> By His divine power, God has given us everything we need for living a godly life. We have received all of this by coming to know him, the one who called us to Himself by means of his marvelous glory and excellence.
>
> 2 Peter 1:3 (NLT)

In order to connect your business to your purpose as an individual, it's imperative to first understand the will of God and His purpose for your life. As stated in Ephesians 5:17 (NKJV), we should "not be unwise, but understand what the will of the Lord is." It's important to note that God's will has two aspects: determined and desired. And both of them represent God's best for us.

In his book, *Living the Extraordinary Life: Nine Principles to Discover It*, Dr. Charles F. Stanley explains that God's *determined* will includes those aspects of your life that are unchangeable because His overruling sovereignty allows nothing to deter these occurrences. Divine promises and prophecy fulfillment are examples of God's determined will.

On the contrary, God's *desired* will involves all the blessings that He wants for you that, with your limited free will, you are able to refuse. A successful career and thriving businesses are examples of God's desired will.

Understanding the will of God might seem like a daunting task, but it's not difficult because the Bible makes it clear for us. According to Genesis 1:27-29 (NKJV), God created us in "His *own* image" and we were created to have "dominion over…all the earth." Scripture says that we "may be called trees of righteousness, the planting of the Lord, *that He may be glorified*" (Isaiah 61:3, NKJV), and, "For it is God who works in you both to will and to do for *His* good pleasure" (Philippians 2:13, NKJV). These scriptures reinforce the fact that we were made in the image of God and we were made to glorify Him.

Your Executive Summary or Purpose Is to Glorify God

God created all of us, including His Son Jesus, to glorify Him. Jesus acknowledges this when He prays: "Father, the hour has come. Glorify Your Son, that Your Son also may glorify You" (John 17:1, NKJV). Our purpose as God's sons and daughters is to glorify Him so that His "name may be declared in all the earth" (Exodus 9:16, NKJV).

Your Purpose Determines Your Profession

We know that our purpose is to glorify God, but what does this mean for our professional pursuits? The Bible tells us that the way we live must honor God (2 Thessalonians 1:12). Everything—including our businesses—has been created by Him and for Him. So our professional and commercial endeavors must also honor and glorify God.

If you're reading this book, then you most likely have a genuine interest in glorifying God in your business ventures. But you might be wondering, *What does honoring God in commercial business really entail? How does the glorification of God become manifested in our business models?* The answer is: It all begins with a covenant.

Establishing a Spiritual Covenant for Your Commercial Business

A covenant is generally defined as an agreement that is legally binding. But God's covenant is spiritually binding. All of God's covenants are outlined for us in His Word. The blood of Jesus serves as His covenant with us for salvation (Mark 14:24; Hebrews 12:24). God tells us:

> Now therefore, if you will indeed obey My voice and keep My covenant, then you shall be a special treasure to Me above all people; for all the earth is Mine.
>
> Exodus 19:5 (NKJV)

God never breaks His covenants with us (Deuteronomy 7:9; Isaiah 59:21). He tells us:

> Thus, I establish My covenant with you: Never again shall all flesh be cut off by the waters of the flood; never again shall there be a flood to destroy the earth...I set My rainbow in the cloud, and it shall be for the sign of the covenant between Me and the earth...and I will remember My covenant which is between Me and you and every living creature...
>
> Genesis 9: 11-15 (NKJV)

Now let's consider the concept of covenant relative to your business. Consider the following questions:

- What is your covenant with God regarding your business?

- How do you plan to honor God's spiritual principles in your commercial endeavors?

- In what ways will your business serve to advance God's kingdom?

By posing these questions, I'm encouraging you to think about how you plan to honor and glorify God vis-à-vis your professional and commercial ventures. I'm asking you to consider some of the mainstay, nonnegotiable godly principles that you intend to incorporate into your business philosophy, plans, management, and operations. Example: How will you leverage your business to:

- Allow others to see the Christ in you?

- Bring others closer to God?

- Demonstrate godly business practices?

- Enhance the lives of future generations?

Pray and strategize about the practical ways in which you can help bring business management and administration to a Higher level. For instance:

- If you are in the financial services industry, how will you minimize the occurrence of corporate financial misdeeds in your organization? How will you set a Higher standard of excellence for other industry players?

- If you are in marketing, what are some of the dishonorable products and services with which you refuse to be associated? How will you exemplify marketing excellence?

There must be certain core spiritual, foundational principles and practices that distinguish our businesses from those of unbelievers. What are those distinguishing factors for your business?

Follow His Kingdom Agenda for Your Business

We must commit to following God's kingdom agenda for our businesses. Remember, our businesses don't belong to us. We are simply stewards over His enterprises. So if we want to achieve the abundant blessings that God has already pre-destined for us, we must adhere to His agenda as opposed to our own.

As His sheep, we are to listen to His voice and follow Him (John 10:27). Ask God to reveal His kingdom agenda of what He desires to accomplish through you and your business. And when He reveals it to you, *do not* attempt to modify what He has told you in any way. Don't add a word to what He commands you to do and don't remove a word from it (Deuteronomy 4:2). Just hand the reins over to Him and follow His lead.

When you begin to appreciate the fact that God controls your business, it takes the pressure of ultimate accountability off you. *What a blessing!* By yielding to God's sovereign agenda and following His divine plan for the business, you no longer have to operate within the confines and limitations of your human capabilities. You no longer have to worry about the economy, competitive threats, and corporate downsizing, because you now have almighty God at the helm of your business, orchestrating His pre-destined agenda. The next step in following His agenda is to allow Him to design your business plan.

Allow God to Develop Your Business Plan

There's a humorous adage that says: "If you want to make God laugh, tell Him your plans." I learned this lesson the hard way, but fortunately, I learned it early in life. During my senior year at U.C. Berkeley as I prepared for graduation, my plan was to get a job with The Coca-Cola Company. Well, my plan didn't come to fruition for eight years! During those years before I achieved my goal of working for the company, I experienced a number of peak and valley periods in my life, and I matured spiritually. I learned that everything revolves around God's plan, not mine. This is when I really came to appreciate the importance of planning prayerfully according to God's will.

I share this testimonial only to introduce the importance of our planning prayerfully about our professional goals and commercial ventures. Allow God to author your business plan. It's important to have a strategic plan, but it's imperative that it be vetted by God. Pray for *spiritual discernment*, which is the ability to hear from God by perceiving His messages and promptings through the Holy Spirit. Spiritual discernment allows us to filter out data from all other sources and simply hear from God.

The Bible tells us:

> The natural man does not receive the things of the Spirit of God, for they are foolishness to him; nor can he know *them*, because they are spiritually discerned. But he who is spiritual judges all things, yet he himself is *rightly* judged by no one.
>
> 1 Corinthians 2:14-15

As Christians, we have the mind of Christ (1 Corinthians 2:16), so we must allow Him to instruct us on how to develop business plans according to God's sovereign plan.

Seek God's will for your business and pray that His will, not your will, be done (Luke 22:42). Always be willing to change your professional course as God prompts you so that your business plan is never stagnate but always dynamically aligned with His plan. The Bible warns us about being too focused on our own personal agenda and plans as opposed to being obedient and following the will of God:

> "Woe to the rebellious obstinate children," says the Lord, "who take counsel, but not of Me, And who devise plans, but not of My Spirit, that they may add sin to sin…"
>
> Isaiah 30:1 (NKJV)

Don't be tied to a specific destination with your business such as going public or capturing a certain percentage of market-share within a certain timeframe. It's all right to have clearly defined goals and objectives, but make sure they are established by God and remain flexible to His timing. He'll let you know what to do and when to do it. Wait for His perfect timing in planning and executing your initiatives.

"Good planning and hard work lead to prosperity, but hasty shortcuts lead to poverty" (Proverbs 21:5, ESV). When you commit your plans to the Lord and allow Him to direct you, your plans are guaranteed to come to fruition (Proverbs 16:1,3,9; 20:5). The Bible says that if you obey God, He promises to make your name great, or enhance your reputation, and make you a blessing to others (Genesis 12:2).

No one has seen what God has prepared for those who love Him, and no one can change the plans of God (1 Corinthians 2:9; Isaiah 43:13). The Lord takes pleasure in those who reverently fear Him (Psalm 147:11). We should have so much reverence for God that we would not want to risk disobeying and disappointing Him. Partial obedience is still disobedience. Be obedient to God. "Whatever He says to you, *do* it" (John 2:5, NKJV). In the business world, go wherever He sends you and speak whatever He commands of you (Jeremiah 1:7).

Your Definition of Success

Is it possible to be successful without allowing God to develop our business plans? Can we be successful while operating outside of God's will and purpose for our lives? Frequently, we encounter people who appear to be successful, but the answers to these questions depend on your definition of success.

If you define success by Western societal standards and metrics such as having professional credentials, an impressive title, an extensive financial portfolio, luxury homes and automobiles, then the answer is *yes*; you can achieve this while operating outside of God's will and purpose for your life and business.

There are countless individuals, both saved and unsaved, in this situation right now. There are plenty of people who are affluent financially but impoverished spiritually. They are wealthy but may also be extremely miserable, lonely, unhappy, angry, and bitter. But more importantly, because they are operating outside of the will of God, they are not experiencing the *peace of God*. Therefore, they are experiencing *less than* God's best for them. They are not making preparations for their eternal destiny. And they are operating at a level that is *below* their potential as individuals. They are not living up to their Highest selves.

God guides us down a path of peace (Luke 1:79; Colossians 3:15; Proverbs 3:24; Isaiah 55:12). Jesus, the Prince of Peace, tells us, "Peace I leave with you, My peace I give to you; not as the world gives do I give to you. Let not your heart be troubled, neither let it be afraid" (John 14:27, NKJV; Isaiah 9:6).

People who are operating outside of God's will and purpose are missing out on the opportunity to have peace and success *in every aspect* of their lives. They are sacrificing and forfeiting the holistically abundant life that God promises for all who believe in Him and receive salvation. You may even find yourself in this situation, where you're doing okay. But here's the key question: Is "okay" enough? You can be materially successful yet spiritually destitute and miss God's purpose or executive summary for your life.

On the other hand, if your definition of success involves not only having life but also having it *more abundantly* as Jesus promised us in John 10:10, then the answer to the initial two questions is *no*; it is *not* possible to be successful while operating outside of the will of God. You may be at the top of your game career-wise, but social status, material possessions, fame, fortune, and power can never be substituted for a personal sense of purpose and spiritual fulfillment in God.

Only God holds the keys to your achieving your full potential as an individual. When we make choices that are displeasing to Him, we consequently sow seeds that have the potential to bring forth a fruitless harvest. There are many people who are successful in the eyes of the world but who are failures in the eyes of God. Some of them are saved and will enter the kingdom of heaven, while others are not saved and will not experience heaven. Jesus makes this clear when He says:

> Not everyone who says to Me, "Lord, Lord," shall enter the kingdom of heaven, but he who does the will of My Father in heaven.
>
> Matthew 7:21 (NKJV)

Furthermore, He goes on to say that:

> Many will say to Me in that day, "Lord, Lord have we not prophesized in Your name, cast out demons in Your name, and done many wonders in Your name?" and then I will declare to them, "I never knew you; depart from Me you who practice lawlessness!"
>
> Matthew 7:22-23 (NKJV)

It is vital that we follow God's will for our lives, because our eternal salvation is at risk. The world's definition of success is limited, short-term, and temporary (Job 5:3), but God's definition of success is for an eternity. Eternal salvation. Life is short. Eternity is forever. Our final Planning Proverb for this chapter will add more perspective around this.

Always Remember: It's Not About You

Initially, this may be a difficult concept to comprehend and embrace, but your life is not about you. Your business is not about you. They are about God and His purpose for advancing His kingdom. Scripture tells us: "For of Him and through Him and to Him are all things, to whom be glory forever. Amen" (Romans 11:36, NKJV).

The Bible teaches us that "we are His workmanship, created in Christ Jesus for good works, which God prepared beforehand that we should walk in them" (Ephesians 2:10, NKJV). Jesus died for us, so we no longer live for ourselves, but we live for Him (2 Corinthians 5: 14-15). We are alive because of Him and for Him. Likewise, our commercial businesses exist because of Him and for Him. Your profession is never about you but always about Him.

You and I were created to play our individual roles in our respective kingdom-building assignments. Your life is precious. Your role in the business world is extremely important. You are the vessel through which God is able to perform miracles. Only God can divinely impart revelations to you that will not only solidify your financial independence while, more importantly, enhancing the business arena and society in unimaginable ways. When you adhere to God's agenda and plans, you position yourself for achieving untold success that will bless you and others for generations to come.

But even though you serve as an important vessel for God, remember that wherever you are in the business world, regardless of your title, position, credentials, and responsibilities, you are still, and will always be, a steward over God's business. So as you progress in your profession and are blessed with extraordinary success, always remember to give God the glory (1 Corinthians 6:20; 10:31) because it's never about you.

Directives for Executing the Divine Executive Summary

Following are nine suggestions for implementing the divine executive summary for your business:

I. Make sure that you believe in God and receive Jesus Christ as your Lord and Savior.

Read and study the Bible and its instructions for receiving salvation from God through belief in Jesus Christ. Meditate on the following scriptures: John 3:16; 10:27-28; Romans 10:9-10; Matthew 6:33; Ephesians 1:13-14; 2:8-9; 1 Corinthians 15:3-4, and 1 John 1:9; 4:14-16; 5:1, 12-13. If you sincerely believe these scriptures and confess them, then you have received salvation.

Commit to the ordinance of baptism, and join and become active in a Bible-based church (Acts 2:41; Hebrews 10:25). If you need support in understanding and seeking salvation in God or honoring God in your lifestyle, reach out to a godly minister for prayer and counseling.

Immerse yourself in the Word of God daily. Keep "His commandments, His judgments, and His statutes"

(Deuteronomy 8:11). And infuse your Christian beliefs into every aspect of your life including your business endeavors.

Pray for God's guidance (Ephesians 6:18). He won't let you down. If you believe in God and are sincere in your quest to understand Him and pursue His will for your life, He will divinely place supportive people and resources to help strengthen your understanding and spiritual walk with Him. God will honor your desire to grow closer to Him, and He will give you everything you need for your magnificent journey.

2. Pray for spiritual discernment and understanding of God's executive summary, or purpose, for your life.

Pray and ask God to reveal to you what He has already planted within you and ordained for you to accomplish in life. Pay attention to His divine methods and vehicles for communicating with you through your feelings and convictions as well as through messages and confirmations relayed through individuals, books, dreams, sermons, and the Word of God. (John 14:14; 1 John 3:2).

3. Pray for God's wisdom in developing the divine executive summary, or purpose, for your business.

Follow the promptings of the Holy Spirit in drafting a divine executive summary that accurately and effectively describes your commercial concept and business model (1 Corinthians 2:10; James 1:5; Luke 4:1).

4. Draft your executive summary last.

Although the executive summary should always appear as the *first* section of your business plan, I recommend that you make it the *last* section you actually draft. The rationale behind this is to give yourself time to hear from God and for Him to reveal some of the other essential elements of His plan for your business (e.g., the divine mission and vision, situation analysis, and the marketing, operations, financial, management and organization plans, and exit strategy). Once you have a better understanding of God's purpose for your business and clarity around some of your critical goals, then you will be in a better position to develop a comprehensive business plan and provide a clear overview of it in the executive summary section of your plan. But always seek His counsel first. (Proverbs 20:18).

5. Make your executive summary brief but impactful.

Throughout the Bible, Jesus spoke in brief but extremely powerful terms and parables. Develop an executive summary that is brief but impactful. Ideally, your executive summary should be no longer than two pages. It should be informative enough for readers to understand your basic business concept and intriguing enough for them to want to read your plan, in its entirety, and ultimately support your venture (Ephesians 3:3; Mark 4:33-34).

6. Stay flexible to God's plans and timing.

Always be willing to change your plans and timing as God leads you. Sometimes we'll misunderstand God's intentions. Example: We might find ourselves pursuing one avenue for venture capital, or funding, while He is actually trying to lead us to another. At times, God will purposely change the direction for your business endeavors. But rest assured, if you stay focused on Him, He will keep you on the right track. You'll find that certain opportunities will be closed to you while others will miraculously open. Just remain flexible to His agenda and follow Him (Exodus 13:17-22).

7. Biblical coaches for implementing the divine executive summary.

The Bible relays fascinating accounts of people who prayed to understand God's executive summary, or purpose, for their lives and who ultimately accomplished what He called them to do. Clearly, the life of Jesus serves as the epitome of such a life (John 6:38; 8:12). You might also consider studying the lives of other disciples such as Mary, the mother of Jesus (Matthew 1:18-25); Moses (book of Exodus); Esther (book of Esther), David (books of First Samuel and Second Samuel), and Joseph (book of Genesis, chapters 39–50).

8. Praise God for the executive summary that He has already written for your life.

   God says: "Giving thanks is a sacrifice that truly honors Me" (Psalm 50:23, NLT). "I will bless the Lord at all times, His praise shall continually be in my mouth" (Psalm 34:1, NKJV). "Let everything that breathes sing praises to the Lord!" (Psalm 150:6, NKJV). Refer to the entire book of Psalms, which includes many powerful praises to God— many of them written by David (Psalm 71:6; 86:12; 92:1-2; 139:1-24; 150: 1-6). Rejoice in the Lord always (Philippians 4:4)!

9. Enjoy the journey!

   You are embarking on a remarkable journey as you follow God's plan for your life and for your business. Not only will you maximize your personal fulfillment and professional success, but, more importantly, you will achieve your purpose in life and be blessed with the gift of eternal salvation (Ecclesiastes 3:13; 5:18; 2 Timothy 2:10; Hebrews 5:9).

In the next chapter, we'll explore how to uncover God's divine mission and vision for your life and business. But for now, we'll end this chapter with a quote from the autobiography, Mary Kay:

> Over the years, I have found that everything seems to work out if you have your life in the proper perspective: God

first, family second, and career third. I truly believe the growth of Mary Kay Cosmetics has come about because the first thing we did was to take God as our partner. If we had not done that, I don't believe we would be where we are today.... He has blessed us...to use the wonderful God-given talents that lie within each of us. I've found that when you just let go and place yourself in God's hands, everything in your life goes right. When you try to do everything and rely on yourself, you begin to make major errors.

—Mary Kay Ash
Founder, Mary Kay Cosmetics

The Divine Mission and Vision

Then the Lord answered me and said: "Write the vision and make it plain on tablets, that he may run who reads it. For the vision is yet for an appointed time; But at the end it will speak, and it will not lie, though it tarries, wait for it; because it will surely come, it will not tarry."

Habakkuk 2: 2-3 (NKJV)

What is your mission as an individual? Does your line of business complement or negate your mission? What's the vision for your business? How does your vision connect with your legacy? Before we consider the specifics around these questions and get into our three Planning Proverbs, let's first take some time to consider: 1) The importance of mission and vision statements from a conventional business planning perspective and 2) What the Word of God says about our mission and vision as believers.

The Importance of Mission and Vision Statements

Most of us are familiar with corporate mission and vision statements and understand their roles in positioning organizations for success. Well-crafted mission and vision statements benefit organizations by communicating corporate goals and aspirations to members of the organization as well as to society at large.

The term *mission* is generally understood as one's business or calling. A mission statement typically describes the fundamental purpose, goal, or philosophy of an organization. A mission statement conveys what the company is trying to accomplish in a particular focus area such as products, services, and industry. A corporate mission statement is short term in that it communicates the primary role of the organization at the *present time*.

On the contrary, the word *vision* is generally defined as the power of seeing; discernment; something seen in the imagination, in a dream, or in one's thoughts. A vision statement describes the *long-term* aspirations of a company and offers direction for the organization by encouraging behaviors that are consistent with the achievement of the corporate mission.

Mission and vision statements communicate what the organization is doing and where it is going. Your mission and vision statements should not be mutually exclusive. Accomplishing one should not preclude achieving the other. Both should be able to coexist. Your vision statement should describe a state that is a natural progression to a Higher level of excellence from the core business focus embodied in your mission statement.

What Is Our Ultimate Mission?

Jesus is a perfect example of an individual who stayed focused on God's mission and vision for His life. Jesus followed God and the Holy Spirit as He pursued His ministry (Acts 10:38; Luke 2:46-49; 3:23; 4:18; Mathew 3:17). Just as God anointed Jesus to do His work, He will also anoint you to do yours.

Jesus tells us that just as God sent Him into the world to spread the gospel, He (Jesus) sends us into the world to spread the gospel (John 17:18; 20:21; Acts 1:8). He declares we are to "go into all the world and preach the gospel to every creature" (Mark 16:15, NKJV). Jesus informs us that our ultimate mission is as follows:

> Go therefore and make disciples of all nations, baptizing them in the name of the Father and of the Son and of the Holy Spirit, teaching them to observe all things that I have commanded you; and lo, I am with you always, even to the end of age.
>
> Mathew 28: 19-20 (NKJV)

As Christians, we are all disciples and ambassadors for Christ as well as ministers of God (2 Corinthians 5:20; 6:4). We have been crucified in Christ and no longer live for ourselves but for Him (Galatians 2:20). For us as Christian business leaders, this means that we are sent to spread the gospel of Christ in the business world. This is our ultimate, collective mission.

Understanding Your Mission and Vision as an Individual

While we have already defined the term mission, I will also refer to your individual mission as your divine calling, anointing, or personal ministry. I'll use these terms interchangeably when describing your mission.

Your purpose precedes your mission. One way to frame this connection is to remember your purpose tells you *why* you were created (i.e., to glorify God) and your mission tells you *how* you will glorify Him (e.g., through your commercial initiatives).

Just as God reveals His mission for us, He will also reveal His vision for our lives and businesses. Vision originates from God (Acts 2:17; Ezekiel 11:24-25). The Bible says that "where there is no vision, the people perish" (Proverbs 29:18, KJV). All of us must have a goal that is meaningful and exquisite to strive for—a dream, a vision.

One way to summarize the connection between *purpose*, *mission*, and *vision* is as follows:

- *Our Executive Summary or Purpose: Is to glorify God.*

- *Our Ultimate Mission: Is to spread the gospel.*

- *Your Personal Mission: Is the unique way in which you as an individual are called to use your gifts to glorify God and spread the gospel.*

- *Your Vision: Is the revelation that God gives you of who you are and what you are to accomplish for His kingdom-building purposes.*

Now you might be thinking, *Well, Shelette, that's all wonderful, but I'm still not sure what my particular mission is as an individual. How do I know what God wants me to accomplish and how my business relates to it?* Glad you asked. We'll explore the answers in the next sections.

Identifying Your Personal Mission: Begin from Within

If you have questions regarding exactly what your calling is as an individual, then the answers are easily accessible. The answers lie within you.

When you accept Jesus Christ as your Lord and Savior, God actually anoints you with the same Holy Spirit with which He anointed Jesus. "This makes it clear that our great power is from God, not from ourselves" (2 Corinthians 4:7, NLT). This is reinforced by Jesus as He declares:

> For indeed, the kingdom of God *is within you.*
>
> Luke 17:21 (NKJV)

The Bible goes on to reinforce the fact that God's Spirit lives within us, in the following passages:

- "But he who is joined to the Lord is *one spirit with Him*" (1 Corinthians 6:17, NKJV).

- "For you were bought at a price; therefore glorify God in your body and *in your spirit* which are God's" (1 Corinthians 6:20, NKJV).

- "And if the Spirit of Him who raised Jesus from the dead is living with you, He who raised Christ from the dead will also give life to your mortal bodies through His Spirit who *lives in you*" (Romans 8:11, AMP).

- "That good thing which was committed to you, keep by the Holy Spirit who *dwells in us*" (2 Timothy 1:14, NKJV).

Following are a few more thought-provoking questions:

- "Do you not know that you are the temple of God and that the Spirit of God dwells *in you?*" (1 Corinthians 3:16, NKJV).

- "Or do you not know that your body is the temple of the Holy Spirit who is *in you*, whom you have from God, and you are not your own?" (1 Corinthians 6:19, NKJV).

- "Do you not know yourselves, that Jesus Christ is *in you?*" (2 Corinthians 13:5, NKJV).

Because God's Holy Spirit resides within each one of us, we only need to look inside ourselves to God, Who resides within us, to discover our divine mission. Pray for His revelation, direction, wisdom, and power to discern the mission that He ordained for you (Proverbs 4: 4-7; Ephesians 1: 17-24; Ephesians 5: 15-17; 1 Corinthians 3:13). Now, you might wonder: *When we look within, what are some of the clues to our personal mission?*

Clues to Your Personal Mission: Your Gifts

One way to uncover your personal mission is by examining your unique gifts, or inimitable talents and innate strengths. "Every good and perfect gift is from above" (James 1:17, NIV) and "each of us has his own gift from God" (1 Corinthians 7:7, ESV). God equipped some of us "to be apostles, some prophets, some evangelists, and some pastors and teachers" (Ephesians 4:11, NKJV).

Although we are blessed with *different gifts*, we all possess the *same Spirit of God* (Romans 12:4; 6-8; 1 Corinthians 12:4-11, 27). Our gifts are "for the equipping of the saints, for the work of ministry" (Ephesians 4:12, NKJV), and we are to use each gift to "minister it to one another as good stewards of the manifold grace of God" (1 Peter 4:10, NKJV). So we must never take our gifts for granted.

In order to discover some of your God-given gifts, you might look to some of your innate talents and the areas in which you naturally excel. These are the abilities for which you constantly receive compliments. People might comment on how great you are at doing something that others may find difficult or daunting, yet it is virtually effortless and quite enjoyable for you!

Another clue to your gifts lies in your interests, intellectual passions, and hobbies. These are the activities that you love to do and that you would gladly do without being compensated for them. These are the hobbies that, while engrossed in them, time just seems to fly because you are enjoying yourself. Pray and ask God to reveal your special talents and areas of anointing, and when He does, the next step is for you to *start stirring*.

Start Stirring

The Bible encourages us to cultivate our gifts (1 Corinthians 14:1) and to not neglect but "to stir up the gift of God, which is in you" (2 Timothy 1:6, NKJV). This means that we are responsible for awakening, rekindling, and continually developing the gifts that God has given us. So start stirring!

In order to start identifying and stirring up your gifts, ask yourself the following questions:

1. What is my passion? (i.e., What excites me in life and in business?)

2. What are my gifts (e.g., natural talents, abilities, and strengths)?

3. What hobby brings me the most joy? How can this hobby be used to glorify God in the business arena?

4. What type of professional products and services interest me the most? Why?

5. What problem do I most want to solve? How can my business or profession be leveraged to offer solutions?

6. For what question is my life or business the answer? What do I feel called to do?

Obey Your Thirst

In the '90s, The Coca-Cola Company launched a national advertising campaign for brand Sprite® with the slogan: "Obey your thirst." Consumers were encouraged to be themselves, do their own thing, and follow their own intellectual and creative interests. Industry experts reported that the campaign and slogan helped to strategically position Sprite® as a brand that encourages consumers to embrace themselves as unique individuals and to obey their own personal thirst for individuality and originality.

Let's take a moment to consider your yearning or thirst as an individual. What do you love to do? What do you thirst for spiritually and intellectually? How can your thirst be leveraged in the business arena for God's glory? God tells us that He "will give of the fountain of the water of life freely to him who thirsts" (Revelation 21:6). Jesus says, "If anyone thirsts, let him come to Me and drink" (John 7:37). The only way to quench your spiritual thirst is through Him. Taste and see that the Lord is good (Psalm 34:8). Obey your thirst. Obey Him.

Your Gifts Are Irrevocable

The late author Leo Buscaglia observed: "Your talent is God's gift to you. What you do with it is your gift back to God." Once God blesses you with gifts and a divine calling, or personal mission, He does not revoke them (Romans 11:29; 1 Timothy 4:14). Unfortunately, so many of us choose to ignore our areas of gifting and anointing out of pure disobedience.

The Bible tells us that we are cursed when we do the work of the Lord negligently or deceitfully (Jeremiah 48:10). But when we are obedient in using our gifts to minister to others (1 Peter 4:10; Ephesians 4:7), our gifts will open up doors of opportunity by bringing us to the attention of influential people (Proverbs 18:16).

Do and Pursue Who You Already Are

Western ideologies and culture place an inordinate amount of focus on what we do for a living, to the point that we almost become defined by our professional occupations and titles. From an early age, we are encouraged to go to school in order to get a "good job," which usually equates to an influential position, which, in turn, equates to great stature, power, respect, prestige, and financial wealth. And most of us, myself included, fall right in line with the rest of the population, buying into this philosophy and methodology.

Many of us then go on to college and attend graduate-level business schools that teach us to excel in business by:

1. Identifying a need, or gap, in the marketplace; and then,

2. Either pursuing a profession or starting a business to fill the market need or gap.

In these ways, we are unfortunately socialized to look outside ourselves to external market opportunities and trends for our vocational pursuits. This whole social inclination and approach of assessing the external market place first and then, secondarily, matching our interests and skill sets to meet an external market niche or need is completely contrary to God's teaching. This approach leads to dissatisfaction with, and disengagement from, our professions because it does not center on our innate talents and natural interests. We need to first look internally to the God within us to understand our divine gifts, calling, anointing, and mission. And once we have a better understanding of them, then we can consider external market needs and opportunities that will facilitate our accomplishing God's will.

Search inside yourself for the gifts, interests, innate talents, and passions that God has given you and pursue them as part of your professional endeavors. This process allows you to do and pursue who you already are and who God made you to be. This is imperative for maximizing your personal fulfillment and professional success in business.

The market will follow your mission. God has already equipped you with everything you innately need to accomplish your calling (1 Corinthians 15:57; Psalm 100:3; 1 John 5:4; 2 Corinthians 5:5). Once we understand who He made us to be and what we are to accomplish with our lives and businesses, then, as Jesus tells us, "whatever you ask in My name that I will do, that the Father may be glorified in the Son" (John 14:13, NKJV).

In an interview with the *Atlanta Journal Constitution*, Christian business executive and former CEO of HomeBanc Mortgage Corporation, Patrick Flood, shares how he felt as a result of not having a profession that was aligned with his genuine interests:

> My schedule was filled with doing things that were incongruent with my first and greatest love, which was investing with people and encouraging them and enrolling them in the idea that they have something special to give to the world...I was sitting in a meeting for six hours close to accountants talking about issues that were necessary and important, but it wasn't really where my heart pounded, and I found myself estranged because of it.[10]
>
> —Patrick Flood, CEO,
> Covenant Mortgage

"To enjoy your work and accept your lot in life—this is indeed a gift from God" (Ecclesiastes 5:19, ESV). We all know that every profession comes with both positive and negative aspects, but the pros should outweigh the cons. This doesn't mean that the path will be quick and easy, but you should have a certain degree of spiritual peace with your chosen vocation and place of employment. In your career, if you don't have an overall sense of peace and feel restless, unsure, or confused, this may be God's way of telling you that you are out of His order for your life's work. "God is not the author of confusion but of peace" (1 Corinthians 14:33, NKJV; Philippians 4:7).

After looking within yourself to understand your God-given calling, you might be led by the Holy Spirit to create a business, with a mission, to help facilitate the achievement of your personal mission. This brings us to our next important point: Don't plan a business venture and ask God to anoint it; first, find out what God has anointed you to do and then plan a business around it if He so leads you.

You are God's divine creation with a special calling in life and in business. Embrace the distinct business plan that God has for you. Don't feel compelled to model your business after another or emulate your colleagues and competitors. You are in a class of your own.

Three Planning Proverbs for the Divine Mission and Vision

Now that we are grounded in both the secular and spiritual aspects of mission and vision, let's move on to the three Planning Proverbs that we'll explore in this chapter:

1. Connect the mission for your business with your mission as an individual.

2. The vision for your business is inextricably connected to your legacy.

3. Performing below God's mission and vision for your business does not advance the kingdom.

Let's proceed with the first Planning Proverb:

Connect the Mission for Your Business with Your Mission as an Individual

· ·

Biblical Guidelines for Implementing Your Mission and Vision

The book of Habakkuk provides excellent guidelines and practical suggestions for putting your God-given mission and vision into action. While the scriptures in Habakkuk refer to our vision, I believe they are also applicable to our mission and vision—for our lives and for our businesses. With this is mind, I will reference both mission and vision as we relate these scriptures to our commercial business ventures.

Let's begin with Habakkuk 2:2-3, where God provides detailed instructions for understanding and executing your mission and vision. For instance, He says that your vision is:

1. To be written down or recorded (v.2).

2. To be made plain so that others can understand it (v.2).

3. To be shared with other individuals (v.2).

4. For motivating others toward a common goal (v.2).

5. To be acted on or implemented (v.2).

6. For a specific time in the future (v.3).

7. Not to be discarded (v.3).

8.   Fail-proof (v.3).

Now, let's dig deeper into each of these scriptures and break each one down into meaningful and actionable steps that you can apply to your business today.

1.   Your vision is to be written down or recorded (v.2).

First, God tells us that our vision is to be written down or recorded. This means that a critical step for us, as business leaders, is to capture our mission and vision statements in documented formats. If you are an entrepreneur, then it's imperative that you create a mission and vision statement for your company that is aligned with your calling as an individual.

If you are an executive with a company that already has an established mission and vision statement, then it's important that you create mission and vision statements for yourself and for your team and connect them to the overall corporate mission and vision.

2.   Your vision is to be made plain so that others can understand it (v.2).

You might consider recording and documenting your corporate mission and vision statements in a myriad of ways including relaying them in your business plan, company manuals, and on your corporate website. You might also reiterate your mission and vision in your public relations and advertising campaigns.

3.   Your vision is to be shared with other individuals (v.2).

This scripture addresses an important concept in accomplishing our mission and vision: *communication*. By communicating your mission and vision with others, you increase the likelihood of you and your team successfully working toward a common goal and ultimately achieving it.

Remember to share your mission and vision with people who are both directly (e.g., stockholders and employees) and indirectly (e.g., family members and professional coaches) vested in the achievement of your business objectives. They will prove critical to your success and are an invaluable support network.

Your mission and vision should be articulated in a manner that is comprehensive but also clear, concise, and succinct so that others can easily understand them. When communicating your mission and vision, *keep it simple*.

4. Your vision is for motivating others toward a common goal (v.2).

5. Your vision is to be acted on or implemented (v.2).

These two points in Habakkuk 2:2 are interrelated and address another critical concept in achieving our mission and vision: *execution*. If you are leading an organization toward a common goal, you must share the mission and vision statement with them to the point that they not only understand it but they are also able to "run with it" or pursue and implement it.

This focus on execution is vital because so many of us are guilty of drafting mission and vision statements as part of a business plan but then filing the plan in our credenzas and not reviewing and updating or even sharing and reinforcing them with our teams periodically.

Keep your corporate mission, vision, and plans fresh, alive, and top-of-mind for you and for your team members at all times. Track your progress both qualitatively and quantitatively. There's an old adage that says you must "plan your work and work your plan," and the Bible tells us "faith without works is dead" (James 2:26, NKJV; 2:14, 18). Your achievement of God's mission and vision for your business depends on the faith and productive performance of you and your team.

If your team does not believe in or embrace the corporate mission and vision, this will negatively impact their productivity and the operational effectiveness of your entire organization. Ultimately, it will hinder the company's bottom-line profitability. Every functional team is integral to achieving the corporate mission and vision.

It is up to you, as their leader, to communicate and show them how important they are as individuals and how what they do every day actually adds value and is critical to the achievement of organizational goals. This may require that you continually reemphasize the corporate mission and vision and how they are integral to it. What would not get done if they were not there? What critical organizational supply chain or marketplace needs are they addressing just by virtue of what they do every day? Tell them. Show them. Remind them.

Don't be frustrated if you have tried these communication methods and some of your team members still do not embrace the mission and vision. While it's possible for God to change the mind-sets of people to allow them to get into agreement with your strategic direction, it's also important to realize that some people are simply in the wrong vocations and organizations.

Some of your team members may be at a point in their lives in which they are out of God's order. He may be in the process of revealing this to them and might be using you as a vehicle for accomplishing this. Trust Him. He may open up opportunities for some of the individuals to be reassigned to new positions or even to new companies.

While dismissing or firing employees is not a positive experience, when you factor God into the equation, it is sometimes the best thing that can happen to you and to the employee because it places them back on track and in alignment with God's divine plans for them. And it opens up an opportunity for you to hire someone who is passionate about your business and who will be a joyful and productive team member.

6. Your vision is for a specific time in the future (v.3).

Habakkuk 2:3 warns us that vision is for "*an appointed time.*" This suggests that the mission and vision that God has given us, for our lives and for our businesses, are for a specific, God-appointed time. We must stop focusing on our own egocentric timetable of when we *want* to accomplish things or when we *think* something should be done and begin to appreciate God's realm of timing, which is completely different from ours.

While we focus on daily results, quarterly earnings, and annual reports, God knows and sees the entire spectrum of our lives from beginning to end. He knows the perfect timing for every aspect of our lives, including our commercial endeavors, because He knows the ending to the remarkable stories of the books that represent our lives. Remember, He wrote the book!

Now this next point might be a difficult one to receive, but stay with me. It's important you realize that the full vision of what God is accomplishing through you may not be realized within the span of your lifetime.

The purpose of the vision He has given you may actually be to bless future generations. Example: God may desire for you to seed, plant, or pioneer a new commercial concept or idea. But His will may be for someone else to develop and execute it in the marketplace. In this scenario, your role is to *vet the vision* to the point that others can understand, embrace, and implement it.

An example of this is seen in the life of Moses when the Lord explained to him: "'This is the land I promised on oath to Abraham, Isaac, and Jacob... I will give it to your descendants... I have now allowed you to see it with your own eyes, but you will not enter the land'" (Deuteronomy 34:4, NLT). While God gave the vision to Moses, He gave the responsibility of accomplishing it to others.

Another good example of this is witnessed in the life of David. In the eighth chapter of 1 Kings, the Bible tells the story of David who, at the time, had a heart, or a passion and a vision, for building a temple to honor God. God acknowledges and confirms his vision by telling David that He indeed knows that it is in his (David's) heart to build a temple for Him. And He also tells David that his plan is actually commendable. However, and interestingly enough, God also tells David that this was actually all that He intended for the temple to be (i.e., in David's heart only).

God informs David that He never intended for him to *build* the temple. He only intended for David to *have a vision for it* or to pioneer the idea and seed the concept. God goes on to say that His intention is for *David's son* to build the temple. And the Lord fulfilled His Word and divine plan when David's son, Solomon, built a temple in God's name (1 Kings 8:17-20; 2 Samuel 7:12-13; 2 Chronicles 6:7-11). In this case, David had the vision, but it was up to his descendent to execute it.

7. Your vision is not to be discarded (v.3).

8. Your vision is fail-proof (v.3).

Here, we receive the best news of all! In the final two points of Habakkuk 2:3, the Lord tells us not to discard or give up and abandon our mission and vision, because if we wait on them, they will certainly come to pass or come to fruition. *Hallelujah!*

When God gives you the mission and vision, He also gives you the *provision* that you need to accomplish them (Psalm 37:5). He will give you all of the necessary resources—both tangible (e.g., professional contacts and financial resources) and intangible (e.g. grace and favor)—to make what you envision a reality. Just as "Jesus increased in wisdom, stature, and favor with God and men" (Luke 2:52, NKJV), the same can and will happen for you and me.

Trust God's infinite provisioning and allow the Spirit of God to work through you (Matthew 10:19-20).

When God gives us a vision, He not only supplies the provision, but He actually goes ahead of us to prepare a way for us to accomplish His will (Exodus 23:20; Matthew 11:10; Isaiah 45:2-3). Just as God strategically placed a mysterious man to help Joshua lead the children of Israel (Joshua 1:1-9; 5:13-15), He will also go ahead of us to place people and resources to help us on our journeys.

Once you understand God's mission and vision for your business, the process of identifying the right goals, objectives, strategies, and tactics for your business plan becomes less of a challenge because you realize that you are already anointed to accomplish them. Whatever God calls you to do, pursue it wholeheartedly with the confidence that you will achieve it "for He who promised *is* faithful" (Hebrews 10:23, NKJV; Numbers 23:19). As Jesus says, "Because of your faith it will happen" (Matthew 9:29).

Honoring Your Spiritual Calling in a Commercial Environment

What are some of the practical ways that you can honor your spiritual calling in a commercial environment? How do you connect your personal mission with your employer's corporate mission? In order to give you some creative ideas that you can apply to your own situation, I'll provide you with an example.

Imagine you are currently a finance manager within the research and development department of a major corporation. You know that your overarching *purpose* is to glorify God. Let's say that you also know that your *personal mission* is to teach and educate others although you often find yourself working solo, crunching the numbers. And you know that the current *corporate mission* of your department is to create new innovative products for the company each year.

In this case, with your employer's permission, there are a number of tactics that you could employ to help you align your personal mission and passion for teaching and educating with the departmental or business mission of product development and innovation. For instance, you might consider:

- Developing and teaching a financial planning workshop, tailored to R&D managers, to offer insights on the financial implications and ramifications of product development initiatives.

- Serving as a liaison to other internal departments in educating them about the bottom-line impact of R&D initiatives and how teams can work together in support of corporate innovation.

- Producing newsletters to educate team members on financial stewardship and share best practices.

- Teaching a lunch-hour Bible study for employees.

These are just a few tactical examples of ways to honor God and your divine calling and spiritual gifts within the context of your employer's corporate mission. Consider your own situation, pray, and brainstorm creative strategies and tactics of your own. This will help you avoid vocational burnout, and it will help position you for maximizing your personal fulfillment and professional success in business.

The Dangers of Operating
Outside of Your Personal Mission

I believe that the single most common source of job and career dissatisfaction, particularly among those of us in Western society, is the pursuit of a profession that is not in alignment with one's God-given mission or calling. People who are the most frustrated with their professions are typically those who are trying to make a living by doing something they are not anointed to do. I always say, "Business people don't plan to fail; they simply fail to follow God's plan."

We are usually called and anointed for a specific discipline or functional area of business such as administration, management, sales, advertising, marketing, finance, and operations. But sometimes we pursue another area of business that we perceive to be more prestigious or financially rewarding. Because our motives are wrong and we are operating out of purely selfish desires and worldly interests as opposed to following God's plan, we become unfulfilled, resentful, frustrated, and ultimately unsuccessful. This occurs because there is no spiritual connection between your professional pursuits and what God ordained as your personal mission. In effect, you are operating outside of God's will and are not in alignment with what He ordained for you.

When you try to operate outside of God's will for your life and business, you're on your own! When you attempt to function outside of your personal mission, gifting, and calling, you begin operating from a position of *weakness* as opposed to a position of *divine strength* and innate ability.

When you try to be someone who God did not create you to be or achieve something that God did not ordain, you actually place yourself in a predicament in which you will constantly have to rely on your own human capabilities and the finite resources of man (i.e., other people) to accomplish and maintain your goals. Consequently, your life and business become a constant struggle and you lack peace, joy, fulfillment, and success. Your goal should be to position yourself to always have access to the divine guidance and infinite resources of almighty God.

The Signs of Operating Outside of Your Personal Mission

If you are in a business that is not remotely related to God's mission for your life, you will find that your work is neither personally fulfilling nor fruitful, and this will cause you to feel constantly frustrated. Your lack of peace and joy in your occupation may actually be signs from God to let you know that you are operating outside of His will. This may be His way of waving spiritual red flags that signal: Stop! Warning! Change course!

When you are operating in a profession that is outside of God's calling for you, usually you are not being spiritually and personally fulfilled and you are not enriching the lives of others in significant and positive ways. Also, you might find that it is quite easy for you to abandon the profession altogether without any sense of loss or disappointment. If you find yourself in this predicament, then it's time for you to pray and perhaps make some significant changes in your life. You are wasting your time on earth. You are dishonoring yourself, your family, your colleagues, the business community, and society in general. But more importantly, you are dishonoring God.

Don't spend your time in a profession that is neither fulfilling nor gratifying (Isaiah 55:2). If you are an employee, then your personal mission and vision should be complementary with, not contradictory to, your employer's mission and vision. Pray and ask God to guide you in making career moves that are in alignment with your calling.

God will use His divine resources to provide you with wisdom and opportunity. He'll speak to you through a myriad of vehicles, including His Word; people; books; sermons; your own thoughts, dreams (Genesis: 20:3-7; Acts 2:17; Job 33:15-20), and visions (Daniel 7:1-28), as well as through the "still small voice" (1 Kings 19:12-13) that we hear from within guiding us in the right direction. He may lead you to explore other jobs, careers, companies, industries, or even entrepreneurship or advanced educational pursuits. And the good news is that this process doesn't have to take a long time (Malachi 3:1)!

God didn't send His innocent Son to teach, liberate, and emancipate us and then sacrifice His life on the cross and raise Him from the dead three days later just so that we could be miserable for most of our waking hours! Remember, He sent His Son so that you and I would lead abundant, Spirit-filled lives—and this includes our *professional lives*.

Is It Possible to Have More Than One Personal Mission?

You might be wondering whether or not it's possible to have more than one personal mission or calling. Well, we know that all things are possible with God (Matthew 19:26; Mark 9:23, 10:27). If you feel that God has given you multiple ministries or areas of calling, then you are well able and well equipped to fulfill them (Exodus 35:31; 36:1) because He gives talents to each of us according to our own individual ability, calling, and ministry (Matthew 25:14; 1 Corinthians 7:17-20; Psalm 86:11; Acts 20:24).

I believe that we each have a core ministry, or calling, but that it can actually take on different variations during different seasons or appointed times in our lives. I also believe that we have a number of activities that we can do well. But it is within the realm of our core ministry and genuine, God-ordained calling that we begin to bear substantial fruit, or godly results, and actually *excel*. Excellence is the distinguishing factor, and it can be difficult to truly excel in a number of different disciplines.

Preparing Yourself for Achieving Your Mission and Vision

We must prepare ourselves spiritually, emotionally, mentally, and physically for accomplishing our divine mission and vision. Spiritually, we must put on the armor of God so that we can withstand evil (Ephesians 6:10-18). This includes the spiritual armor of salvation, peace, prayer, faith, and fasting as well as reading and studying the Bible daily.

Strengthen yourself emotionally by making time for people and activities that bring you joy. Fellowship with other Christians, and become an active member of a Bible-based church. Do your best to manage stress by keeping your priorities in the right order: Keep God first in your life, followed by family, friends, career, or business. If you are struggling in this area, reach out to a minister or a wise and godly professional counselor for support (Proverbs 20:18; 11:14).

Challenge yourself mentally. Never stop learning. Cultivate new interests by enrolling in classes and attending cultural and educational functions that are outside of your area of expertise. Finally, take good care of your physical body (1 Corinthians 6:19). See health care professionals on a consistent basis and ask them for advice on preventive care and for a healthcare program that is customized for you and your lifestyle. Follow a daily regimen that includes a nutritional diet, physical exercise, rest, and relaxation to ensure that you are in the best possible shape for God to use you in accomplishing His divine mission and vision for your life.

Real-Life Examples: Successful Companies with Mission and Vision Statements that Glorify God

For us as Christian business leaders, the mission and vision for our businesses should always be for a Higher purpose that will enhance society and ultimately exalt God. But here's a key point to keep in mind:

> You don't necessarily have to use biblical terminology in your corporate name, philosophy, mission, and vision statements for them to glorify God. They simply need to exemplify and reinforce His principles and teachings, not contradict them.

The former chairman of the ServiceMaster Company, C. William Pollard, sums up the importance of taking your business mission and vision to a Higher level with the following observation: "If the firm does not have a moral reference point, it has the potential to contribute to the bankruptcy of the human soul."[11]

Fortunately, there are still business leaders around who understand and appreciate the importance of having a moral compass for their organizations and who are not afraid to acknowledge God publicly in their corporate philosophy and statements of purpose, mission, and vision.

Chick-fil-A

Chick-fil-A is a $3.5 billion privately owned restaurant chain with over 1,300 locations in the U.S. Founded by Truett Cathy almost sixty years ago, Chick-fil-A is now the nation's second-largest quick-service chicken restaurant chain based on annual sales. Yet, even with all of their success in the marketplace, as stated on their corporate website: "From the beginning, the first priority for Truett and Chick-fil-A has never been just to serve chicken. It's to serve a Higher calling…we're here to serve…and not just sandwiches." Chick-fil-A publicizes their purpose and mission as follows:

Chick-fil-A Corporate Statement of Purpose:

"We exist to glorify God by being a faithful steward of all that is entrusted to us and to have a positive influence on all who come in contact with Chick-fil-A."

Chick-fil-A Corporate Mission Statement:

"Be America's Best Quick-Service Restaurant"

In these ways, the leaders of Chick-fil-A make no qualms about to Whom they belong and why they exist. Let's break down the key elements of their statements and explore the ways in which they reinforce godly principles:

- "We exist to glorify God."

  This reinforces our purpose as Christians, which is to glorify God so that we "may be called trees of righteousness, the planting of the Lord, that He may be glorified" (Isaiah 61:3, NKJV).

- "Being a faithful steward of all that is entrusted to us."

  This supports the biblical teaching that "all things were created through Him and for Him" (Colossians 1:16, NKJV). So we are to be faithful stewards over all that God has given us (Matthew 25:23).

- "Have a positive influence on all who come in contact with Chick-fil-A."

  This aligns with the teachings of Jesus Christ that we "are the light of the world" and are to let our light shine "before men, that they may see your good works and glorify your Father in heaven" (Matthew 5:14-16, NKJV).

- "Be America's Best Quick-Service Restaurant."

  This reinforces God's teachings that we are to pursue excellence in all that we do (Philippians 1:10) and strive to show the world "a more excellent way" (1 Corinthians 12:31, NKJV; Romans 2:18) because we are working for the Lord and not for men (Colossians 3:23).

Republic Airways

Republic Airways, based in Indianapolis, Indiana, is an airline holding company that owns Chautauqua Airlines, Frontier Airlines, Lynx Aviation, Midwest Airlines, Republic Airlines, and Shuttle America. Reflecting the sentiments of Genesis 1:27 (NKJV), which describes how "God created man in His own image," the Republic Airways vision statement is as follows:

> We believe that every employee, regardless of personal beliefs or world-view, has been created in the image and likeness of God. We seek to become stronger from our diversity. We seek personal respect and fulfillment from

our work. Most of all, we seek to recognize the dignity and potential of each member of our Republic Airways Holdings family.

ServiceMaster Company

The $3 billion ServiceMaster Company controls many well-known brands such as ServiceMaster Clean, Merry Maids, TruGreen, and Terminix. On their corporate website, they are forthright in acknowledging that their company was built on a biblical foundation. Each of the company's publicized objectives correlates to a number of biblical principles. For instance:

- To honor God in all we do.

  This relates to 1 Peter 1:15-16 (NKJV): "But just as he who called you is holy, so be holy in all you do for it is written: 'Be holy, because I am holy.'"

- To help people develop.

  This alludes to Hebrews 6:10 (NIV): "God is not unjust; He will not forget your work and the love you have shown him as you have helped His people and continue to help them."

- To pursue excellence.

  This reflects Romans 2:18 (NKJV): "And know His will, and approve the things that are excellent, being instructed out of the law." And 1 Corinthians 12:31 (NKJV): "But earnestly desire the best gifts. And yet I show you a more excellent way."

- To grow profitably.

This aligns with Proverbs 14:23 (NLT): "All hard work brings a profit, but mere talk leads only to poverty."

AES Corporation

Business Week featured an insightful interview with Dennis Bakke, who, at the time, was CEO of the $12 billion AES Corporation. Bakke describes how he and his business partner, Roger W. Sant, founded the company in 1981 and based it on the following unique philosophy: "First, people should be trusted. Second, businesses don't exist to make money. They exist to serve."[12]

Their corporate philosophy is centered on serving others, which is in alignment with God's teaching that each of us is a "servant of the Lord" (Judges 2:7-8) and that He has called us to serve one another (Galatians 5:13).

Timberland

In the book, *The Business of Changing the World: Twenty Great Leaders on Strategic Corporate Philanthropy*, Timberland, the $1.6 billion global leader in the design and marketing of premium-quality footwear, apparel, and accessories, is highlighted as one of several progressive companies.

Timberland president and CEO, Jeffrey Swartz, states: "The notion of interdependence—that you are your brother's or sister's keeper—was always part of our business model."[13] In this way, the description of Timberland's corporate philosophy alludes to Genesis 4:9 in which the Lord questions Cain as to where his brother, Abel, is, and Cain answers, saying, "Am I my brother's keeper?"

Timberland's corporate website relays their mission as follows:

> Our mission is to equip people to make a difference in their world. We do this by creating outstanding products and by trying to make a difference in the communities where we live and work.

Timberland's reference to "making a difference in their world" equates to the biblical references of being the light of the world by being a shining example of God (Matthew 5:14; John 9:5). Also, Timberland's focus on "creating outstanding products" aligns with God's teachings on the importance of performing "good works" (Ephesians 2:10; Titus 3:8).

Hewitt Associates

Hewitt Associates, a $2 billion publicly traded company that was founded in 1940, is one of the world's foremost providers of human resources outsourcing and consulting services. Hewitt Associates relays their mission, via their corporate website, as follows:

> "To make the world a better place to work, our organization is guided by three fundamental objectives:

- To serve our clients exceptionally well;
- To enhance associate engagement;
- To strengthen our business."

In this way, the company's mission statement is focused on serving and improving, which reflect God's commandment to "serve wholeheartedly, as if you were serving the Lord, not men" (Ephesians 6:7, NLT).

Hobby Lobby

Another powerful mission statement comes from the $1 billion Hobby Lobby, which operates creative craft centers nationally in thirty-two states. Hobby Lobby communicates their statement of purpose as follows:

> In order to effectively serve our owners, employees, and customers the Board of Directors is committed to:
>
> • Honoring the Lord in all we do by operating the company in a manner consistent with biblical principles.
>
> • Offering our customers an exceptional selection and value.
>
> • Serving our employees and their families by establishing a work environment and company policies that build character, strengthen individuals, and nurture families.
>
> • Providing a return on the owners' investments, sharing the Lord's blessings with our employees, and investing in our community.
>
> • We believe that it is by God's grace and provision that Hobby Lobby has endured. He has been faithful in the past, we trust Him for our future.

Interstate Battery System of America, Inc.

The $650 million Dallas-based Interstate Battery System of America, Inc. states their company's mission as:

> To glorify God as we supply our customers worldwide with top quality, value-priced batteries, related electrical power-source products, and distribution services. Further, our mission is to provide our partners and Interstate Batteries System of America, Inc. (IBSA) with opportunities that are profitable, rewarding and growth-oriented.
>
> To treat others as we want to be treated: treating all our business associates with respect, fairness, and integrity; caring for and listening to them; professionally serving them; always being a model of working hard and striving toward excellence.

Auntie Anne's, Inc.

Auntie Anne's, Inc., the $252 million Pennsylvania-based franchisor that supports over 925 Auntie Anne's Pretzels locations worldwide, also glorifies God in their corporate purpose and philosophy. In the book, *Executive Influence*,[14] Anne Beiler, the founder of the company, shares the corporate statement of purpose, which they commonly refer to by the acronym LIGHT:

- Lead by example

- Invest in employees

- Give freely

- Honor God

- Treat all business contacts with integrity

Now that we've explored the importance of connecting the mission for your business with your mission as an individual, let's move on to our second Planning Proverb.

The Vision for Your Business Is Inextricably Connected to Your Legacy

· · · · · · · · · · · · · · · · · · · ·

You Don't Need Sight to Have Vision

Helen Keller, the famous blind author and activist, was once asked if there is anything worse than being blind. She responded by saying, "It is terrible to have sight and no vision." In other words, it would be a tragedy to have natural eyesight yet have no clear spiritual direction, destination, or long-term goals and aspirations for your life.

Although Helen Keller did not have natural eyesight, she still had a remarkable vision for her life. While her point was first shared decades ago, it still remains relevant today: You do not need sight to have vision. In business, divine vision compels you to take your business in a certain direction. Like the Apostle Paul, we must also press toward the divine goal and vision to which we are called (Philippians 3:12-14).

Another good example of a person who stayed focused on the vision God gave him is seen in the life of Abraham. The Bible tells us that "by faith Abraham obeyed when he was called to go out to the place where he would receive an inheritance…and he went out, not knowing where he was going" (Hebrews 11:8, NKJV).

Abraham followed God's instruction even though he had no idea where God was taking him. And more importantly, Abraham's obedience to God resulted in blessings for multitudes of future generations of people long after he died (Hebrews 11:12). Just as God guided Abraham, He will also guide you toward the vision He has for your business.

The Connection between Vision and Legacy

As you make progress in pursuing the divine vision for your business, you also become more strongly positioned to inherit the promises of God. And when you inherit His promises, you also leave blessings for others that last long after you are gone (Hebrews 6:17-18). These residual blessings form the foundation of legacy—your legacy as an individual and the legacy of your business.

Legacy is generally defined as an inheritance or anything handed down from an ancestor or predecessor. Your legacy is what others will *inherit* as a result of your life and business. A legacy can include tangibles (e.g., real estate) and intangibles (e.g., ethics). And depending on your level of obedience to God, your legacy may be one of blessings or curses (Deuteronomy 30:19; Isaiah 46:11). Make sure you equip and position yourself to leave a legacy of blessings.

Performing below God's Mission and Vision for Your Business Does Not Advance the Kingdom

Performing below God's mission and vision for your business does not advance the kingdom. God gives us the power to accomplish our work, and He is able to do exceedingly above and beyond all that we can think or ask (Ephesians 3:20; Isaiah 26:12). As stewards over His enterprises, we have a High calling. Honoring God's kingdom mandates requires that we perform at a Higher level than our colleagues and competitors. We are to "walk worthy" of our calling and show the world "a more excellent way" (1 Corinthians 12:31, NKJV; Romans 2:18; Ephesians 4:1; 2 Peter 1:3; Philippians 1:10-11). And excellence is simply doing your best.

God's Agenda

God has His own agenda for calling us to accomplish extraordinary goals (Ephesians 3:20). The Bible tells us that one aspect of God's agenda is that He will call us to accomplish extremely difficult goals so that we, and everyone else, will know that they could have only been accomplished by Him working through us.

Furthermore, in order to make His plan even more illuminating, God will purposely choose the least likely candidates to achieve a particular mission and vision. Remember how God chose and anointed David, the youngest of his brothers and a mere sheepherder, to be king? The Bible reveals:

> But God has chosen the foolish things of the world to put to shame the wise, and God has chosen the weak things of the world to put to shame the things which are mighty; and the base things of the world and the things which are despised God has chosen, and the things which are not, to bring to nothing the things that are, so that no flesh should glory in His presence. 1 Corinthians 1:27-29, NKJV)

Let's break down the four key points of this scripture. It tells us God will deliberately choose:

1. People who the world considers *foolish* to put so-called *wise* people to shame by proving them wrong.

2. People who the world considers *weak* to put the supposedly *strong* people to shame by proving them wrong.

3. People who the world considers *lowly, insignificant, and worthless* "*nobodies*" to put the purported *influential people* or "*somebodies*" to shame by proving them wrong.

    And God does this so that:

4. We have to depend on Him and not on any human being so *only He will get the glory*.

I once heard a television evangelist say, "God doesn't call the equipped; He equips the called." God uses ordinary people to do extraordinary things. So "that they may see and know, and consider and understand together, that the hand of the Lord has done this, and the holy One of Israel has created it" (Isaiah 41:20, NKJV). God is not focused on your ability and disability; He's focused on your *availability*. God doesn't require *perfect* people to do His perfect work. He only requires *willing* people (Mark 8:34). God is an equal opportunity employer to those who obey Him, saying, "Here am I! Send me" (Isaiah 6:8, NKJV).

No Limits

It's never too early or too late to manifest what God ordained for you. Regardless of your circumstances, you are still in prime position to achieve His vision for your life and for your business. Now, you may be saying, "That's all well and good, Shelette, but I'm middle-aged, married, with three kids in college, a mortgage, and two car payments."

Or you might be lamenting, "I'm a Hispanic woman who's completely fed up with the constant battle against racism and sexism in corporate America." Or, you may be saying, "But I'm a single parent whose every minute is accounted for with children, household chores, and work-related responsibilities. How can I possibly attain the awesome vision God has given me?"

These are all common situations that include valid concerns. Each case is unique in that they highlight different personal and professional challenges. However, all of these scenarios are the same in one respect: they each attempt to place limitations on a limitless God.

Stop placing limitations on a limitless, all-powerful God. "He does great things too marvelous to understand. He performs countless miracles" (Job 5:9). Stop putting shackles on yourself. We are all guilty of doing this, and it's been going on for centuries (Psalm 78:41). You are never too young or too old to accomplish your personal mission and vision. Example: Jesus, Joseph, and David were all around thirty years old when God appointed them to their formal, public ministry (Luke 3:23; Genesis 41:46; 2 Samuel 5:4).

When God told Jeremiah that He ordained him to be a prophet to the nations, Jeremiah's immediate response was that he was too young and the Lord reprimanded him for using his youth as an excuse (Jeremiah 1:6-8). Paul coached his protégé Timothy on this same topic by telling him not to let anyone look down on him because he is young (1 Timothy 4:12).

Moses was eighty years old when God called Him into his personal mission (Exodus 7:1-13). But when God asked him to share his testimony with others, Moses responded by telling God how he stutters and stammers and can't speak eloquently. God reminded Moses that it is He who grants the ability to speak, hear, and see (Exodus 4:1-17). He asked Moses, "Has my arm lost its power? Now you will see whether or not my word comes true!" (Numbers 11:23, NLT).

Fast forward a few centuries and we find that Colonel Harland Sanders was sixty-five years old when he founded Kentucky Fried Chicken. And Ray Croc started the McDonald's restaurant franchise at the age of fifty-nine.

Too often we place self-imposed confinements on ourselves by saying, "But I'm just _____." You fill in the blank (e.g., I'm just a high school graduate; an administrative assistant; single parent; blue-collar worker, etc.) There is no "But I'm just" in God's realm. What you are is just a child of the Most High God!

Think Outside the Box

God is concerned with our hearts, or our thoughts and intentions, and not with our outward appearances (1 Samuel 16:7). So we must think outside the proverbial box of gender roles, racial concepts, cultural stereotypes, religious paradigms, social constructs, economic barriers, and political obstacles. "Is anything too hard for the Lord?" (Genesis 18:14, NKJV; Jeremiah 32:27). Of course not. God resides in eternity, and His reach transcends infinity. There are no limits with God; therefore, you can be:

- Humble and powerful

- Youthful and wise

- Elderly and thriving

- Gorgeous and brilliant

- Female and mighty

- Sensitive and strong

- Ethnic and exquisite

- Compassionate and competitive

- Ambitious and sanctified

- Wealthy and godly

- Poor and prominent

- Blind and a visionary

Indeed. There is no "glass ceiling" with God. When we walk in all that God ordained for us, we begin to shift the world's limited definitions and paradigms by introducing them to the truth of what can actually be with, and through, the power of God. Expand your vision. Think outside the box.

Self-Efficacy and Self-Actualization through God

Norman Cousins, the late journalist and author, observed that: The tragedy of life is not death; rather, it is what we allow to die within us while we live.

What dreams do you need to actualize in order to live a life of no regrets? What do you need to do to reach your full potential? These questions allude to the concepts of *self-efficacy* and *self-actualization*.

Self-efficacy is generally defined as the belief that one has the power to impact change and control their environments. *Self-actualization*, as defined by Abraham Maslow in his renowned psychological theory, Maslow's Hierarchy of Needs, is referred to as the highest form of human development or the state of reaching one's fullest potential.

I propose we take both concepts to a Higher level and place them within the context of an omnipotent, omniscient, and omnipresent God without whom we can do *nothing*. Phenomenal vision precedes extraordinary achievement, but so few of us are willing to take accountability and responsibility for what God has called us to achieve. As Jesus tells us, "Many are called, but few chosen" (Matthew 20:16, NKJV); "the harvest truly is plentiful, but the laborers are few" (Matthew 9:37, NKJV; Luke 10:2). It is only by submitting ourselves to God's plan that we will reach our maximum potential as individuals.

God May Want to Do Something New Through You

The Lord may desire to do a "new thing" (Isaiah 43:19, NKJV; Habakkuk 1:5) in the business world through you. It's easy for us to assume that this new thing is for only our benefit, but it may be for the benefit of a department, company, industry, nation, bloodline, or even a generation.

This notion of doing something the world has never seen may seem outlandish to us, but this is only because we fail to realize the power of our own significance as God's vessels (Acts 17:25-27; Isaiah 52:11; 64:8). If you find yourself with a God-given vision that is extremely innovative, don't worry and don't be afraid. When others don't encourage you, be like David and encourage yourself (1 Samuel 30:6). "For, eyes have not seen, ears have not heard, and minds have not conceived the things God has prepared for those who love Him" (1 Corinthians 2: 9, NIV).

Refuse to Rob Others

The Bible says that when we enlarge the place of our tent, stretch out the curtains of our dwellings, lengthen our cords, and strengthen our stakes, we will then expand to the right and to the left and our descendents will inherit nations and be blessed (Isaiah 54:1-3; Genesis 28:13-15). Similarly, in order to fulfill our God-given vision, we must expand our mental models and perspectives. We must strengthen our faith so that we can serve as vehicles for God's miraculous work. And when we do this, we motivate and liberate others to walk in their predestiny all because we were bold enough to walk in ours.

Don't get too comfortable or complacent with your current lot in life when you know that you were created to achieve more. Rise to your magnificence. There are people who are living in spiritual darkness but are watching you and waiting to witness God's miraculous work in your life so that they may come to know Him and be emancipated. They are waiting for you to fulfill your divine vision so that they can walk in theirs. Refuse to rob others of this tremendous blessing. Understand and acknowledge your kingdom role. Play your role and play it well.

Favorable Conditions

Don't wait for all of life's conditions to be favorable before you step out on faith and pursue your divine vision. We live in a dynamic society. If we wait for a utopian environment, you and I will never achieve what God has ordained for us (Ecclesiastes 11:4).

Also, don't wait until the people closest to you begin to understand and appreciate your God-given vision. When Jesus told His mother that He had to be about His Father's business, the Bible says that even His mother and the other adults who heard Him "did not understand the statement which He spoke to them" (Luke 2:50, NKJV).

The Bible says: So what if the people around you don't understand or believe in your vision (Romans 3:3-4)? This has no impact on the power of God! Their faithlessness doesn't nullify God's faithfulness! If God is for you, who can be against you (Romans 8:31)? The Bible says that the Lord will withhold no good thing from those who do what is right (Psalm 84:11). "Arise, shine; for your light has come! And the glory of the Lord is risen upon you" (Isaiah 60:1, NKJV) because you have been raised up "for such a time as this" (Esther 4:14, NKJV).

Don't Settle for Less Than God's Best

When you pursue *less* than God's vision for your life and business, you are doing a profound disservice to yourself and to others; more importantly, you are being disobedient to God. Settling for less than God's best will cause you to feel regret and possibly, at the end of your days, to wonder what your life could have been had you followed God's plan.

Because of the personal commitment and the pursuit of vision of numerous pioneers, the lives of countless persons have been forever enhanced in profound ways. Consider these visionaries and trailblazers: Plato, Michelangelo, Shakespeare, Rembrandt, Issac Newton, Bach, Beethoven, Mozart, Henry David Thoreau, Susan B. Anthony, Florence Nightingale, Louis Pasteur, Thomas Edison, Booker T. Washington, Henry Ford, George Washington

Carver, Madam C.J. Walker, Orville and Wilbur Wright, W.E.B. DuBois, Mahatma Gandhi, Mary McLeod Bethune, Albert Einstein, Amelia Earhart, Ernest Hemingway, Walt Disney, Ray Kroc, Rosa Parks, Nelson Mandela, Billy Graham, John H. Johnson, Alex Haley, Truett Cathy, Shirley Chisholm, Dr. Martin Luther King Jr., Gloria Steinem, Kenneth Chennault, Oprah Winfrey, Bill Gates, and Barack Obama.

All of these individuals have served as vehicles of unique and inspired contributions to the world. And I would venture to say that most of them, in the early stages of their lives, had no idea how much of a positive impact and sustaining imprint they would have on the world. Many people who lived during and after them have, and will, become emancipated, liberated, and blessed because of their thirst for purpose and quest for vision.

You may be asking yourself, *Who am I to have such an extraordinary vision from God? Why me?* My response is: Why not you? Who are you *not* to have such an extraordinary vision? You are a child of the Most High God! Who else is better equipped and able to carry out God's phenomenal kingdom vision for the business world than one of His own children? If not you, then who?

Jesus encouraged His disciples to go out into the deep water (Luke 5:4). What is your deep water? What will be your extraordinary contribution to the world at large or to the business arena in particular? Helen Keller said, "One can never consent to creep when one feels an impulse to soar." For us as Christian business leaders, operating within the realm of sub-excellence is simply unacceptable.

In an excerpt from Marianne Williamson's insightful and inspirational book, *A Return to Love*, she eloquently captures the sentiment that performing below God's vision for your life and business does not advance the kingdom when she asserts:

Our deepest fear is not that we are inadequate.
Our deepest fear is that we are powerful beyond measure.
It is our light, not our darkness, that most frightens us…[15]

Keep Raising the Bar

"Whatever you do, do it all for the glory of God" (1 Corinthians 10:31, NKJV). Romans 12:11 instructs us to never be slothful in business but to be fervent in spirit, serving the Lord. Stay true to your calling and steadfast in your efforts to achieve what God has purposed for you. After you have the job, envision a career. After you have the career, envision an empire. After you have the empire, envision a nation. Go ahead and patent your invention; start the ministry; write the book!

Go forth with your kingdom-building business initiatives. Run your race and run it well (1 Corinthians 9:24). Prepare to pass the baton of wise corporate governance, principled planning, entrepreneurial excellence, and corporate social responsibility to future generations of business leaders who will continue running the race long after your days on earth have ended. For Jesus said:

Most assuredly, I say to you, he who believes in Me, the works that I do he will do also; and greater works than these he will do, because I go to My Father. And whatever you ask in My name, that I will do, that the Father may be glorified in the Son. If You ask anything in My name, I will do it.

John 14:12-14 (NKJV)

In this statement, Jesus tells us that, through His sovereign power, we are not only able to do what He has done but greater works than these we will do if we believe. Amen.

Directives for Executing the Divine Mission and Vision

Following are six suggestions for implementing the divine mission and vision for your business:

1. Create your own personal mission and vision statement.

    Pray and ask God to reveal His mission and vision for your life through Jesus Christ (John 14:6). Consider keeping a journal of the insights and ideas that the Lord gives you. As you become more aware of your calling, take time to create a personal mission and vision statement for yourself. Mine are as follows:

    My mission is to take business to the Highest level by creating empowering products and services to help business leaders connect their business plans with God's purpose and plan for their lives so that they maximize their personal fulfillment and professional success.

    My vision is to become the worldwide leader in empowering business leaders with products and services for achieving their spiritual goals and individual purpose in cadence with their professional objectives and business imperatives.

2. Connect your personal mission and vision statement with the mission and vision for your business.

If you are a business owner, make sure your personal mission and vision complement the mission and vision for your business. If you are an employee, make sure your personal mission and vision align spiritually and philosophically with your employer's mission and vision. If your spiritual calling is not in alignment with your professional endeavors, ask God for wisdom in connecting them (Colossians 1:9; James 1:5)

3. Communicate your corporate mission and vision.

Make sure that you effectively communicate your corporate business mission and vision to key internal constituencies (e.g., employees and board members) and external constituencies (e.g., customers and suppliers). Refer back to the second chapter of Habakkuk for instructions in doing this (Habakkuk 2:2-3).

4. Establish SMART business objectives.

The Holy Spirit leads you in identifying the right goals, objectives, strategies, and tactics to fulfill the path that God has ordained for you (Proverbs 3:5-6). As you identify your professional objectives, make sure that they are SMART, which is the commonly used acronym for:

- *Specific* (i.e., be precise about what you intend to achieve)

- *Measurable* (i.e., ensure that your objectives are quantifiable)

- *Attainable* (i.e., make sure that your goals are achievable)

- *Realistic* (i.e., confirm that your objective is one that you are willing and able to pursue)

- *Time-bound* (i.e., identify the timeframe or deadline for achieving the stated objective)

Example: A SMART objective might be: To gain 25 percent of the U.S. market for designer handbags by December 31, 2020.

5. Biblical references of coaches who embraced their divine mission and vision include a number of God's apostles such as Jesus, David, Ruth, Joseph, Esther, and John. The book of Jonah offers a fascinating account of the consequences of trying to avoid the mission and vision God gives you.

6. Pursue the divine mission and vision God has given you, and praise Him for them (Proverbs 19:15; 20:4; Habakkuk 3:18-19; John 2:5)!

In the next chapter, we'll discuss how to achieve God's mission and vision for your life and business in an ever-changing world.

The greater danger for most of us lies not in setting our aim too high and falling short; but in setting our aim too low, and achieving our mark.

—Michelangelo

III

The Divine Situation Analysis

Now may the Lord of peace Himself give you his peace at all times and in every situation. The Lord be with you all.

2 Thessalonians 3:16 (ESV)

How do we accomplish our mission and vision in the midst of an ever-changing marketplace and intense competition? As business professionals, we know that when developing a business plan, it's important to have a thorough understanding of the external threats and opportunities facing our business as well as the internal strengths and weaknesses that are inherent to our organizations. This assessment is included within the section of the business plan commonly referred to as the situation analysis.

The purpose of the *situation analysis* is to position a business for success by identifying key external trends and internal factors that may impact a company either positively or negatively. This section of a business plan is also sometimes referred to as the situation assessment, market analysis, competitive analysis, or industry outlook. But for our purposes, we'll refer to it as the situation analysis.

A comprehensive situation analysis includes the social, political, economic, and organizational factors potentially affecting a business and usually covers such topics as industry and market trends, competitive landscape, regulatory environment, new technology, and company culture.

Most of us wouldn't dream of starting a business without first conducting a thorough analysis to help insure commercial viability. Many of us have been taught how to assess our business models, the market, and competitive threats in an effort to predict the probability of commercial success.

Most of us are familiar with the SWOT framework, which was introduced in the late 1960s by Edmund P. Learned, C. Roland Christiansen, Kenneth Andrews, and William Guth in the book *Business Policy, Text and Cases*. SWOT, an acronym for strengths, weaknesses, opportunities, and threats, is still a popular framework used by organizations to help dimensionalize the strengths and weaknesses of their internal organizations as well as the opportunities and threats of the external marketplace.

Many of us have also leveraged the groundbreaking contributions of Michael Porter, one of the world's leading authorities on the competitive strategy of companies and countries. Porter's innovative "Five Forces" model for industry analysis helps managers determine the type of market force posing the greatest threat to a company. Examples of these forces include rivalry among competitors, barriers to market entry, the threat of substitute products and services, and the bargaining power of buyers and suppliers.

Three Planning Proverbs for the Divine Situation Analysis

An accurate and comprehensive situation analysis can help us in understanding and addressing a myriad of commercial challenges and opportunities. But what does the Word of God say about how we are to perceive and respond to these challenges and opportunities? What are some of the biblical-based principles for dealing with competition? How do we maximize our success in an ever-changing marketplace? We'll answer these questions and more as we explore the following three Planning Proverbs for the divine situation analysis:

1. God is the Supreme Analyst and Sovereign Forecaster.

2. You have no real competitors.

3. Remember, the battle is not yours.

Now let's proceed with the first Planning Proverb:

God Is the Supreme Analyst and Sovereign Forecaster

· · · · · · · · · · · · · · · · · · · ·

God Designed Situation Analyses

You may be surprised to learn that situation analyses including market reports and competitive assessments are not just modern-day inventions and practices endemic to the business world. They are not new to God. He designed them!

When Moses led the Israelites into the land that God promised them, he was directed by God to be proactive in assessing the situation, including the environment, or market, as well as the competition. The Lord told Moses:

> Send some men to explore the land of Canaan, which I am giving to the Israelites. From each ancestral tribe send one of its leaders.
>
> Numbers 13:1-2 (NIV)

Moses, being obedient to God, promptly instructed his men to go out and:

> See what the land is like and whether the people who live there are strong or weak, few or many. What kind of land do they live in? Is it good or bad? What kind of towns do they live in? Are they unwalled or fortified? How is the soil? Is it fertile or poor? Are there trees on it or not? Do your best to bring back some of the fruit of the land.
>
> Number 13: 18-20 (NIV)

After observing the land, the men returned. They brought samples of "the fruit of the land" and reported that although the towns were large and the land was fruitful and flowing with milk and honey, the people who lived there were much stronger and powerful than them (Numbers 13: 21-28).

God, the Supreme Analyst and Sovereign Forecaster, then instructed Moses to send a few men to go into the land, ahead of the broader team, to evaluate and analyze the market before the entire team proceeded to enter it. In these ways, the disciples were actually conducting a situation analysis. In order to be prepared for the market situation and position themselves for success, they were doing preliminary research, gathering data, assessing the external threats and opportunities, and evaluating their own internal strengths and weaknesses.

God Ordained Seasons in Business

God has a term for the constant market fluctuations and industry trends we see every day in the business world. He calls them "seasons." A *season* is generally defined as events taking place over a period of time. The Bible says that "to everything *there is* a season, a time for every purpose under heaven" (Ecclesiastes 3:1, NKJV) and that there are signs and seasons for everything (Genesis 1:14), including the ebb and flow of the business world.

But Jesus tells us in Acts 1:7 (NKJV): "It is not for you to know times or seasons which the Father has put in His own authority." Applied to the commercial arena, this scripture asserts that it's not necessary for us to know or understand all of the times and seasons we go through in business. We just need to know the Father—the Supreme Analyst and Sovereign Forecaster.

Jesus lectured His disciples about the importance of being able to discern the time and seasons (Luke 12:54-56). He admonished the Pharisees and Sadducees, saying, "Hypocrites! You know how to discern the face of the sky, but you cannot discern the signs of the times" (Matthew 16:3, NKJV). Similarly, we as Christian business leaders must also discern the signs of the times relative to our commercial endeavors. Are you in a season of sowing and planting? Or one of reaping and harvesting?

In order to excel in business, we must allow God, through the Holy Spirit, to help us understand both our current and upcoming seasons. God expects for us to look to Him first for spiritual discernment, wisdom, and guidance. And this requires establishing a solid relationship with Him and maintaining a strong prayer life.

God controls the course of world events. He gives us knowledge and wisdom and "He reveals deep and mysterious things and knows what lies hidden in darkness, though He is surrounded by light" (Daniel 2:21-22, ESV). God knows exactly when social, political, and economic shifts will occur as well as their potential impact on your business both positively and negatively. He knows about the upcoming technological advancements, international market shifts, consumer trends, government regulations, and corporate alliances that are not even at the conceptual stages of development today but will prove to be major forces impacting your business in the future. God knows the real financial future of the companies with which you are interested in investing or partnering. And He can reveal all of this to you if you look to Him first.

Primary Versus Secondary Data Sources

When we think of primary versus secondary data sources, we typically think of marketing research. Primary research consists of experiments, investigations, or tests that involve data observed or collected directly from firsthand experience. Secondary research, on the contrary, involves a review or study of published data that has been collected in the past. Let's consider the notion of primary and secondary data sources from a spiritual perspective.

As Christian business professionals, we must ensure that we keep the conventional aspects of business research and support systems in the proper perspective. From a spiritual standpoint, they are all *secondary* data sources and tools. Our *primary* focus must be on God and His divine plan for our business. He should always be our Primary Data Source and Ultimate Resource for industry and market information because He is the Supreme Analyst and Sovereign Forecaster.

"Faith is the substance of things hoped for, the evidence of things not seen" (Hebrews 11:1, ASV). We are called to walk by faith and not by sight, being led by the Spirit of God (2 Corinthians 5:7; Galatians 5:16). The Bible tells us that it is "by faith that we understand that the worlds were framed by the Word of God, so that the things which are seen were not made of things which are visible" (Hebrews 11:3, NASB). Said differently: the visible comes from One who is invisible.

The concept of walking by faith and not by sight is a direct contradiction to many of the conventional methodologies, processes, and tools that we use to conduct situation analyses for our business ventures. We must change the way we think about business support resources. We have to transform our perspectives and reprioritize our focus areas so that we concentrate on:

- Spiritually discerning God's will *first*

- Incorporating conventional data and information *secondarily*.

This approach is necessary in order for us to achieve all that He has predestined for us. Let's consider a practical example involving the stock market. When you get up in the morning, do you immediately check the financial market results, or do you seek the Word of God first? The stock market should not be your primary source for information, data, and guidance.

Don't become so preoccupied and obsessed with the stock exchange to the point that it becomes the first thing you focus on every day and the core of every major business decision you make. When this occurs, you, in effect, have begun to worship, idolize, and follow the promptings of the stock market as opposed to God's Holy Spirit. This is a dangerous situation and one you want to avoid at all costs because our God is a jealous God and He does not tolerate our worshiping anything over Him (Exodus 20:5; 34:14).

Now, keep in mind that this doesn't mean that we, as Christian business professionals, should completely disregard, divorce, or isolate ourselves from the myriad of reputable market resources and reporting tools available in the commercial sector. If you work for a publicly traded company, it's natural for you to be interested in your company's financial performance in the marketplace. It would be unwise for you to completely ignore the stock market, because it serves as one of many vehicles and barometers for gauging the financial progress of your company and its stance in the industry.

Wall Street analysts, industry experts, business consultants, economic reports, market studies, information technology (IT) systems, and corporate decision-support models and systems serve as critical resources for business analysis and assessment. They are all valid and extremely useful for supporting our business plans and positioning our companies for success. But they are inferior to God. They should be consulted as *secondary* resources that are to be leveraged *after* we have first consulted God for His divine insights into our careers and commercial endeavors. Jesus reinforces the importance of this approach when He prays on our behalf to God:

> I do not pray that You should take them out of the world,
> but that you should keep them from the evil one. They are
> not of the world, just as I am not of the world. Sanctify
> them by Your truth. Your word is truth.

John 17:15-17 (NASB)

In this way, don't ignore the resources and productive protocols of the business world, but realize that the truth of your current business situation must be revealed by God and your future business ventures must be sanctified by Him. Remember, our goal is to transcend from basic information to divine revelation and transformation.

God desires for us to seek Him, pray, study, and obey His Word using spiritual discernment first and conventional data sources secondarily as we develop the divine situation analysis for our business plans. By taking this approach, we are able to accurately evaluate and forecast our commercial endeavors because we are initiating the process by incorporating the perfect wisdom and guidance that come only from God.

While the Business World Is Ever Changing, God Remains the Same

As Christian business leaders, we have to remind ourselves that although the business world is ever changing, God and His Word are not. He remains the same and serves as the one constant in our constantly changing lives. God declares: "For I am the Lord, I do not change" (Malachi 3:6; Exodus 3:14).

Not only does God remain steady and stable for us, but so does His Son. Scripture says, "Jesus Christ *is* the same yesterday, today, and forever" (Hebrews 13:8, NKJV). Because God and His

Son do not change, we must seek their wisdom and direction in planning for imminent marketplace changes.

Pray for Wisdom and Direction, Not Opportunity

When planning the strategic course for our business endeavors, godly wisdom and direction, not opportunity, should be the focus of our prayers. It's important that we don't become so preoccupied with praying for opportunities in the forms of new business accounts, financial rewards, material wealth, power, and fame. God is not in the business of building our personal empires. Remember, our commercial pursuits are linked to His kingdom agenda.

So as stewards over His enterprises, you and I must pray for wisdom and direction in terms of where *He desires* to take our business ventures. Choose God's "instruction rather than silver, and knowledge rather than pure gold. For wisdom is far more valuable than rubies. Nothing you desire can compare with it" (Proverbs 8:10-11, NLT; 18-21). "That's the value of wisdom; it helps you succeed" (Ecclesiastes 10:10, NLT).

Now, I know that following divine direction is easier said than done when you are faced with a myriad of business challenges—from hostile takeovers and organizational restructuring to declining market share and just trying to make payroll. But remember that following God's direction is not only possible, it's *mandatory* in order for you to maximize your personal fulfillment and professional success. Once you are in alignment with His plans, He will present the right opportunities for you at the right times. Now, let's turn our attention to one of the main topics addressed in virtually all situation assessments: *competition.*

You Have No Real Competitors

No, I have not lost my mind. I know this statement runs counter intuitively to everything you and I have been taught to believe, but stay with me. Remember, one of the main goals of this book is to help us transform our mind-set, reorient, reconceptualize, and recontextualize commercial business and take it to a Higher level of excellence. In order to do this, we have to change some of our conventional perspectives, and one of them has to do with the concept of competition.

Competition is generally defined as a state of trying to somehow win or gain something that is either possessed or wanted by others. It's the idea that we are striving to outdo another for some particular prize or profit. We'll start the process of tearing down some of our traditional mental models of competition by first considering what the Bible says about the concept of competition.

Beware of Comparisons

In the Western world, we have been indoctrinated with the idea that we are always competing against someone or some entity for happiness, fame, and fortune. In business, we compete for rewards and prizes that consist of everything from job promotions and executive compensation packages to record-breaking earnings, industry accolades, and market share. This preoccupation with competing against other individuals and entities results from our tendency to constantly compare ourselves with others.

The Bible cautions us against comparing ourselves with others to the point of provoking one another and becoming conceited and envious of others, because envy is like cancer in our bones (Proverbs 14:30; Galatians 5:26). It's important to note that these biblical admonishments against comparisons are applicable to not only comparisons made between *individuals* but also to comparisons made between *enterprises*. It doesn't matter whether we are comparing ourselves with our colleagues or comparing our company with another company. The core issue is that constant comparisons tend to be problematic from a spiritual perspective because they take our focus off God.

The Bible also warns us against coveting, or longing for, what others possess (Exodus 20:17; Deuteronomy 5:21; Ecclesiastes 4:4). In these ways, we should never be jealous of the talents, gifts, abilities, possessions, and success of others. Being overly concerned with other people's success is counterproductive. So do your best not to be envious others, because what God has for you is truly for you. No one can stop the plans of God (Isaiah 14:27; James 4:2). As Jesus encourages us: "Whatever things you ask when you pray, believe that you receive them, and you will have them" (Mark 11:24, NKJV).

When Jesus Is Your Standard, You Have No Real Competitors

God grants wisdom to the righteous and protects those who walk in integrity (Proverbs 2:7). As Christian business professionals, we are to examine and evaluate our own individual conduct and work standards (Galatians 6:4), not based on comparisons against others but based on God's principles and how He made us.

Jesus teaches us to be free of men and liberated to be who God made us to be as individuals (1 Peter 2:15-16; John 8:26-29). In Psalm 119: 97-99 (NKJV), David eloquently proclaims:

Oh, how I love Your law!
It is my meditation all the day.

You, through Your commandments, make me wiser than
my enemies;
For they are ever with me.
I have more understanding than all my teachers,
For Your testimonies are my meditation.

When our focus is on God and Jesus, there's no need to compete
by comparing ourselves, our lives, and our businesses with others. When your role model, or your ultimate standard, is Jesus,
then you have no real competitors. As God's children, we have no
real competitors in the business arena. No one can compete with
us and the divine wisdom, guidance, favor, and protection that
we have through Him. By adopting this perspective, focusing on
God, and following His sovereign plans, we free ourselves from
unnecessary stress and strife and ultimately position ourselves to
perform at unprecedented levels of kingdom excellence.

Isn't Competition Sometimes a
Positive Force in Business?

While intellectually we may understand and appreciate biblical warnings against the concept of competition, we may still be
grappling with deep-rooted attitudes and ideologies about competition. While some of us perceive competition as a negative or
necessary nuisance that we have to deal with in business, many
of us may see it as a positive force inspiring us to perform better.
Some of us may be thinking: *Isn't competition a good thing, especially when it causes us to strive for excellence?*

It's certainly acceptable to appreciate the fruitful, kingdom-
building works of others. I am not suggesting that we shouldn't
allow the success and blessings of others to inspire and moti-

vate us to achieve our personal best and professional excellence. I believe in striving for self-improvement.

I am simply advocating that the *primary* way to excel is not by comparing ourselves and competing against others but by following God's principles for how we should lead our lives and govern our businesses. The world will always make comparisons between us. It's just a function of human nature and social dynamics. But we are never to idolize people and look to them as the standard keepers and ultimate leaders for our lives and businesses.

As Christians, our interest must be centered on a lifestyle and a business protocol that glorifies God. We are called to a Higher level of authority and standard of excellence because we serve an excellent God and have a perfect role model in Jesus (Psalm 8:1; Romans 2:18; Philippians 1:10-11). This is why we are encouraged to "press toward the mark for the prize of the high calling of God in Christ Jesus" (Philippians 3:14).

Keeping Performance Indicators and Measurement Tools in the Right Perspective

You may be wondering just how feasible it is for us to employ divine judgment and honor Biblical admonishments against comparisons in today's workplace and marketplace where cutthroat comparisons between the performance of both individuals and organizations are customary. Performance indicators and measurement tools are a way of life for us.

Case in point: In the workplace, we compare individuals via employee performance evaluations, 360-degree feedback, sales incentive programs, industry awards, and recognition programs. In the marketplace, we compare companies via Wall Street brokerage reports, consumer ratings, customer service indices, quality awards, and stock market performance. Not only do these resources serve as commonly accepted standards for measuring professional, commercial, and economic progress, but also they are also fundamentally *comparison oriented.*

With comparisons being such an integral part of the business arena, is it even feasible that we as Christian business professionals can honor biblical warnings against comparisons? Good question.

Here's the answer: Again, as Christian business leaders, we should not, and cannot afford to, ignore historical, commonly accepted performance indicators and measurement tools. Earnings reports, market indices, industry growth rankings, stock performance evaluations, and employee performance ratings are all critical aspects of business. Once again, the key is to keep them in the proper perspective.

The wisdom of God is not necessarily found in conventional performance indicators and measurement tools. Spiritual discernment and divine judgment require that we operate at a Higher level than the rest of the business world. We must base our individual performance and business initiatives *first* and *foremost* on His principles and on what He prompts us to do, not on what is reflected by performance indicators, measurement tools, and market indices.

What Happens When We Fail to Keep Performance Indicators and Measurement Tools in the Right Perspective?

Obsessing over performance and market indicators can distract you from the path of fulfilling God's purpose for your life. Oftentimes, God leads us down avenues of opportunity and direction that are completely contrary to conventional wisdom and what market research indices and industry reports support. But whose report will you believe?

Example: You might find that the Lord is leading you to make a career move to a company that has a *declining* stock value. The devalued stock may cause you to become cautious, discouraged, and reluctant to seek employment with the company. Consequently, your focus on outward appearances may result in your missing out on the marvelous blessings that God may have had in store for you at the company. Furthermore, the company may miss out on the enormous contributions that you could have made to the organization, which may have ultimately helped to quadruple not only their stock value but also your personal net worth!

Here's another example: You might be an entrepreneur who feels led by God to open up a particular type of apparel shop in your city when, in the past, several similar establishments have failed and many of the market indicators suggest that yours would also have a similar fate. Don't follow market research and forecasts. Follow God. Remember, He may be trying to do "a new thing" (Isaiah 43:19, NKJV) at this time in the market through you and your business.

Our Threefold Competitive Intelligence Network

God tells us: "I will instruct you and teach you in the way you should go; I will guide you with My eye" (Psalm 32:8, NKJV). For us, as Christian business leaders, the holy Trinity serves as our divine threefold competitive intelligence network, or spiritual intelligence network, providing us with wisdom and direction for our commercial endeavors. Jesus tells us:

All authority has been given to Me in heaven and on earth…go therefore and make disciples of all the nations, baptizing them in the name of the Father and of the Son and of the Holy Spirit.

Matthew 28:18-19 (NKJV)

In this statement, Jesus references the holy Trinity, which includes: 1) God, the Father; 2) Jesus Christ, the Son; and 3) the Holy Spirit.

The Apostle Paul also references the holy Trinity in his benediction to the Corinthians, saying, "The grace of the Lord Jesus Christ, and the love of God, and the communion of the Holy Spirit *be* with you all. Amen" (2 Corinthians 13:14, NKJV).

The key point I'm making here is that it is important to remember that as a child of God, you have the power of the holy Trinity on your side to lead and guide you in all of your business endeavors. When you find yourself going through difficult seasons in your business, you will find this spiritual network to be invaluable.

Our Six Divine Competitive Advantages

"Spirituality could be the ultimate competitive advantage,"[16] observes Dr. Ian Mitroff in his book, *A Spiritual Audit of Corporate America*. As God blesses His enterprises to launch, prosper, and remain viable in the marketplace, He gives us divine competitive advantages and response tactics to help us serve as effective stewards over His businesses. Let's consider some of the practical ways in which God gives us favor in the marketplace.

1. God covers us with grace and mercy.

One competitive advantage that God gives us is His ongoing covering of grace and mercy over us and our business initiatives. If you find yourself saying, "I just don't see how my business can survive," the Word of God answers by saying, "Let us therefore come boldly to the throne of grace, that we may obtain mercy and find grace to help in time of need" (Hebrews 4:16, NKJV). Let's take a moment to explore the concepts of grace and mercy.

Grace is broadly defined as "unmerited or undeserved favor," and it is the gift of God (Ephesians 2:8; Psalm 5:12). The Bible states that as Christians we have been "justified freely by His grace through the redemption that is in Christ Jesus" (Romans 3:24, NKJV) to the extent "that having been justified by His grace we should become heirs according to the hope of eternal life" (Titus 3:7, ASV).

Jesus tells us in 2 Corinthians 12:9 (NKJV): "My grace is sufficient for you, for My strength is made perfect in weakness."

When we pursue God's will for our lives and businesses, we become the recipients of God's grace through Jesus Christ. Following are a couple of examples of having the grace and favor of God:

- When your firm is *not* the lowest bidder but is still awarded the lucrative contract, this is the grace of God at work.

- When you are not the most qualified candidate for the job but are still awarded the position, this is the grace of God literally at work!

Now that we've explored the competitive advantages inherent in God's grace, let's now consider the power of His mercy.

Mercy is generally defined as "kindness and forgiveness given to one who does not necessarily deserve it."

As in the case of grace, the Bible makes it clear that it is through the resurrection of Jesus Christ that we have been given God's mercy, which never ceases (1 Peter1:3; Lamentations 3:21-23). God says, "I will have mercy on whom I have mercy, and I will have compassion on whom I have compassion" (Romans 9:15, AMP). "So then, *it is* not of him who wills, nor of him who runs, but of God who shows mercy" (Romans 9:16, NKJV).

Therefore, our ability to receive mercy does not depend on our desires or actions but on *God's* desires and actions. *His mercy*. Following are a couple of illustrations:

- When you exaggerate your firm's clientele and annual revenue, yet you still win the lucrative account, this is God's mercy at work.

- When you have criticized and gossiped about your manager to others, yet you still get promoted, this is God's mercy literally at work!

We are all daily recipients of God's constant grace and mercy in every aspect of our lives. As we operate within the business arena, it is God's grace and mercy that provide us with the only real, sustainable, long-term, competitive advantage in the marketplace. God's competitive advantages are ones that will never change and will endure until the end of time. This is our true edge in the marketplace.

2. God gives us spiritual weapons as response tactics.

Our struggles in the business world are not against evil humans but against evil spirits. Our battles in the workplace and marketplace are not with *physical* opponents (i.e., flesh and blood or people). But they are against *spirits of wickedness* in the supernatural sphere (i.e., demonic forces). This point is illuminated in Ephesians 6:12 (NASB), which states:

> For our struggle is not against flesh and blood, but against the rulers, against the authorities, against the powers of this dark world and against the spiritual forces of evil in the heavenly realms.

This means that as we go about our day-to-day operations, our struggles are not with our customers, clients, employees, managers, suppliers, union leaders, corporate board members, regulatory officials, business partners, government officials, attorneys, and media representatives. Our primary struggle is with Satan. Jesus describes Satan, our enemy, as a liar and a thief who comes only to steal, kill, and destroy (John 8:44; 10:10; Genesis 3:1-5).

It's also important to note here that often our struggles in business come from our struggles *within ourselves*. By this, I mean that we fight against our own personal doubts, fears, and insecurities—all of which are planted in our minds by Satan. Hence, the old adage "sometimes we are our own worst enemies." I once heard a minister capture this notion by saying, "I'm not worried about *an enemy*; I'm worried about *the enemy that is the inner me*" (i.e., the enemy in me). *The enemy within.*

How do we protect ourselves when we are under attack by Satan? When faced with adversity in our professional lives, God gives us *spiritual weapons* to use as response tactics. Scripture tells us that "though we walk in the flesh, we do not war according to the flesh" (2 Corinthians 10:3, NKJV). The weapons that we use are not the same as the weapons used by the secular world. "Our weapons are not carnal, but mighty in God for pulling down strongholds," (2 Corinthians 10:4, NKJV), or areas in which we are held in bondage due to a certain way of thinking or mental model.

Our spiritual weaponry has the power to demolish corporate corruption and tear down barriers against the truth of God in the workplace and marketplace. Our spiritual weapons consist of godly principles and practices as outlined in the Bible. They include the Word of God, prayer, praise, obedience, and manifesting the fruit of the Spirit, such as love, joy, peace, longsuffering, kindness, goodness, faithfulness, gentleness, and self control (Galatians 5: 22-23). Of course, we will still have to employ some of the conventional, ethical competitive response tactics such as price reductions, increased media expenditures, and damage control campaigns. But our first response should always be spiritual.

3. God gives us authority over Satan.

Genesis 3:1 (NKJV) states: "The serpent was more cunning than any beast of the field which the Lord God *had made*." God made Satan. Satan, our demonic enemy, exists only because God has a reason for him to exist. Therefore, Satan is under the authority of God.

God gives us authority over Satan. Scripture says that although we struggle against satanic forces, God has already given us power and authority over demons or evil spirits (Matthew 10:1; Mark 6:7). So when you find yourself under various attacks in the workplace and marketplace, just remind yourself of what Jesus tells us:

> I give you authority to trample on serpents and scorpions, and over all the power of the enemy, and nothing shall by any means hurt you.
>
> Luke 10:19 (NKJV)

The only power Satan has is the power that you give him. Refuse to grant Satan any power in your life. Satan uses a variety of individuals and circumstances to try to not only thwart your business plans but also destroy your personal relationship with God.

When you find yourself attacked by the enemy, remember God is still in control. His permissive will always reigns (Lamentation 3:37-39). Even Satan recognizes the power of God through Jesus. Let's consider the story of Job. Before Satan could attack Job, Satan had to first *get permission* from God (Job 1:6-22; Mark 1:27). And Satan had to *adhere* to the parameters and limitations that God placed on him when it came to the attacks on Job. For instance, "the Lord said to Satan, 'Behold all that he (Job) has is in your power; only do not lay a hand on his person'" (Job 1:12, NKJV) and, "And the Lord said to Satan, 'Behold, he (Job) is in your hand, but spare his life'" (Job 2:6, NKJV).

God places limitations on our adversity. God gave Satan permission to put Job through various trials, but He did not give Satan permission to cause him bodily harm. Likewise, when we're under Satan's attack in our professional endeavors, God still has our best interests in mind, and He is still covering us.

Do as the Bible instructs: submit yourself to God and resist the devil, and he will flee (James 4:7; 1 Peter 5:8-9). You have God-given authority, so exert it by trusting in the Lord and ensuring that your thoughts and behavior are in alignment with His principles. When you do this, God promises to keep you in perfect peace in *any* situation (Isaiah 26:3-4).

4.   God anoints and blesses our business initiatives.

God gives us the competitive advantage of having business plans and initiatives that are already blessed and anointed by Him to succeed. If you know that God has called you to pursue a particular commercial initiative, rest assured that He has already blessed it, conducted a divine market assessment, scouted out your territory, designed your professional networks, orchestrated your business contacts, and sent His designated angels to protect you during the journey. You only need to follow the promptings of the Holy Spirit.

Example: God may lead you to pursue an untapped market, create a new market niche, or simply abandon an industry altogether. Or, as was the case when Moses led the Reubenites who renamed the cities they rebuilt (Numbers 32:37-38), God may lead you to redefine, or *rename*, a certain product, service, or market sector. Don't remain stagnate with a "better safe than sorry" mentality. Because you are following God's plan, "He will be with you, He will not leave you, *nor* forsake you; do not fear nor be dismayed" (Deuteronomy 31:8, NKJV; Psalm 46:2; Lamentations 3:31).

There will also be times when God desires for you to simply stand still and not make any major moves with your business regardless of the changes occurring in the marketplace. Sometimes, neither you nor your team members will understand the path that God is leading you down. At times, the course may seem questionable or even unconscionable to you, and you might not even want to share some of these radical plans with your shareholders for fear of appearing foolish. But remember that it is God to whom you will ultimately have to give an account (Romans 14:12). Follow Him and He will provide all of the necessary content and data that you need for your business case because He has already anointed and blessed you to accomplish what He has ordained.

5. God paves a way for us in the marketplace.

Another competitive advantage that we have as Christian business leaders is that when we pursue what God ordained for us in business, He will always proceed ahead of us to establish a pathway of divine favor, protection, and support (Deuteronomy 31:3; Isaiah 52:12). He goes ahead of us and paves a way for us in the workplace and marketplace. Example: When his leaders expressed fear of treading into the new land or territory, Moses responded by telling them to not be afraid because God had already gone ahead of them to fight and make a way for them (Deuteronomy 1: 29-30).

Moses encouraged them to be strong, confident, and courageous by telling them that as long as they were being obedient to God, He would always go ahead of them, clear a pathway, and protect them as they pursued His will. This type of divine guidance and intervention is available for us today. God did it for them, and He will do it for you. Trust God. Even when conditions appear most grim, He is still able to modify situations and open up countless opportunities for you.

6. God reveals upcoming market trends.

Whoever is of God listens to God (John 8:47). One of the ways in which God strengthens our situation analyses and allows us to have a competitive advantage in the marketplace is by showing and telling us about upcoming social, political, cultural, and economic trends. This in reinforced in a number of scriptures. For instance, God tells us:

- "For I alone am God! I am God, and there is none like me. Only I can tell you the future before it even happens. Everything I plan will come to pass, for I do whatever I wish" (Isaiah 46:9-10, NLT).

- "Call to Me, and I will answer you, and show you great and mighty things, which you do not know" (Jeremiah 33:3, NASB).

Similarly, Jesus tells us in John 16:13 (NLT):

When the Spirit of truth comes, He will guide you into all truth. He will not speak on his own but will tell you what he has heard. He will tell you about the future.

In these ways, God reinforces the fact that He will inform us of upcoming seasons in life and in business (Isaiah 44:7). He is well able to alert us of upcoming demographic trends, technological advances, industry alliances, and financial market shifts before they actually occur! Who else can do this with perfect accuracy? Wouldn't you want your business plans and situation analyses to reflect the most profound knowledge and perfect data that can only be derived from God?

Sometimes God will reveal future trends to you directly through His Spirit, His Word, dreams, and visions. Other times, He'll work through other individuals to get the information to you. One biblical example of God's ability to reveal the future to us is described in the book of Hebrews and involves Noah.

The Bible tells us that God instructed Noah to build an ark because He planned to do away with all of the corrupt people by bringing floodwaters on the earth (Genesis 6:1-22). We learn that:

> By faith Noah, when warned about things not yet seen, in holy fear built an ark to save his family. By his faith he condemned the world and became heir of the righteousness that comes by faith.
>
> Hebrews 11:7 (NASB)

God forewarned Noah of upcoming events for which there were no visible signs. Noah obeyed God. He immediately followed God's divine instruction by taking heed to His warning of upcoming market trends and diligently constructing an ark that the world had never seen. Because of his faith in God, Noah received righteousness in God.

What upcoming trends has God warned you about? How are you obeying His warnings? What is your ark? Take some time to contemplate these questions. Then proceed to the final Planning Proverb for the divine situation analysis.

Remember, the Battle Is Not Yours

In the business world, as in every aspect of our lives, we will face adversity. Jobs become jeopardized. Business owners file for bankruptcy. Companies are sued by their employees. And the unfortunate list goes on. But we must keep adversity in the proper perspective. "Cast your burden upon the Lord and He will sustain you; He will never allow the righteous to be shaken" (Psalm 55:22, NKJV). The Bible says that when we, as His righteous sons and daughters, cry out to Him, not only will He hear us, but He will deliver us out of our troubles (Psalm 34:17-22; 94:13).

Because we have the power of the Most High God living within us, we don't need to worry about professional barriers or commercial threats of any type. We just need to position ourselves to allow the Lord to guide and fight for us. Remember, the battle is not yours. The battle belongs to God. The Word of God makes this clear for us:

> *Thus says the Lord to you: 'Do not be afraid nor dismayed because of this great multitude, for the battle is not yours but God's.'*

> 2 Chronicles 20:15 (NKJV)

You will not have to fight this battle. Take up your positions; stand firm and see the deliverance the Lord will give you, O Judah and Jerusalem. Do not be afraid; do not be discouraged. Go out to face them tomorrow, and the Lord will be with you.

2 Chronicles 20:17 (NASB)

Scripture also tells us:

> Do not be terrified; do not be afraid of them. The Lord your God, who is going before you, *will fight for you*, as He did for you in Egypt, before your very eyes, and in the desert. There you saw how the Lord your God carried you, as a father carries His Son, all the way you went until you reached this place.

Deuteronomy 1:29-31 (NIV)

These passages confirm for us that no battle, regardless of whether it's personal or professional, is ever ours to fight. Psalm 9:9 (NKJV) says, "The Lord is a shelter for the oppressed, a refuge in times of trouble." He is our refuge and our fortress (Psalm 91:2).

Whenever we attempt to venture into a marketplace battle without God, we will be defeated (Numbers 14: 42-43).

You Already Have the Victory!

As God's disciples, we already have victory over every battle through His Son Jesus Christ (1 Corinthians 15:57; 2 Corinthians 2:14). Furthermore, the Bible tells us that God will perfect that which concerns those of us who love Him and cause everything to work together for our good (Psalm 138:8; Romans 8:28). This is wonderful news for those of us in business, because as long as we follow Him, we'll be victorious regardless of our challenges!

And even if the situation doesn't turn out exactly as we hoped, God will still use it for our good!

When facing seemingly insurmountable challenges in business, don't be afraid, dismayed, or overwhelmed. Although we may feel troubled and oppressed, we are never driven to despair because God "has not given us the spirit of fear, but of power and of love and of a sound mind" (2 Timothy 1:7; 2 Corinthians 4:8-9). In Genesis 15:1 (NKJV), God appeared to Abram in a vision, telling him, "Do not be afraid, Abram, I am your shield, your exceedingly great reward."

God also makes this clear for us in Isaiah 41:10 (NKJV):

> Fear not, I am with you; Be not dismayed, for I am your God. I will strengthen you, yes, I will help you. I will uphold you with My righteous right hand.

Now, take this statement and insert your name:

> Fear not, _____, I am with you; Be not dismayed, for I am your God. I will strengthen you, yes, I will help you. I will uphold you with My righteous right hand.

Meditate on your personalized scripture. Keep it readily available for viewing because this is exactly what the Lord wants you to remember when facing challenges in business. God is your shield. And like a shield, He will cover and protect you.

God is a "shield to those who put their trust in Him" (Proverbs 30:5, NKJV), so put on the armor of God (Psalm 33:20; Ephesians 6:13; Romans 13:14). As David acknowledges: "But You, O Lord, *are* a shield for me, my glory and the One who lifts up my head"

(Psalm 3:3, NKJV). "Take up the shield of faith" (Ephesians 6:16, ESV). At times, the only action God wants us to take is *no* action. Sometimes, He simply wants us to "Be still, and know that I am God" (Psalm 46:10, NKJV).

If the Battle Isn't Mine, then Why Do I Find Myself Struggling in Business?

God promises to fight your battles for you, give you grace to endure them, and deliver you out of them. But Jesus makes it clear when He tells us: "In the world you will have tribulation; but be of good cheer, I have overcome the world" (John 16:33, NKJV). "Yes, and all who desire to live godly in Christ Jesus suffer persecution" (2 Timothy 3:12, NKJV). So even when we are following God's counsel in business, we will still have periods of tribulation or severe hardship.

When considering the question of *why* God allows adversity in business, we are not privy to the rationales and ways of God (Isaiah 55:8). Sometimes He uses our professional struggles to mature or discipline us. Other times, He uses them to show and remind us and others of the magnitude of His power and glory. Regardless of the reasons behind the struggles, as the Apostle Paul said, we should:

> Count it all joy when you fall into various trials, knowing that the testing of your faith produces patience. But let patience have its perfect work, that you may be perfect and complete, lacking nothing.
>
> James 1:2-4 (NKJV)

"You therefore must endure hardship as a good soldier of Jesus Christ" (2 Timothy 2:3, NKJV). As the Apostle Paul observes in Philippians 1:12, even your most adverse situations can be used to further the gospel. If you find yourself struggling today in business, just know that your present hard times and sufferings don't even compare to the marvelous times and glory that He will reveal in you (Romans 8:18).

He Gives You Double for Your Trouble

Jesus says, "Give and it shall be given to you; good measure, pressed down, shaken together, and running over" (Luke 6:38, NKJV). When you are obedient to God in your commercial endeavors, He will not only restore, or make up for, the time that you feel you may have lost struggling against Satanic attacks in the business arena, but He will also "restore double to you" (Zechariah 9:12, NKJV; Joel 2:25)!

God gives us a twofold recompense, or double blessings, for our trouble. Scripture tells us: "Instead of your shame, *you shall have* double *honor*" (Isaiah 61:7, NKJV). One example of receiving double for trouble involves God's servant Job. After going through a season of profound trials and loss, "the Lord gave Job twice as much as he had before" and "the Lord blessed the latter *days* of Job more than his beginning" (Job 42:10,12, NKJV).

Another example of receiving a twofold recompense is relayed in Joshua 21:43-45. In this passage, we learn that the Lord not only gave the people of Israel all of the land He promised their forefathers and protected them from their enemies, but He also helped them conquer all their enemies!

Greater Is He Who Is in You Than He Who Is in the Business World

When we're trying to stay motivated during times of professional tests and trials, we must take the Word of God and apply it to our situations. The Bible tells us that "He who is in us is greater that he who is in the world" (1 John 4:4, NKJV)—and this includes the *business* world. "We are more than conquerors through Him who loved us" (Romans 8:37, NKJV). This means that we are more than victors!

David declared, "The Lord *is* my light and salvation; whom shall I fear? The Lord *is* the strength of my life; of whom shall I be afraid?" (Psalm 27:1, NKJV). What can mere mortals do to us (Psalm 56:3-4; Hebrews 13:6)? If God is for us, then who can be against us (Romans 8:31)? When we take these same scriptures and relate them to the business arena, they might be interpreted and translated as follows:

- Greater is He who is in me than he who is in the business world.

- We are more than conquerors, in the marketplace, through Him who loved us.

- The Lord is my light, salvation, strength, and the creator of my business. Of whom, in the marketplace, shall I be afraid?

- If God be for me, then who in the business world can be against me?

Let these scriptures encourage and inspire you during times of challenge and adversity. Don't be intimidated, worried, or angry when you find yourself under attack. These negative feelings and emotions lead to depression and will only get you off track from what God wants to accomplish through you (Philippians 1:28; Proverbs 12:25; Matthew 6:25-34).

"Do not fret because of evil men or be envious of those who do wrong; for like the grass they will soon wither, like green plants they will soon die away" (Psalm 37:1-2, NIV). Just be obedient to what God has called you to do, and remember that He will be the ultimate judge and jury (John 8:50; 1 Peter 1:17). "Who will bring any charge against those whom God has chosen? It is God who justifies" (Romans 8:33, NLT).

When you are in the will of God, He will not allow your enemies to overtake you (Psalm 41:11; 18:3; 2 Samuel 22:18-20). He watches over you and sends His angels to protect you from the devious schemes of your adversaries in the workplace and marketplace. He will cause them to stumble and fall even to the point of making them your footstool (Psalm 91:11, 27:2, 110:1)!

Your Most Important Preemptive Strategy

Prayer is one of our most powerful weapons in spiritual warfare. Prayer isn't a last resort; it's a preemptive strategy. In fact, prayer should be your first line of defense. It should be your first response. Prayer allows you to be proactive in defending yourself and your business against imminent attacks in the marketplace. Don't wait until your business is in a state of chaos and then say, "Oh, well, there's nothing else I can do, I guess I might as well start praying."

Prayer should be the first action you take in *every* situation. Pray when business is good and pray when it's bad. Give all of your fears and concerns over to God. Trust that He will resolve them and resist the temptation to take the issues back from Him.

This is particularly important for those of us who are proactive and get impatient when we don't get a quick resolution.

The Bible gives us a number of scriptures to use in our preemptive prayer strategies. For instance, the Bible tells us to:

- "Seek the Lord and His strength" (Psalm 105:4, NKJV).

- Recall the words of Jesus: "Let not your heart be troubled; you believe in God, believe also in Me" (John 14:1, NKJV).

- "Take the helmet of salvation and the sword of the Spirit which is the word of God" (Ephesians 6: 17, NKJV).

- "Pray in the Spirit on all occasions with all kinds of prayers and requests" and "with this in mind, be alert and always keep on praying for all the saints." (Ephesians 6:18, NIV).

- Know that "no weapon formed against you shall prosper" (Isaiah 54:17, NKJV).

- Know that God says, "When you pass through the waters, I will be with you; And through the rivers, they shall not overflow you. When you walk through the fire, you shall not be burned, nor shall the flame scorch you. For I am the Lord your God…" (Isaiah 43:2-3, NKJV).

- "…be strong and of good courage, do not be afraid, nor be dismayed, for the Lord your God is with you wherever you go" (Joshua 1:9, NKJV).

These are just a few of thousands of scriptures that will minister to your heart and remind you of God's loving grace and kindness. I encourage you to read the Bible and cull out the ones that particularly resonate with you personally. You will find, like I have, that when faced with seemingly insurmountable barriers in the turbulent business arena, God will still bless you with peace, confidence, and resources to overcome every obstacle. Don't wait until you face a crisis to begin strengthening your faith by immersing yourself in the Word of God.

Is there something pressuring or worrying you in your professional life? If so, take a moment to consider your issues of concern. List them. Now take a deep breath, close your eyes, pray, and simply ask God for wisdom in dealing with the situation according to His will (James 1:5; Matthew 6:9-15; Luke 11:2-4). And then wait on His instructions and follow them. Regardless of the situation, just do your best, sit back, relax, and let God be God.

Real-Life Examples of the Divine Situation Analysis

Sometimes you know deep down inside your heart and spirit that the Lord is telling you to pursue a particular business initiative, but all the market research and data reports indicate that it won't be successful. Your situation analysis and competitive market assessments all point to potential failure for a host of reasons. Or you might feel that you are just not personally, or professionally, ready to take on the challenge. Question: What do you do? Answer: You obey God. You press on.

It's not easy to say yes when all market and performance indicators say no. But you are *not* saying yes to them. You are saying yes to God. You are honoring Him. When you honor God, He will honor you. God tells us in 1 Samuel 2:30 (NKJV): "Those who honor Me I will honor." There is no failure in honoring God.

I experienced these same feelings when I felt led to resign from a six-figure corporate position to honor God's promptings and commit myself to writing this book. So I know it's not easy, but you have to be obedient and press on. God will give you the grace, favor, protection, and peace that you need to accomplish what He calls you to do. And He'll provide angels to support you while He opens up an array of opportunities for you. Remember, "without faith it is impossible to please Him" (Hebrews 11:6, NKJV).

Mrs. Fields Cookies®

Many of us have had to ignore what market research and analysts have said about our business plan and just proceed with God's plan. Case in point: Debbi Fields, a young mother with no business experience, opened her first cookie store in Palo Alto, California, in 1977. People told her she was crazy and that no business could survive by just selling cookies. But Debbi Fields was obedient and pressed on. Today, Mrs. Fields Cookies® is a $500 million chain of cookie and baked goods stores with nearly 390 locations in the U.S. and over eighty locations internationally. There is no failure in honoring God. As stated on their corporate website:

> The important thing is not being afraid to take a chance. Remember, the greatest failure is to not try. Once you find something you love to do, be the best at doing it.
>
> —Debbi Fields
> Founder, Mrs. Fields Cookies®

Chicken Soup for the Soul

After working on their book for three years, Jack Canfield and Mark Victor Hansen began approaching publishers with their project. They were rejected by 140 publishers who undoubtedly relied on their market analysis and performance indicators to conclude the following about the project: Anthologies don't sell; it's not topical enough; there's no market for the book; it will never sell; and—my favorite excuse of all—it's "too positive"!

So what did the authors do? They were obedient and pressed on. They kept reaching out to publishers and eventually contacted the president of Health Communications, Inc. who caught the spirit of the project and agreed to publish their book. What was the result? With over 112 million copies sold, 170 titles in 40 languages, the authors' project, *Chicken Soup for the Soul*, has made international publishing history! There is no failure in honoring God.

The Passion of the Christ

No motion picture studio or film distributor would touch Mel Gibson's project, *The Passion of the Christ*. Industry executives, referring to their market research and metrics, claimed the following about the project: It was too controversial; the general public wouldn't support it; it wouldn't be profitable; and it would probably even destroy his career.

So what did Mel Gibson do? He was obedient and pressed on. He invested over $25 million of his own money into the project and filmed the movie himself. What was his *financial* return on his investment? To date, the epic film has grossed over $600 million worldwide. What was his *spiritual* return on his investment? *Priceless*. Again, there is no failure in honoring God.

Directives for Executing the Divine Situation Analysis

Following are five suggestions for implementing the divine situation analysis for your business:

1. Pray for God's wisdom and direction in understanding the current and upcoming seasons of your life and business.

    Ask God to give you an understanding of the current season of your life and business as well as upcoming opportunities. Pray for His guidance in preparing for new seasons and finding the appropriate data and information sources for your business plan. God is the Rock for your business, and His ways are perfect for enabling you to attain and maintain a strong position in the marketplace (Deuteronomy 20:1-4; 32:4; Isaiah 26:4).

2. Develop an accurate and comprehensive situation analysis for your business plan.

    Make God your Primary Data Source. Honor the seasons in business to which He calls you (1 Corinthians 7:24). Synthesize all of your information and data into an accurate and comprehensive situation analysis section for your business plan. Be sure to include the following information:

    - General market or industry assessment

    - Market share analysis

    - Competitive assessment

    - Your company's competitive positioning (SWOT Analysis)

- Barriers to entry

- Strategic business opportunities

Also incorporate pertinent information from conventional primary market research (e.g., consumer focus groups and customer surveys) as well as from secondary market research (e.g., published empirical studies).

3. Stay focused on God's constant presence in a constantly changing business arena.

    God is the one aspect of business that never changes. While your commercial initiatives are constantly changing, He is constant. His Word never changes and His strength is everlasting. Remember, the joy of the Lord is your strength (Nehemiah 8:10).

4. Biblical coaches who exhibit and embody the revelation of how to analyze their divine situation or season include: a number of disciples such as Jesus, David, Paul, Mary (the mother of Jesus), Esther, Ruth, Job, and Joseph. Review some of their stories in the Bible and cull out the ones that minister to your heart. When going through extremely challenging seasons in business, the entire book of Psalms is full of inspirational scriptures such as Psalm 23:1-6; 37:1-40; 41:1-13; 55:22; 62: 1-12; and 91:1-16.

5. Praise and press on.

    Continue to praise God for what He has shown you about your current business situation and about your upcoming seasons of opportunity (Psalm 113:3). Praise God during both peaks and valleys in business (1 Peter 4:16). Encourage yourself by recalling previous victories and the ways He has delivered you from difficult circumstances (Deuteronomy 8:14-16; Psalm 77:11). Thank Him for His protection and keep reminding yourself that your present

troubles don't compare to the glory that lies ahead for you
(2 Corinthians 4:17; Psalm 15:17; 18:3; 40:1-4; 150:1-6;
Habakkuk 3:17-19)!

In the next chapter, we'll discover how to glorify God in our
marketing initiatives. But for now, we'll end this chapter with a
quote from the book *The Business of Changing the World*, which
really puts performance and market indicators in the proper
perspective:

> In God we trust; everything else we measure.[17]
>
> —Michael L. Eskew, Former Chairman and Chief
> Executive Officer, UPS

IV

The Divine Marketing Plan

"Come, follow me," Jesus said, "and I will make you fishers of men."

—Matthew 4:19 (NLT)

How can the Word of God help us in the marketing function? Is it possible to glorify God through our marketing initiatives? The American Marketing Association (AMA) defines marketing as "the activity, set of institutions, and processes for creating, communicating, delivering, and exchanging offerings that have value for customers, clients, partners, and society at large." Based on this definition, we are all marketers to a certain degree. As employers and entrepreneurs, we market our expertise and reputation in the form of our products and services. As employees, we market our knowledge, skills, and professional experience.

The marketing plan serves as the primary section of your business plan for outlining how you plan to promote and sell your products and services. While every marketing plan is different, most of them address the basic elements of the marketing mix, which include the infamous 4Ps: product, price, place, and promotion.

Your marketing plan should clearly describe your *product* or *service* offerings including *price* points, associated fees, and any important justifications or rationales. Your marketing plan should also include data regarding the typical *places* in which your product or service will be offered as well as the ways in which you plan to sell, advertise, or *promote* your offerings.

Most marketing plans include topics such as marketing goals, objectives, strategies, tactics, consumer demographics and psychographics, target consumer markets, marketing research, advertising messages, intellectual property, media vehicles, sales structure, and public relations platforms. These are the secular aspects of marketing. But what are the spiritual aspects of marketing? Let's address this question before we proceed with our Planning Proverbs.

You Are God's Marketing Vehicle

Fundamentally, marketing is a means for influencing others to buy into lifestyle enhancement regardless of whether the benefits take the form of a product or service. Similarly, as Christians we are also charged with reaching and encouraging others and influencing them to embrace a lifestyle enhancement—a spiritual lifestyle enhancement. We are living epistles and advertisements for God in the marketplace. Jesus didn't demand that people come to Him in order to hear the gospel. He went to them. He went into the marketplace and through towns teaching the gospel (Matthew 4:23).

There are a number of classic questions that continue to be debated among academicians: Is marketing an art or a science?

Does marketing create consumer need? Or, does consumer need create marketing? I won't go into the valid arguments that have been presented for both sides. But let's reframe this question from a spiritual perspective: What spiritual need does marketing for God address? The Bible is clear on the answer: *Salvation*.

Clarifying Points

Before we proceed with our three Planning Proverbs, it's important that I take a moment to acknowledge a couple of viewpoints. Both relate to the fact that there are, unfortunately, negative connotations associated with the marketing profession just as there are with other vocations.

The first point is that some people may actually question whether or not the marketing profession is fundamentally deceptive in practice because its core objective involves persuading others to purchase products and services that they may or may not need. I will address this notion by first saying that commerce, i.e., buying and selling, is a vital aspect of our society and of the world economy. For ages, and even during biblical times, virtually all cultures around the world have participated in some form of bartering, selling, and consuming.

There is nothing inherently deceptive about marketing *in theory*. However, there is always potential for deception in marketing, as in any other profession, *in practice*. For us as Christians, it is imperative that our business practices are in alignment with the Word of God.

The second point is that some of us may object to the use of the terms *marketing* and *selling* within the context of God's holy Word. The terminology of this chapter is in no way intended to be irreverent or disrespectful to God. We are just taking another common business term and commercial function and applying the Word of God to them in ways that resonate with business professionals.

As Christians, we are authorized by Jesus Christ to represent God here on earth, making disciples of all the nations by teaching the Word of God and leading others to salvation (John 8:31-32; 14:6; Matthew 28:19; Mark 16:15). We serve as ministerial vessels that God uses to inform others that *He is the answer* for every situation they encounter in business and in life in general. God sends us out into the world as His sheep among wolves, and we are called to be innocent and harmless, yet shrewd and wise (Matthew 10:16; John10:4), as we oversee His commercial enterprises. Regardless of our specific occupation or functional area, as Christians we are first and foremost kingdom ambassadors, or marketing vehicles for God (2 Corinthians 5:20).

Three Planning Proverbs for the Divine Marketing Plan

Following are the three Planning Proverbs that we'll explore in this chapter:

1. Recognize your superior brand value.

2. Marketing is fishing.

3. Know the fifth "P" of marketing.

Let's proceed with the first Planning Proverb:

Recognize Your Superior Brand Value

The American Marketing Association defines a brand as "a name, term, design, symbol, or any other feature that identifies one seller's good or service as distinct from those of other sellers." A brand is often referred to as the sum total of every experience that consumers have with your product or service. Brands are integral elements of most marketing plans. And those of us in American society can certainly attest to the global reach and influence that Madison Avenue has had on numerous brands.

Some of the most ubiquitous and powerful brands have risen to a level of not only prevailing as part of our social nomenclature but actually redefining the product category. Case in point: Kimberly-Clark Corporation's Kleenex® brand. Kleenex has transcended traditional branding parameters and its initial brand footprint, or the essence, meaning, and personality of the brand. Kleenex has become so much of a mainstay in the social vernacular and nomenclature used by the general public that it practically defines the entire facial tissue category! Instead of asking for a tissue, we simply ask for a Kleenex. I share this example of a brand that has transcended beyond traditional brand limitations to define or redefine a category to make the following point:

We as Christians should become so much of a mainstay for God, His principles, and His sovereign brand that we begin to transcend conventional marketing parameters to redefine the function of marketing and take it to a Higher level. But in order to accomplish this, we must first understand and embrace our brand value in God.

A New Brand

As Christians we are inextricably linked to the Creator of the universe, the King of Kings, and the Lord of Lords (1 Timothy 6:15). The Bible tells us that God made us in His own image (Genesis 1:27; Psalm 139:14) and that His Spirit lives within each of us (Romans 8:11; 1 Corinthians 3:16; 2 Corinthians 13:5). So we are already made in the magnificent and holy image of an omnipotent, omniscient, and omnipresent God.

When we dedicate our lives to God through Jesus Christ, we do away with our former selves, renew our mind-sets, and become members of God's kingdom and extensions of Him (Isaiah 42:9; Revelation 21:4; Ephesians 4:21-23). The Bible tells us that if anyone is in Christ, then he is a *new creation* and is given a new heart and spirit (2 Corinthians 5:17; Ezekiel 36:25-29; Romans 6:4). When we accept the Lord Jesus Christ as our personal Savior, we become *brand new*. A new brand. A new brand of people. A new brand of business leaders.

The Word of God declares that, "We may have boldness in the day of judgment; because as He is, so are we in this world" (1 John 4:17, NKJV). *As God is, so are we in the business world.* As His ambassadors, we are not only blessed with the attributes and characteristics of the living God, but we also stand for Him and His principles. We are extensions of Him, His kingdom, and *His holy brand*.

God's brand line extensions are endless. They transcend all human notions of time and space. I once heard a sermon by Pastor Joel Osteen of Lakewood Church, in which he ministered on how we are born from God's sovereign DNA and how it flows in our bloodline. Indeed, we are members of God's family and come from extraordinary ancestry. This is superior brand value.

Let's consider God's holy DNA within the context of a divine marketing plan. Let's begin to think of our holy bloodline and heritage as our holy brand architecture, an amazing and unparalleled lineage of sovereign brand attributes. Consider the fact that:

- Our Father created the universe. *There is amazing creativity in our brand architecture.*

- Jesus, who was the firstborn among many, defeated Satan and was brought back to life. *There is victory in our brand architecture.*

- The Holy Spirit is our helper and comforter. *There is constant help and support in our brand architecture.*

- Abraham had faith. *There is faith in our brand architecture.*

- Solomon was wise. *There is wisdom in our brand architecture.*

- Job was devoted to God and had integrity. *There is devotion to God and integrity in our brand architecture.*

- Esther had a sense of purpose and mission. *There is a sense of purpose and mission in our brand architecture.*

- Jeremiah had prophetic vision. *There is prophetic vision in our brand architecture.*

- Ruth had tremendous tenacity. *There is tenacity in our brand architecture.*

- Samson had enormous strength. *There is strength in our brand architecture.*

- The Queen of Sheba was highly intelligent. *There is brilliance in our brand architecture.*

- Nehemiah had a plan for rebuilding Jerusalem. *There is divine planning in our brand architecture.*

- David was a great leader. *There is great leadership in our brand architecture.*

- Paul was a tentmaker who employed others. *There is entrepreneurship in our brand architecture.*

- Boaz was wealthy and successful. *There is wealth and success in our brand architecture.*

- Abraham was redeemed. *There is redemption in our brand architecture.*

These are just a few examples of the distinguished pedigree and phenomenal brand architecture from which we originate.

We must always remember who we are and Whose we are. Remember your true God-given identity. We are a part of God's awesome brand. Consider yourself as a brand in God's kingdom. A kingdom brand. Think about how you would answer the following questions:

1. What do you stand for?

2. What are your personal brand attributes? How do they permeate the business world?

3. What is your value proposition to yourself? To your employer? To your employees? To your customers?

It's important that you take the time to pray and answer these questions, because you represent God in the business arena. It's imperative that you understand your brand identity and value in

Him and realize that they go far beyond your credentials, professional titles, and career.

The Brand Names that God Gives Us

Through His Word, God reminds us of who we are in His sight (Hebrews 13:21). Do you know your God-given brand names? If not, then please allow me to introduce you to some of them. God says we are:

1. Gods (Psalm 82:6; John 10:34; Genesis 1:27)

2. God's Elect People (1 Peter 1:1; Psalm 100:3; Deuteronomy 14:2)

3. God's Workmanship (Ephesians 2:10; 1 Corinthians 3:9,16)

4. Children of God (1 John 3:1-2; Matthew 5:45; 10:16; Psalm 82:6; 100:3)

5. Blessed (Genesis 26:29; 1 Peter 3:14; 4:14; Exodus 19:5)

6. Kings and Priests (Revelation 1:6; 5:10; 1 Peter 2:5, 9)

7. Family of God (1 Peter 4:17; Romans 8:14; Galatians 3:26; John 12:36)

8. The Body of Christ (1 Corinthians 3:23; 4:1; 12:27; 2 Corinthians 3:3; John 15:5-6)

9. Saints (1 Corinthians 1:2; Matthew 5:48; 1 Peter 2:9)

10. Special People (Deuteronomy 26:18; 1 Peter 2:9)

11. Ambassadors (2 Corinthians 5:20; 1 Corinthians 3:9; 4:1; John 8:31-32; 1 Peter 5:2; Luke 10:2)

12. Salt of the Earth (Matthew 5:13)

13. Light of the World (Matthew 5:14)

14. Eagles (Isaiah 40:31; Exodus 19:4)

15. More than Conquerors (Romans 8:37)

16. The Lender…not the borrower (Deuteronomy 28:12)

17. The Head…not the tail (Deuteronomy 28: 13)

18. Above…and not beneath (Deuteronomy 28: 13)

19. Chosen Generation (1 Peter 2:9)

20. Heirs to all of God's Promises (Galatians 3:29)

As Christians, we should relate to all of these kingdom-based brand names. As Christian business leaders, we are to embody and exemplify them in the workplace and marketplace. Print a copy of this listing of your godly brand attributes and place it where you will see it daily to remind yourself of who God says you are. This is by no means an exhaustive list, so feel free to search the Bible for more brand names to add to it. Take a look at the following, and you'll see what I mean: Ephesians 5:8; Luke 10:3; John 15:14; and 1 Thessalonians 5:5.

Refuse to dilute or pollute your powerful God-given brand. Always remember who God says you are, and never let others define you. He has already defined you. You have greatness within you. You are part of an elite brand. So embrace your kingdom lineage, respect your heavenly titles, and ensure that your godly brand attributes permeate every aspect of your commercial endeavors. Now that we have a better understanding of our godly brand attributes, let's move on to our second Planning Proverb.

Marketing Is Fishing

· ·

Fishing for Others to Bring into the Kingdom

Jesus gives us a great commission: "Go therefore and make disciples of all the nations, baptizing them in the name of the Father and of the Son and of the Holy Spirit" (Matthew 28:19, NKJV; 1 Timothy 2:3-4). Jesus tells us, "Follow Me and I will make you become fishers of men," and, "Do not be afraid. From now on you will catch men" (Mark 1:17, NKJV; Luke 5:10, NKJV). We are charged with seeking, or fishing for, and catching individuals to bring into the kingdom of God for salvation (1 Corinthians 9:22). In this way, marketing is analogous to fishing.

Marketing is fishing from a kingdom perspective. For instance, both fishing and marketing involve skillfully and strategically:

- Targeting a certain area or audience.

- Casting a line with a hook or slogan.

- Offering an enticing bait or benefit.

- Reeling in or recruiting.

Fishing with the Right Salt

Jesus says, "You are the salt of the earth; but if the salt loses its flavor, how shall it be seasoned? It is then good for nothing but to be thrown out and trampled underfoot by men" (Matthew 5:13, NKJV; Luke 14:34). Salt is one of our earliest preservatives. As a compound and ingredient, it enhances the flavor of foods and is known to stimulate thirst. It makes us thirsty. So as the salt of the earth and of the business world, we must also stimulate a thirst in others. A thirst for God. A thirst to know the secret to our commercial success. A thirst to know how we can be at peace during times of economic turmoil. When we stimulate a thirst for God in others, Jesus says He will do the rest by providing the water of life (Revelation 21:6).

Fishing in the Right Light

Jesus says, "You are the light of the world...let your light shine before men that they may see your good works and glorify your Father in heaven" (Matthew 5:14-16, NKJV). He encourages us to give light to those who are in spiritual darkness because they do not know Him (Luke 1:79; John 12:36).

It's important that we acknowledge our God-given role as the light of the world. The purpose of light, as a form of energy, is to make things visible or to illuminate and make them brighter. Light drives out darkness. You can't have light and darkness in the same place. In the commercial arena, we are called to illuminate and enhance the business world. We are called to drive out darkness, or anything ungodly, in the workplace and marketplace. We are to be the moral, ethical, and spiritual leaders in society. So the light of your personal character and integrity should shine brightly and consistently both during and after business hours.

How many people are being illuminated by their exposure to the Spirit of God in you? How brightly does your light shine in the workplace and marketplace? When we live and conduct business righteously, we allow our light to shine, attracting others and ultimately winning souls for God's kingdom (Proverbs 11:30). Do your best to ensure that everyone who encounters you also encounters the God in you. Commit to honorable business conduct (1 Peter 2:11-12). Dishonesty, gossip, hypocrisy, arrogance, racism, and sexism are never options for us as Christians.

Your True Target Audience

Your true target audience is always watching you. Some of them don't know God and are unsaved, while others are believers who simply need to strengthen their spiritual walk. These people represent your true target audience, or target market, as a fisher of men in the business arena.

Our *primary* target audience, which was given to us by Jesus Christ, is the world at large (Matthew 13:38; 28:19; Mark 16:15). Our *secondary* target market may be unsaved individuals, and our *tertiary* target audience might be lukewarm Christians (Revelation 3:16) who may be vacillating between living a life that glorifies God and one that does not. But ultimately, you and I have a target audience that is an audience of One: *God.*

In the commercial sector, your target audience is comprised of a myriad of individuals from associates, colleagues, employees, and managers to customers, clients, suppliers, strategic partners, and even competitors. They are watching you at work, in meetings, in the boardroom, at conventions, in class, in church, on flights, on the golf course, and in every aspect of life.

You might be wondering, *Why are they watching me? What are they looking for?* The answer is they *should be* watching you. Remember, you are the salt and the light of the business world! They need to observe you in order for them to see the God in you and ultimately grow closer to Him. They are looking for examples of the Highest forms of personal character, integrity, ethics, and professionalism in business. As God's ambassadors, we are called to be the spiritual leaders and the unequivocal marketing trendsetters of the business world.

Just Be Like Him

How do we serve as effective marketing vehicles for God? The Highest form of marketing for God is to just be like Him. We serve Him best when we emulate Him. Now, you might be wondering exactly how we mere humans could even entertain the notion of being like almighty God, especially in the ruthless and cutthroat world of business. Well, this may not be as much of a quantum leap as you might think.

First, we must remember that God created us in His own image (Genesis 1:26). He calls us "gods" and we are instructed to be imitators of God (Psalm 82:6; John 10:34; Ephesians 5:1). So we must leverage our godly brand attributes and obey His commandment to imitate or be like Him. Fortunately, God has already given us a professional coach to help us with this. God declares that we are to be "conformed to the image of His Son" (Romans 8:29, NKJV; 2 Corinthians 3:18).

Jesus Christ is our ultimate role model and coach. He is the Benchmark. The Standard. The Bible tells us that we have the mind of Christ (1 Corinthians 2:16) and Christ has the mind of God, so being like Him is not impossible. Jesus tells us:

> Don't you believe that I am in the Father and the Father is in me? The words I speak are not my own, but my Father who lives in me does his work through me.

> John 14:10 (NLT)

The Bible says that "Jesus went around doing good" (Acts 10:38, NLT). Just by reading the Bible and learning more about Jesus and His leadership practices, we can learn so much about how to be ambassadors for God, particularly within the commercial arena. In the Foreword for the book, *Church on Sunday, Work on Monday*, Ken Blanchard, world-renown leadership expert, states that "Jesus was a leadership model for all leaders" and that "business leaders need help and they need the kind of help that they can get from the leadership message of Jesus."[18]

We are to share God's blessings and anointing in our lives with others so that we can give our target audience a preview of Jesus and God's redemptive power (Revelation 1:1-5). Jesus tells us, "I have set you an example that you should do as I have done for you" (John 13:15, NLT). He is saying that He has given us an example and a pattern to follow so that we can serve as effective ambassadors and marketing vehicles for God. You don't have to lecture or preach about God at work. The only thing you need to do is just be like Jesus.

Just be like Him in the workplace and in the marketplace and you will attract the attention of your target audience. Just being like Jesus equates to leading and ministering to others *by example*. We are to exemplify godly principles in our business philosophy and practice. We are to be holy because He is holy (Leviticus 20: 7-8; 1 Peter 1:14-16). Example: The Bible relays the account of Jesus washing the disciples' feet (John 13:1–17). They are astonished that their Lord would perform this humble and submissive act. But Jesus patiently responds by telling them that just as He washes their feet, they should also wash one another's feet.

When we commit to being like Him, we are committing to be role models in our conduct (1 Timothy 4:12). We are committing to show others how to be "a pattern of good works; in doctrine *showing* integrity, reverence, incorruptibility, sound speech that cannot be condemned" (Titus 2:7-8, NKJV) putting our opponents to shame to the point that they have nothing negative to say about us! We are committing to set the Highest standards for others to follow by allowing our business practices to give credence to our belief in God. But does this mean that we have to be perfect?

The Bible tells us in Ephesians 4:1 (NKJV) that we must mature as individuals and "grow up in all things into Him who is the head—Christ." We are to be obedient to God and live and mature by following the example of the life of Jesus Christ. But this doesn't mean that we have to be perfect. We just need to exemplify excellence and wisdom. Remember, excellence is doing your best. Excellence is not perfection. We will *never* be perfect, for we all sin and fall short of the glory of God (Romans 3:23). We just need to do our best to live the Christian life we espouse so that God can use our faith, testimonies, and blessings to bring others closer to Him.

The God Effect

Your true target audience is looking for the evidence of God in you. They want to see the extraordinary effect of God in your life and in your business. The God effect. They are watching to see how you react to the peaks and valleys of life and business. They are looking to see how you respond to the positive peaks of job promotions, growing market share, and industry awards as well as to the negative valleys of job layoffs, lawsuits, and corporate scandals.

We know that success and prominence in the commercial arena attracts attention. But do you realize that your prominence as a proclaimed Christian business leader often attracts even more attention? Once others know that you are a highly successful Christian business leader, they become even more interested in and intrigued by you. Why is this the case?

I believe that this is partly due to a couple of reasons. The first is that it is, unfortunately, uncommon for a business leader in Western society to publicly profess his or her devotion to God. So when one does, there is an initial surprise factor and a certain level of curiosity and mystique that comes with the admission.

The second reason is that when a business leader takes a stand for God, others become inquisitive as to what will be different about his or her leadership philosophy, style, and business results as compared with their non-Christian or non-professed Christian counterparts. In the country club of prominent, yet non-professed Christian business leaders, what will be different about the self-proclaimed Christian leader? They want to know the God effect. And you are the sermon for communicating it.

You Are the Sermon

As a Christian business professional, the extent to which you are able to effectively market in both the traditional sense (i.e., commercial) and spiritual sense (i.e., as a fisher of men) depends largely on who you are as an individual. It begins with your character and integrity as a person and who you are in Christ. Your lifestyle and approach to business speak louder than your words. Stephen Covey captured this sentiment very well in his best-selling book, *The 7 Habits of Highly Effective People*, when he says, "In the last analysis, what we are communicates far more eloquently than anything we say or do."[19]

Make sure that your conduct does not cause others to perceive God unfavorably or give unbelievers a reason to reject Him (Psalm 39:1). At work, you may be the only representation of God that your unsaved colleagues will encounter for the week. They may not know any other Christians personally, but they know you. They may not go to church, but they go to work with you. They may not hear a sermon, but they hear you. They may not read the Bible, but they can read you. Remember, we win people over by our godly lives (1 Peter 3:1).

Being godly will gain you even more respectable and dependable employees, customers, board members, and lucrative business opportunities than you can ever imagine. People are more likely to follow what you *do* as opposed to what you *say*. Don't just lecture and give sermons about God to others, but commit to being a *living* sermon and testimony for God.

St. Francis of Assisi said, "Preach the gospel at all times and when necessary use words." The sermons that we live out in the workplace and marketplace are much more powerful and compelling than the ones we preach. *Who* you are as a person and *how* you conduct business are more poignant and profound than any sermon from a pulpit. Anyone can say anything. But how are you living your life? It's critical for others to witness the God in you because you are the sermon for those who do not go to church. You are the living Word for those who do not read the Bible. You are the testament, and your lifestyle is the testimony.

Your Slogan: "My Success Begins and Ends with God"

Most people, myself included, are intrigued by socially prominent, highly successful business people with their prestigious titles, extensive staff, country club memberships, private jets, beachfront mansions, yachts, and couture wardrobes. We want to know: What's the secret to their success?

Wouldn't it be a powerful testimony if these successful business leaders confessed that the true secret of their success begins and ends with God (Revelation 21:6; Isaiah 44:6)? It is only through the strength and power of God that we are able to achieve success. It is the *God in us* (1 Peter 4:11; 2 Corinthians 9:14)! Most of us have been abundantly blessed. One way for us to honor our position as God's marketing vehicles is by sharing our testimonies of how God is the secret to our blessings and success. Being exceedingly grateful and humble, we must *decrease* our role in our success so that God may be exalted and *increased* (John 3:30). Don't be ashamed, but be bold for Christ (Philippians 1:20) and boast only in the Lord (Psalm 34:2). Begin today by making this your slogan and motto: "My success begins and ends with God." I love the way Oprah Winfrey captured this sentiment on the last day of her extraordinary show's twenty-five-year run:

> People often ask me what is the secret to the success of this show. I non jokingly say, 'My team and Jesus,' because nothing but the hand of God has made this possible for me.

My Success Begins and Ends with God, but What about My Failures?

In Job 36:15, the Bible tells us that God gets our attention through adversity. God allows us to fail in order to discipline us and build our character so that ultimately He may be glorified. The Bible tells us that God uses adversity to benefit those He loves by strengthening them and chastising or correcting them

(Proverbs 3:12; Hebrews 12:5-11). Even while we're doing our best to be like Him, God will humble us by allowing us to fail. Sometimes, He will indirectly test us by allowing the enemy to put us through trials as in the case of Job (book of Job). Other times, He will directly test us Himself as in the case of Joseph who loved and honored God yet had to endure many trials, including being sold into slavery and falsely imprisoned (Genesis 37:36; 39:1-23).

After Job and Joseph went through their trials and passed their tests, God blessed and promoted them (Job 42:10; Genesis 41:44). He blessed Job with twice the fortune he had previously, and He appointed Joseph to a powerful position as administrator over Egypt. Similarly, God uses our failures to test our faith before He blesses and promotes us to Higher levels in life and in business to see if we will continue to follow Him in spite of the difficult circumstances.

Sometimes God permits us to fail privately, while other times He allows us to fail right in front of our target audience. He will: "Do this right in front of the people so they can see you. For perhaps they will pay attention to this, even though they are such rebels. Bring your baggage outside during the day so they can watch you" (Ezekiel 12:3-4, NLT). In these instances, we go through adversity while members of our target audience have a front row seat to view it! Life's public trials. These are the times we are fired from the job; passed over for the promotion; lose the lucrative account; are sued; have to file for bankruptcy; go through a public scandal, divorce, or life-threatening illness. These times are living nightmares wrought with pain, fear, anger, embarrassment, and profound disappointment.

During these times we find that not only are our personal character and professional reputations called into question, but they are called into question on a public stage for the world to witness. Why would our loving God allow this to happen to us? The surprising answer is because He loves us. When God allows you to fail publicly, it accomplishes two feats simultaneously:

1. He shows His love for you by developing your character so that you can serve as a more effective marketing vehicle for Him

2. He shows His love for your target audience by allowing them to witness God's redeeming power in your life.

Regarding the first point, the Word of God says, "Behold, I have refined you, but not as silver, I have tested you in the furnace of affliction" (Isaiah 48:10, NASB). When we are going through trials, God is refining and strengthening us as individuals (2 Corinthians 4:15-16). Our trials provide an opportunity for us to strengthen our individual character by humbling ourselves before God and trusting Him.

Our trials also allow us to be able to relate to and comfort others who are going through similar ordeals. How will we ever witness God's power to save us from harm if we never face danger? How will we ever share our powerful testimonies of how God brought us through trouble if we never experience trials? As the Apostle Paul explains:

> All praise to God, the Father of our Lord Jesus Christ. God is our merciful Father and the source of all comfort. He comforts us in all our troubles so that we can comfort others. When they are troubled, we will be able to give them the same comfort God has given us.
>
> 2 Corinthians 1:3-4 (NLT)

In reference to the second point, God will sometimes allow us to fail so that He can save us and raise us to a Higher level of redemption and success for our target audience to witness. This may take place on a public platform, such as in the media, so that others can witness the magnificent work of God in our lives and so that everyone, including us, will know that it was *only* by His mighty works, mercy, and grace that we survived (1 Corinthians 1:27-29; John 9:3; 2 Kings 19:19). In these cases, our trials become our testimonies for others so that they too may become believers or strengthen their faith in God (John 1:7). And all "will know that it is I, the Lord, who cuts the tall tree down and makes the short tree grow tall. It is I who makes the green tree wither and gives the dead tree new life" (Ezekiel 17:24, NLT).

We are to count it a joy when going through trials because God is revealing what is really in our hearts (2 Chronicles 32:31) and we are maturing in the process (James 1:2-4). Scripture tells us that we should not give up because even though "our outward man may appear to be perishing, yet the inward *man* is being renewed day by day" and that our affliction, "which is but for a moment, is working for us a far more exceedingly *and* eternal weight of glory" (2 Corinthians 4:16-17, NKJV).

Although God will test and refine us through our adversities, in the end, we will come out like pure gold (Job 23:10; Malachi 3:3; Psalm 66:10-12). So don't be dismayed by what may seem to be a *public* failure. But realize that you are being strengthened *privately*, on the inside, relative to your character, integrity, and overall relationship with God.

Ultimately, one of the main purposes of our trials is for God to be glorified (2 Corinthians 4:15-17; 1 Peter 1: 6-7). The children of Israel wandered through the wilderness for forty years, yet God never allowed their clothes and shoes to wear out! Furthermore, He sent food from heaven for them and caused water to gush from a rock so they would remain nourished (Exodus 16:35; 17:6; Numbers 11:9; 20:11)! God was constantly showing them and others that *He is Lord God* (Deuteronomy 29:5-6). So as devastating as these wilderness experiences or life trials may be, they are necessary for reminding us and showing others the sovereign power of God in our lives.

Remain faithful to Him, and He will bring you through the valley periods in life and in business. You are one of His important evangelists. But you still have to "endure afflictions, do the work of the evangelist, fulfill your ministry" (2 Timothy 4:5, NKJV). Stay encouraged. And remember that God desires all the glory, and in the end He will get all the glory.

Pull Strategies Versus Push Strategies

In the field of marketing, we employ push strategies and pull strategies to influence consumers to purchase various products and services. A pull strategy is generally defined as a marketing strategy in which a company relies mainly on product advertising or consumer sales promotions aimed at creating consumer demand and motivating consumers to pull the product through the channel. A push strategy, on the contrary, is broadly defined as activities aimed at getting products into the dealer pipeline and accelerating sales by offering incentives to dealers, retailers, and salespeople. So the product is pushed through the channel. These incentives might include introductory price, distribution, and advertising allowances.

Which marketing strategy proves more effective for us as ambassadors for God in the workplace and marketplace? The answer is that it depends entirely on the situation and the individuals involved. Some of us may be more comfortable with one strategy over another. In some business situations, pull strategies are more effective, while other circumstances call for more of a push strategy. Let's continue exploring these two strategies and how we might leverage them in our role as marketing vehicles for God.

Jesus says, "Blessed are those who hunger and thirst for righteousness, for they shall be filled," and we are encouraged to always be prepared to share our testimony for God with others (Matthew 5:6, NKJV; 1 Peter 3:15). Our success and failures in life and in business get people's attention and cause them to ask questions. When people begin to inquire about how we achieved our success or how we made it through adversity, it shows that they are eager to learn more about the secret to our success. They are *thirsty* for knowledge; they are looking for *light*. It is at this point that they may be most receptive to hearing our powerful testimonies. They are primed and positioned to learn more about God and His kingdom-centric principles for success. And this is the perfect opportunity for us to share our testimony for God.

During my last week at The Coca-Cola Company, one of my colleagues took me out to lunch. As we sat in the chic restaurant chatting about the business, our teams, jobs, and career goals, the conversation turned to spirituality. We openly discussed the ways in which we felt God was leading us in our careers.

The conversation shifted to the topic of whether or not people in corporate America should be open about sharing their religious and spiritual beliefs. We both agreed that many of our saved colleagues feel their religious beliefs are private and are reluctant to share their Christian values with their coworkers. I believe that this is contrary to the Word of God.

If you are a Christian, then you are called to be an ambassador for God, a fisher of men. One of the best ways to bring others into the kingdom is by sharing your faith. This is not a choice. It's a mandate from God and a directive from Jesus to share our faith with others. In fact, the Bible says that we should be so on fire for God that "we cannot stop telling about everything we have seen and heard" (Acts 4:20)!

The business sector, particularly in Western society, has a history of being religion-adverse. Speaking about spirituality and religion, within the context of commercial business and within the walls of corporate America, is considered taboo and shunned upon. Nevertheless, I believe that you don't have to mask or hide your spiritual beliefs in the business arena. You just have to use spiritual discernment and wisdom and be strategic and respectful in the manner in which you share your faith with others.

Let's consider some examples of pull and push strategies within a spiritual context. As He predicted His death on the cross, Jesus said, "And I, if I am lifted up from the earth, will draw all peoples to Myself" (John 12:32, NKJV). If we were to consider this statement in the context of a marketing strategy for us as ambassadors for God, the core message would be that when we as Christians lift Jesus up or glorify Him in life and business, then we consequently draw or pull people to Him. So this is more of a pull, versus a push, marketing strategy in the sense that we are pulling or drawing others into the kingdom by exhibiting a lifestyle and business conduct that generates intrigue among members of our target audience.

Pull strategies manifest themselves when we are *just being* who we are in God during the peaks and valleys of our lives and in business. There should be something about you that others find so positively intriguing that it draws or pulls them to you. It may be the wisdom, confidence, peace, and joy that emanate from you. Both saved and unsaved people will recognize the special anointing that is on you to the point that it pulls them to you and causes them to want to learn more about you and proactively reach out to you with questions. This equates to opportunity for you to respond by sharing your faith with them.

Pull strategies are effective for people who are not positively predisposed to religion because they allow you to *expose* your beliefs to others rather than *impose* them on others. One example of a powerful pull strategy would be a situation in which you continue to keep an optimistic attitude even during one of your public failures. Or a situation in which you are positive, calm, and peaceful in the midst of a corporate downsizing while your colleagues are negative, worried, and stressed. By displaying the peace of God, you evoke their interest in learning why you are so joyful and calm in the midst of turmoil and how they too can reduce their stress and be joyful.

If a coworker asks you for advice about a personal problem or professional challenge, this is the time to offer *spiritual, practical solutions* and to share your testimony for God. This is the time for you to share the good news and to comfort and console the brokenhearted and glorify God (Isaiah 61:1-3). This is the time to witness to them! This is an excellent opportunity to pull them into the knowledge of God. The key point here is that they asked you; hence, they opened the door for an invitation for you to share your faith with them.

Now let's consider a *push strategy*, which is when we proactively encourage others to know God without any initial inquiry from them. In this case, you simply take it upon yourself to gently nudge members of your target audience into learning more about God through appeals such as invitations to visit your church or join the company's lunchtime Bible study. The key point here is that they *did not* show any initial interest in learning more about God or your spiritual beliefs. You are attempting to gently push them closer to Him without any initial interest on their part.

A push strategy may not be the most effective one for witnessing to others, particularly in a business setting. A push strategy may prove problematic and counterproductive should your colleagues start to feel that you are forcing your religious beliefs on them, and they may begin to resent you for it. Even though your intentions are good and sincere, they could become so offended that they file religious-based discrimination charges against you. This is not to suggest that this could not also occur with the pull strategy. But at least with the pull strategy, the other individual is the one who expressed initial interest in your lifestyle. They opened the door for you as opposed to you just barging in.

It's important to note, however, that when done appropriately in a kind, considerate, and nonthreatening way, a push strategy can still be a valid approach for witnessing to others. Some of us are more receptive to invitations to religious events as well as consistent encouragements to strengthen our relationship with God.

You must pray and ask God for spiritual discernment and wisdom regarding which strategy you should employ in a business environment. Regardless of the strategy you use, you should never share your spiritual and religious beliefs in ways that are overbearing, critical, and judgmental. Talking in tongues or chanting to colleagues and trying to force them to read biblical scriptures are counterproductive in the business arena and might get you fired!

God desires for you to share His Word with your colleagues (Acts 4:17-20). He will reveal the appropriate timing, approach, and strategy for sharing your testimony. Just focus on being like

Him. Plant the seeds to bring others closer to God, and He will take care of the harvest (Matthew 9:37-38; Luke 10:2).

Real-Life Examples of Ambassadorship

We must be spiritually discerning, respectful, strategic, and tactful in our evangelistic approach and service as an ambassador for God. Ray Berryman, the former CEO of Berryman & Henigar Enterprises, offers this advice to other Christian business owners:

> Be open about your belief in God. Don't be intimidated or hesitant to express your faith in ways like opening a meeting in prayer when this is appropriate. Just be consistent. Our practices need to be in agreement with the principles we say we believe. This means being open to anybody who sees something that's not in line with our profession. Public faith invites public scrutiny.[20]

Now, you may be wondering, What if I manage a team of other individuals who don't share my spiritual beliefs? Won't my being open about my Christian values make my team intimidated or concerned that I might consciously or unconsciously discriminate against them because they don't share my beliefs?

In America, each person has a right to his or her religious convictions and pursuits. If you are a manager of others, you can be open about your own faith while still being respectful of others' spiritual beliefs even if you don't necessarily agree with them. You should never give your employees the impression that they must agree with your beliefs, religious or otherwise, in order to keep their jobs or get promoted.

As Dennis Bakke, the former CEO of the $12 billion AES Corporation explains in *Executive Influence*:

> It is not a requirement that people share my Christianity in order to work at AES. However, they do have to adopt our way of doing business, and they should know that our corporate values are consistent with biblical faith.[21]

The cofounder of Inmac and Ariba Technologies, Inc., Ken Eldred, also shares:

> Believers should not be afraid to be public about their faith. Yes, I've taken flack for being so open about what I believe. However, I've also had people who have given me a bad time come back privately and say they respect the fact that I'm not ashamed of my faith.[22]

In her autobiography, the founder of Mary Kay Cosmetics, the late Mary Kay Ash, also echoes these sentiments:

> I never try to impose my personal religious beliefs on anyone. I do let it be known, however, that God is a very important part of my life.

You can combat potential feelings of intimidation, on the part of your employees, by treating them fairly based on their professional performance regardless of their spiritual beliefs. You might even consider sharing the fact that your Christian values actually denounce showing favoritism (Acts 10:34-36; Isaiah 61:8). When necessary, you may need to articulate the fact that Christian values are a foundation for inclusion, not exclusion.

Several years ago, I worked with a young lady who served as an administrative assistant for our team. She was at a point in her career where she was dissatisfied with her job and desperately wanted to change industries and relocate to another state. I knew from our personal conversations that she was not living a saved life. I also knew that she believed in God, but, as she said, she "hadn't read the Bible in years."

As an ambassador for God, I had to select the best marketing strategy—either a push strategy or a pull strategy. I prayed for discernment and was led to follow more of a pull strategy. So when she would ask me about how I was able to get a job in another state, I simply shared my testimony of how God made a way for me to relocate by blessing me with the right professional contacts. I told her about how God led me to take practical measures such as identifying my career goals, developing a career plan, updating my resume, and reaching out to the right professionals in my field. I also encouraged her to ask Him for guidance.

One day, I mentioned to her that one book that really helped me was *The Purpose Driven Life* by Rick Warren. I told her how much I appreciated the book because of its focus on God's purpose for us as individuals and mentioned that I refer back to it during different seasons in my life. Surprisingly, she was so intrigued that she went out and purchased the book and read it for herself.

Interestingly enough, I had actually prayed and asked God if I should loan her my copy. He spoke to me, not aloud, but deep down in my spirit with His still, quiet voice and told me to allow her to go and purchase it herself because then it would actually mean more to her because she would have invested her hard-earned money into it and would be more apt to read it. And so she did.

Today, she is well on her way to achieving not only her career goals but, more importantly, God's purpose for her life. Just let the Holy Spirit lead you, and He will provide the right opportunity to bring about His will. Your only job is to allow yourself to serve as God's marketing vehicle.

Corporate Guidelines

The Bible says we are to submit to our employers (1 Peter 2:18). So it's important that we adhere to workplace guidelines and procedures, as set by our employers, even as we seek to serve as effective ambassadors for God.

Every workplace has its own unique business codes of conduct. Some organizations embrace the sharing of spiritual beliefs, while others prohibit it. I encourage you to investigate your organization's rules and regulations around religious practices. If you are prohibited from verbally witnessing for God, then just continue to pray and *be like God*. If you can't vocalize God, then allow your target audience to visualize Him through you.

Know the Fifth "P" of Marketing

Most of us are familiar with the 4Ps of marketing: Product, Price, Place, and Promotion. In this section, we'll consider some of the practical ways to execute the 4Ps in ways that are reflective of God's principles. But before we get to these traditional marketing mix elements, we'll introduce a new one: the fifth "P" of marketing: your kingdom platform.

Your Kingdom Platform

In marketing, the concept of a brand platform is generally defined as all of the tangible and intangible aspects of a brand. A brand platform includes elements such as brand name, vision, mission, values, and personality and can evolve into unique selling points or promotional angles such as quality, value, prestige, and expertise. Example: BMW's brand platform centers on being the ultimate driving machine, while Volvo's brand platform is focused on safety.

The brand platform for your product or service plays a critical role in informing and facilitating your marketing goals and strategies. Now, let's consider your brand platform from a spiritual standpoint. What is your kingdom platform?

Your kingdom platform is defined as what you and your business stand for from a kingdom, or a godly, perspective, and it should always reinforce God's principles such as the fruit of the Spirit: love, joy, peace, patience, kindness, goodness, faithfulness, gentleness, and self-control (1 John 4:8; Galatians 5:22-23). Your kingdom platform should serve as the overarching theme from which your marketing strategies and tactics are spawn.

Example: You might be an interior decorator. Because, for you, interior decorating is a Higher calling than just making a room look pleasant and inviting, your kingdom platform may be centered on creating joy and peace for people within their living spaces. In this way, your platform reinforces godly principles and, consequently, serves as a strong spiritual foundation for your marketing initiatives.

You don't necessarily have to advertise your kingdom platform unless you feel led to do so. You just need to identify it, commit it to God, and ensure that the remaining 4Ps of your marketing plan align with it. Having a kingdom platform is just another way to bring your marketing plans and programs to a Higher level of success and significance.

Product

We equate a product with an item or service that is bought and sold. From a marketing perspective, a product or service is viewed as the sum of the intrinsic (e.g., physical and psychological) and extrinsic (e.g., sociological) consumer benefits the buyer derives from purchase, ownership, and consumption. For instance, marketers of luxury automobiles might design their strategies in a way that addresses not only the basic utilitarian and safety needs of consumers but also the social prestige and psychological benefits of owning a certain luxury vehicle.

As Christian business professionals, we must ensure that we market superior products and services that are not contradictory to the Word of God. Clearly, we know that they should be legal, moral, and ethical consumer offerings. But they should also be positive and edifying for consumers. The intention behind the creation of our products and services should be for good, not evil, purposes (Amos 5:14).

If you feel any sense of spiritual dissention about the products and services that you are promoting, these feelings are not a coincidence. They may be indicative of the Holy Spirit making you aware of the fact that you are out of alignment with God's plan, and He may be leading you to make the necessary changes in your business or career. Pray for guidance and an understanding of God's will, and be obedient to Him, because first and foremost you represent Him in the business world—not a particular company, product, or service.

Price

We know that price equates to the assigned monetary value of a product or service. Most of us certainly appreciate pricing strategies and methodologies for identifying appropriate price points for goods and services given factors such as supply, demand, and a variety of other market influences. The Bible warns us about dishonest and unfair pricing strategies. Scripture says that we should not steal from others (Ephesians 4:28; Leviticus 25:14) but are to work to provide useful products and services to share with others. This reference to stealing also includes robbing consumers, customers, and clients out of their hard-earned money by implementing unfair pricing strategies.

In the U.S., there have been instances in which minorities have been targeted with unfair pricing strategies. Case in point: A number of empirical research studies, such as ones conducted by the National Community Reinvestment Coalition (NCRC), have reported racial inequities in real estate rates and housing fees in which African-American homebuyers have been charged significantly more in fees than their Caucasian counterparts.

Targeting certain consumer groups with unfair fee structures and pricing strategies is never justified. If you find that your pricing strategies are questionable, then I encourage you to reevaluate them and institute a fair and equitable system so that you are not only in alignment with national laws and the market but, more importantly, you are in alignment with God.

Place

Place commonly refers to where a company's offerings will be available for sale to consumers. Retail establishments such as grocery stores, mass merchandisers, and retail malls continue to serve as common places or outlets for selling an array of products and services. And now the World Wide Web or Internet also serves as a formidable and prominent virtual place through which a multiplicity of products and services are offered.

For us as Christian business leaders, the notion of place denotes the locales in which we have the opportunity to not only sell our goods and services, but also serve as marketing vehicles for God. In this respect, we must remember that for us as God's ambassadors, the concept of *place* extends far beyond sales outlets to include the entire *workplace* and *marketplace*. It includes the *world* at large.

Promotion

The final element of the traditional marketing mix is promotion, which refers to the ways in which information about a firm's products and services will be communicated to the target market. We know that customary promotional vehicles include advertising, media, public relations, and publicity as well as elements such as media reach and frequency and gross rating points (GRPs). But as a Christian business leader who is applying promotional concepts at a Higher level, it's important to ask yourself a few key questions:

1. What am I really promoting? (e.g., Is it a product or a status symbol? Is it a service or an experience?)

2. Is my promotional message appropriate, positive, and edifying for the target audience?

3. Are my promotional strategies in alignment with God's principles?

Because of the multitude of diverse products and services available with their own underlying promotional strategies, it would be impossible for me to offer a biblical litmus test for each one. But let me share a few examples of promotional strategies and tactics that do not exemplify biblical principles.

First, let's consider a few basic biblical premises. We know that the Word of God teaches us that God does not show favoritism (Acts 10:34); that we are all God's children (Romans 8:16); and that whatever we do, we should do it for God and with Him in mind (Colossians 3:23). Being cognizant of these principles, following are a few examples of promotional strategies and tactics that are *out of alignment* with God's teachings:

- Only featuring models of a specific race or ethnic group as the epitome of beauty in advertisements, as opposed to showcasing a diversity of racial and ethnic groups, is *out of alignment*.

- Perpetuating negative racial and ethnic stereotypes in advertisements is *out of alignment*.

- Degrading women in advertisements is *out of alignment*.

- Building up one group of consumers by denigrating another in the name of humor is *out of alignment*.

- Advertising pathologically thin models as opposed to featuring a variety of healthy physical shapes and sizes is *out of alignment*.

- Directly or indirectly promoting alcohol to underage youth is *out of alignment*.

- Directly or indirectly promoting tobacco products to minors is *out of alignment*.

- Conveniently failing to disclose the known adverse side effects of prescription drugs in advertising is *out of alignment*.

- Incorporating negative or misogynistic lyrics into promotional jingles is *out of alignment*.

- Promoting violence, criminal activity, and sexually explicit content vis-à-vis advertising and promotions is *out of alignment*.

These are just a few commonly witnessed examples of marketing practices that do not embody truth and excellence in marketing and advertising. Consequently, they are not reflective of God's principles.

Corporate Versus Kingdom Philanthropy

Corporate social responsibility (CSR) is generally defined as the integration of business operations and values in such a way that the interests of all of a company's stakeholders (e.g., investors, customers, employees, and the community) are reflected in the company's policies and practices. Most of us are familiar with two common initiatives within CSR plans: corporate philanthropy and cause-related marketing (CRM), or cause marketing.

Corporate philanthropy refers to charitable initiatives that help a company increase visibility, attract loyal customers, and offer employees the opportunity to band together in support of major social and civic concerns. A number of companies oversee corporate philanthropy through their corporate foundation, public relations, or external affairs department.

Leading companies have discovered that there is a strong business case for corporate philanthropy and community involvement. Empirical research studies have shown that people look-ing to work for a particular company have actually admitted that they factor in whether or not they view the company as a good corporate citizen. Studies have also shown that employees feel good in knowing that their company is engaged in giving back to the community.

In recent years, cause marketing has become more prevalent in business. Cause marketing is defined as a commercial activity by which businesses and charities form partnerships with each other to market an image, product, or service for mutual benefit. It's an initiative for addressing social causes and issues by provid-ing resources and funding while simultaneously addressing busi-ness objectives.

Cause marketing programs frequently link the purchase of a product with fundraising. Example: Let's say you own or manage a fast-food restaurant. Your cause-marketing offer to the con-sumer might be: "Purchase a combo meal and a percent of the proceeds will be donated to the local children's hospital." As a result of your cause marketing program:

- Your restaurant benefits from:

    - Increased sales particularly among socially con-scious customers.

    - Enhanced corporate image in the local community and marketplace.

    - Improved employee satisfaction and engagement as a result of your team working for a socially respon-sible company.

- The local children's hospital benefits from additional financial contributions.

- The cause (i.e., children's health care) benefits from heightened publicity.

Corporate social responsibility initiatives can generate significant rewards for all involved. But as Christian business leaders, we must consider the following: How can we leverage corporate social responsibility for the Highest good? How do we extend our philanthropic initiatives from merely building up a company to building up the kingdom of God? How do we pursue kingdom philanthropy?

Given rampant cases of terrorism, starvation, domestic violence, and health-related epidemics including HIV/AIDS, cancer, diabetes, and obesity, there is certainly no scarcity of viable civic and social causes for any company interested in philanthropy. While many of these epidemics are at national proportion, when it comes to addressing victims at the local grassroots community level, it's usually up to the neighborhood churches and other civic organizations to support individual victims and their families. So where is the significant, public outpouring of support for churches from the business community particularly in Western society? It's important to note here that when I speak of support for churches, I am referring to churches across all types of denominations that believe in God and Jesus Christ.

When we as Christian business leaders began to include formal support of God's churches and Christian organizations within the context of our marketing plans and philanthropic outreach efforts, we will have begun the process of bringing corporate philanthropy and charitable giving to a Higher level. And when we are brave enough to publicly proclaim our support of these alliances and how we are working to glorify God in our marketing practices, then we will have truly begun to establish and execute a divine marketing plan.

To whom much is given, much is required (Luke 12:48). Don't ever be ashamed of the gospel of Christ because it is the power of God, which brings about salvation for everyone who believes in Him (Romans 1:16). When you use your marketing influence to help advance worthy causes, the Lord will reward you (Matthew 19:17; Galatians 6:9). Have the courage and fortitude to support churches and civic organizations in ways that are important and necessary, even if they are not always high profile and publicity generating.

By pursuing kingdom philanthropy, your company will serve as a model corporate citizen for others in the community and a catalyst for drawing more attention to, and support for, important charitable initiatives. And for this, you and your organization will also be tremendously blessed by God.

Example: Sam Walton, the founder of Wal-Mart and Sam's Club, established the Sam and Helen R. Walton Award in 1991 when the Waltons made a gift of $6 million to their church, the Presbyterian Church (U.S.A.) Foundation. This donation included a $3 million endowment to be used by new church developments with a strategic focus on site acquisition as a means of sharing the Christian faith in local communities.

By incorporating God's kingdom principles in our divinely inspired marketing plans, we become the magnificent trendsetters and market innovators God created us to be. Remember, God says we are the head and not the tail (Deuteronomy 28: 13). We should not be following the world; the world should be following us.

Now, you might be wondering, *Who's doing it right? What are some of the successful companies with marketing initiatives that are actually in alignment with God's teachings?* Well, I am so glad you asked! There are a number of successful companies that glorify God through their marketing initiatives. We'll explore some of them in the following sections.

Real-Life Examples: Companies That Glorify God with Their Marketing Initiatives

· · · · · · · · · · · · · · · · · · · ·

In & Out Burger

In & Out Burger is a California-based fast-food chain that has been operating for over fifty years. In the past, In & Out Burger has been known to promote the Word of God by simply imprinting Biblical scriptures on various packaging elements, cups, and containers. This is a subtle, yet extremely effective, tactic, because when people see the imprints, many of them will undoubtedly become intrigued enough to look up biblical references if they are not already familiar with them.

In & Out Burger's marketing tactics might actually encourage some people to open up a Bible for the first time in their lives! They may encourage people to take their first step in establishing a relationship with God and ultimately gaining eternal salvation. Because the company's leadership team made a concerted effort to glorify God through simple marketing tactics, they have the potential to positively impact the spiritual lives of thousands of people every day.

Forever 21

As one of the fastest-growing retail clothing chains with over 456 stores in the U.S., Forever 21 was launched by Don and Jin Sook Chang, natives of South Korea who migrated to Los Angeles and opened the first Forever 21 store in 1984. In the past, the Forever 21 team has printed "John 3:16" on the bottom of shopping bags. Bibles are also often on display at the company's corporate headquarters in Los Angeles. "It's a proclamation of my parents' faith, not them saying you all have to believe,"[23] says Esther Chang in a recent interview with the *Los Angeles Times*. Esther and her sister, Linda, are executives in the family business.

Chick-fil-A

Throughout this book, I've referenced many ways in which Chick-fil-A, the $3.5 billion restaurant chain, continues to glorify God in the commercial arena. Another example is through their marketing promotions that target children. For example, in an effort to reinforce education, character, integrity, and moral values, the company designed Kid's Meal bags to include activities, games, and facts that stimulate young minds and help plant the seeds of good character. In past years, Chick-fil-A created illustrated, age-specific card sets, which answer questions on a myriad of topics such as "What happens to food once it hits the stomach?" and "How does a 4.5 million-pound space shuttle fly?" The card sets were developed to explain the uniqueness of how things work while demonstrating the importance of science and technology.

On their corporate website, Chick-fil-A provides an overview of their Kids & Family initiative, explaining that "in order to grow up strong, kids need both good nutrition and good values" and how "Chick-fil-A is dedicated to providing both in a way that is delicious and fun." The company is also a national sponsor of Core Essentials®, which is an educational program that gives teachers and parents a number of creative tools for imparting key values to elementary-age kids. For over twenty-five years, Chick-fil-A has also sponsored a scholarship program at Berry College in Rome, Georgia, which includes a summer camp for two thousand children. Chick-fil-A also operates twelve foster homes and a marriage conference center.

Interstate Battery System of America, Inc.

The $650-million Dallas-based Interstate Battery System of America, Inc. is an example of another highly successful company that has implemented marketing initiatives that are in alignment with the Word of God. On their corporate website, Interstate Batteries offers a link to their Chaplain's Department, indicating, "We are pleased to provide an opportunity to present biblical truths and tools to an array of people within and outside our company."

Interstate Batteries also invites the public to learn more about their philanthropic initiatives, which include "serving hot meals to the less fortunate in downtown Dallas to sponsoring orphans in Galich, Russia." The company provides details on many of their outreach programs, including Corporate Chaplain, Angel Tree, Circle of Light, Children's Hope Chest, and Union Gospel Mission.

The company's website states that their chairman, Norm Miller, "makes time to speak to a variety of audiences interested in how he found the truth of Christianity and how he learned to effectively apply biblical principles to create a more successful business." Anyone viewing the website is invited to download and watch a video clip to learn more.

The phenomenally successful movement, *I AM SECOND* (www.iamsecond.com), which inspires people, of all walks of life, to live for God, was founded by Norm Miller. The initiative started as a conviction in his heart and a directive by the Bible verse, John 13:6, which encouraged Norm to look for ways to lift up Christ around the Dallas-Fort Worth area so that he might draw the people of his city to Jesus. What began as Norm Miller's vision for a local geography now spans international markets.

Hobby Lobby

Since 1997, Hobby Lobby, the $2 billion arts and crafts center chain store, has placed full-page holiday message advertisements in leading news publications, including the New York Times, the Los Angeles Times, and USA Today. The ads are usually targeted for Easter, Christmas, and Independence Day and feature headlines such as "Because He Lives, You Can Have Eternal Life"; "The Way in a Manger!"; "He is Risen"; and "In God We Trust." During Easter of this year, ads were placed in 290 newspapers in thirty states with a readership in excess of 47 million.

Grace 17:20

I love trying new restaurants and recently decided to have lunch at one by the name of Grace 17:20 located in a suburb of Atlanta, Georgia. While the European architecture and ambiance were inviting and the food was delicious, I was still most intrigued with the name of the restaurant. What did it mean? What's the story behind it?

I finally gave into my curiosity and asked my waitress, who promptly shared that Grace 17:20 is based on the Bible verse found in Matthew 17:20. She showed me where the reference "Matthew 17:20" was inscribed in small typeface at the bottom of the menu, but the actual scripture in its entirety was *not* printed. And with that, she offered no additional information. And with that, it was clear that the onus was on me to look up the scripture for myself. What a profound marketing strategy for God!

I am certain that multitudes of people continue to inquire about the name of their restaurant. And they continue to lead people, both saved and unsaved, to the Word of God for the answer. Poignant. And with that said, I will, in turn, leave it up to you to look up Matthew 17:20. Enjoy!

Directives for Executing the Divine Marketing Plan

Following are six suggestions for implementing the divine marketing plan for your business:

1. Pray for God's wisdom in identifying and communicating your kingdom platform and marketing goals, objectives, strategies, and tactics. Ask Him to reveal His plan for enabling you to market your products and services in ways that glorify Him (1 Chronicles 17:25).

2. Remember you are a marketing vehicle, ambassador, and fisher of men for God. Ask that He remind you of this on a daily basis and provide opportunities for you to bring others into the kingdom (Matthew 4:19; Mark 1:17; Matthew 28:19).

3. Make sure that your marketing and advertising messages are in alignment with godly principles (Colossians 3:23).

4. Make kingdom philanthropy a part of your divine marketing plan (Deuteronomy 15:11). Develop a plan for how your organization can facilitate sustainable social development, meeting the needs of the present generation while anticipating and planning for the needs of future generations. Make kingdom philanthropy one of your business objectives, and develop your own scorecard for measuring the benefits to your bottom line—both quantitative and qualitative. Partner with local churches. Some of your initiatives might include:

- Executing a cause-marketing program for a charitable organization.

- Implementing an employee volunteerism effort in the community.

- Conducting corporate fundraisers for charitable causes.

- Disseminating Public Service Announcements (PSAs) to bring awareness to an important civic or social concern, and highlight some of the ways in which your company is working to combat it.

5. Biblical marketing coaches: Include a number of disciples such as Jesus, who was the Ultimate Fisher of Men using both pull and push strategies with everyone from believers to unbelievers, criminals, and prostitutes (Matthew 4:18-25; 21:32; Luke 2:41-52); Mordecai, who coached Esther on how to market herself to be chosen as queen (book of Esther); Naomi, who coached Ruth on how to present and market herself as a suitable wife for Boaz (Ruth 2:22; 3:1-

5); and, Paul who founded and promoted many churches (book of 1 Corinthians; book of 2 Corinthians).

6. Praise God for your divine marketing plan (2 Corinthians 9:19)!

In the next chapter, we'll explore how to ensure that our business operations, practices, and protocols are reflective of godly principles. But for now, let's end this chapter with a couple of quotes from David Rockefeller Sr. and Anne Beiler:

> I don't use my platform to directly evangelize people, but I do speak openly about God's goodness and love. I'm a firm believer in walking before talking. As Christians, if we live our lives as unto the Lord, this will create opportunities to share. To be salt, you have to be tasty. To be light, you have to shine. I've always said, "Light shines, it doesn't speak.[24]
>
> —Anne Beiler, Founder
> Auntie Anne's Pretzels

> The Christian ethic played an essential part in my upbringing...I suspect that many corporations have begun to understand that they have an important role to play in the lives of their communities, and that allocating funds to support local groups helps them discharge that function and also burnish their image.[25]
>
> —David Rockefeller Sr.
> Philanthropist

V

The Divine Operations Plan

And there are diversities of operations, but it is the same God which worketh all in all.

1 Corinthians 12:6 (KJV)

How do you run your business? How can the Word of God enhance your commercial operations? How can spiritual principles inform your commercial operations?

The operations plan is the section of a traditional business plan that describes the day-to-day operations of a company or department. The information included in your operations plan will certainly vary according to the type of business venture and industry sector. But an operations plan typically includes topics such as: production, supply and distribution, order fulfillment, customer service, inventory management, quality control, regulations and guidelines, safety and health procedures, facilities, utilities, maintenance, and contingency planning.

For purposes of this chapter, we'll consider the term *operations* in the broadest sense to include how we *operate* and *behave* in a business environment. So by definition, *operations* will include business practices and protocols as well as behavioral dimensions.

Now, let's consider your operations plan from a spiritual perspective. How does the way you operate your business differ from that of an unbeliever? Are your operations worthy of one of God's enterprises? As we seek to connect our business plans with God's purpose and plan for our lives, we must ensure that we are operating our businesses according to His principles so that we "may walk worthy of the Lord fully pleasing Him, being fruitful in every good work and increasing in the knowledge of God" (Colossians 1:10, ESV).

According to Psalm 34:16 (ESV), "the Lord turns his face against those who do evil; He will erase their memory from the earth." Many of us are aware of the unfortunate scandals that have occurred over the past few years involving prominent companies and executives who have been indicted for a myriad of misdeeds, including financial mismanagement and accounting irregularities. Well-established companies such as Arthur Andersen and Enron have gone out of business as a result of unethical, illegal, and immoral business practices and operations.

In business, we deal with a multitude of behavioral and operational issues. But for us as Christian business professionals, the Bible serves as our ultimate business-planning guide and our ultimate code of conduct manual. We just have to make a concerted effort to be proactive and purposeful in incorporating spiritual principles into our commercial operations. In short, we have to be intentional in making sure that our operational procedures glorify God.

So how do we intend to accomplish this, particularly when we are often dependent upon other individuals to honor their roles and responsibilities along the proverbial supply chain? Our

Planning Proverbs will help us uncover the answers to many of our questions.

Regardless of the various commercial concepts, business models, and religious beliefs of your colleagues, you'll find that there are three critical points to consider when it comes to creating the divine operations plan for your organization. The process:

- Starts with you as an individual.

- Subsequently transcends to your environment.

- Ultimately impacts all of your operational protocols and organizational procedures.

Three Planning Proverbs for the Divine Operations Plan

When we as *individuals* begin to take inventory of our thoughts and make the appropriate changes in our mind-sets, then we as collective *organizations* will begin to improve our *environment* and ultimately enhance our *operations*. Hence, our three Planning Proverbs for the divine operations plan are as follows:

1. Take inventory of your thoughts.

2. Employ quality control measures for your environment.

3. Operate *in* the business world without being *of* the business world.

Let's begin with our first Planning Proverb:

Take Inventory of Your Thoughts

Change your thoughts and you change the world.

—Norman Vincent Peale

As Christians, we are called to seek, love, and serve God with all of our heart, soul, strength, and mind (Psalm 119:2; Luke 10:27; Deuteronomy 11:13; Joshua 22:5). When it comes to operating at a Higher level in business and specifically within operations, it's imperative that we take inventory or set certain criteria for the types of thoughts that we will entertain. And these criteria must come from the Word of God.

God's Criteria for Our Thoughts

The Bible teaches us that one of our goals should be to have the same mind-set as Jesus Christ (Philippians 2:5). Being carnal or sinful-minded leads to death, but being spiritually minded leads to life and peace (Romans 8:6). We must take captive every thought to make it obedient to Christ (2 Corinthians 10:5). This means that we must examine and evaluate the quality of our thoughts to ensure that they are in alignment with God's teachings.

The Word of God also tells us that if we set our minds to be morally alert and keep our faith in God, as revealed through Jesus Christ (1 Peter 1:13), then our *thoughts* will consequently be established. But in order to do this, we have to first take inventory of our thoughts.

Taking inventory of our thoughts means that we must have standards set and a screening process in place for what we *will* and *will not* allow ourselves to dwell on mentally. During the course of a day, numerous thoughts flow through our minds. Yet, it is liberating to know that we have the ability to select which ones we will allow to remain and which ones we will consciously disregard. It is up to us to be proactive and diligent in monitoring the quality of our thoughts.

Take inventory of your thoughts. What are you focusing on mentally? Are these thoughts and mental images positive and edifying? Or are they negative and self-defeating? Are you constantly worried about the economy, declining revenues, competitive threats, job loss, gossip, or rumors? Or, are you focused on God's plan for your life and for your business regardless of the pressures you may be experiencing?

Given the various personal and professional challenges we face daily, it is difficult not to succumb to negative thoughts that eventually lead to anxiety, worry, and depression. But with concerted effort, we can effectively manage our thoughts. We have to be like King David, in the book of Psalms, who praised God as a means of creating and sustaining a positive thought process.

In Philippians 4:8-9, the Bible instructs us to think about whatever is:

- True

- Respectful

- Honorable

- Noble

- Just

- Pure

- Lovely

- Loveable

- Kind

- Pleasant

- Gracious

- Virtuous

- Excellent

- Praiseworthy

These scriptures give us specific criteria and critical standards that serve as the foundation and parameters for us in formulating an effective screening process for our thoughts.

Thoughts Determine Your Behavioral and Operational Responses

In business, we face a multitude of professional challenges—everything from making payroll and dealing with competition to managing employees and navigating our careers during corporate restructuring and impending downsizing and layoffs. During these times, it's normal to feel worried, anxious, frightened, angry, stressed, and depressed. But it is important for us to realize the following: It is not the nature of what is actually happening to us that causes anxiety but it is actually how we perceive what is happening to us that causes anxiety.

Your situation or circumstance does not cause your fear and anxiety. It is the way you *think about* or *perceive* your situation or circumstance that causes fear, anxiety, and a host of negative emotions.

Example: Let's say you are a business owner and you're worried about a pending lawsuit against you and your firm. The lawsuit does not in and of itself cause your anxiety. Your anxiety stems from the pessimistic perception of the situation and the underlying *negative thoughts* that you have about the lawsuit and the overall predicament. And these thoughts are likely grounded in feelings of fear, anger, cynicism, and frustration. *Your thoughts cause anxiety.*

Your thoughts determine how you perceive challenging situations, and they determine how you will respond to them *behaviorally* as an individual. And this will affect the overall operations of your business. Individual behavior impacts corporate operations. So it's imperative that our mind-sets and thoughts line up with the Word of God.

The Bible teaches us that a "double-minded" or anxious and worried person is unstable (James 1: 7-8, NKJV) and that we are to cast our cares on God (1 Peter 5:7) and be anxious for nothing (Philippians 4:6). But in order to do this, we must change our way of thinking and *renew our minds* (Ephesians 4:23).

Renew Your Mind

The Bible encourages us to not to be conformed to this world but to be transformed by the renewing of our minds (Romans 12:2). We are to assume the same humble attitude and positive mindset that are embodied in Jesus Christ (Philippians 2:5). The Bible provides us with a number of simple, straightforward, and practical guidelines for renewing our minds.

In Mark 7:14-23, Jesus tells us that defilement comes from within. It originates in our hearts and subsequently infiltrates our minds. He says:

> There is nothing that enters a man from outside which can defile him; but the things which come out of him, those are the things that defile man.
>
> Mark 7:15 (NKJV)

Jesus goes on to tell us:

> For from within, out of the heart of men, proceed evil thoughts, adulteries, fornication, murders, thefts, covetousness, wickedness, deceit, lewdness, an evil eye, blasphemy, pride, foolishness. All these evil things come from within and defile a man.
>
> Mark 7: 21-23 (NKJV)

The Bible states that the thoughts of the righteous are right, which means that they are honest, just, and reliable (Proverbs 12:5). Therefore, we must do our best to entertain only the right types of thoughts. Scripture reinforces this by telling us to: "Set your minds on things above, not on things on the earth" (Colossians 3:2, NKJV). This means that we must raise our level of thinking to a more positive, spiritual level. A level aligned with godly principles. A Higher level. And we are to keep our thoughts at this Higher level.

The Benefits of Thinking at a Higher Level

What are the benefits of thinking at a Higher level? When we think at a Higher level, we also begin to behave and operate at Higher levels, which not only helps us to succeed in business but also leads to the greatest benefit which is revealed in Philippians 4:9 (NLT):

> Keep putting into practice all you learned and received from me—everything you heard from me and saw me doing. Then the God of peace will be with you.

When we meditate on positive, spiritually edifying thoughts, the peace of God will be with us. Peace of mind. Don't we all want to have peace of mind? Don't we all just want to be happy? Well, happiness starts with having peace of mind, which comes only from God (Romans 5:1). And, achieving peace of mind starts with taking inventory of your thoughts by establishing godly criteria and a spiritual screening process for them.

How to Establish a Screening Process for Your Thoughts

• • • • • • • • • • • • • • • • • •

Line Your Thoughts up with the Word of God

If your thoughts do not meet the criteria set by the Word of God, then refuse to harbor them. Instead, commit to substituting negative thoughts with positive ones that embody godly characteristics because the Bible says, "as he thinks in his heart, so is he" (Proverbs 23:7, NKJV). In order to maintain a Higher level of thinking, we have to make concerted efforts daily to focus on thoughts that edify, encourage, uplift, and exemplify godly principles. We have to refrain from harboring evil or negative thoughts (Jeremiah 4:14).

The Bible instructs us to guard ourselves against thoughts and works of the flesh, or our human nature and selfish desires, such as adultery, fornication, uncleanness, lewdness, idolatry, sorcery, hatred, contentions, jealousy, wrath, selfish ambitions, dissensions, heresies, envy, murder, drunkenness, and revelries, because anyone living this type of lifestyle will not inherit the kingdom of God (Galatians 5:19-21).

On the other hand, the Bible encourages us to focus our minds on positive thoughts that embody the fruit of the Spirit, which are love, joy, peace, longsuffering, kindness, goodness, faithfulness, gentleness, and self-control (Galatians 5: 22-23).

Replace Negative Thoughts with Positive Ones

Following are three examples of negative thoughts and corresponding ways that they might be screened and replaced with positive ones that are reflective of godly principles:

Instead of Thinking:	Begin Thinking at a Higher Level:
I hate my job.	*I am thankful to God and blessed to have a job.* (Psalm 100:4)
I can't afford to lose my business or job.	*I can't afford to lose or miss God's purpose for my life.* (Revelation 17:17) *When one door closes, He will open another.* (Revelation 3:8) *Like everything else, my business and job belong to God and He is in control of them.* (Romans 11:36)
We'll never be able to win this account.	*If it is God's will for us to win this account, then we will certainly win it, for what God has for us is for us, and no one can stop the divine plan of God.* (Proverbs 19:21)

We can take control of our negative thoughts by transforming them into positive ones by acknowledging God's Word, having faith in what He has already predestined and preordained, surrendering to His control of the situation, and praising Him throughout the process.

Remind yourself daily to take inventory of your thoughts. When negative ones begin to infiltrate your mind, just refuse to entertain them. Tune them out. Change the channel. Flip the switch. De-program. As we begin taking inventory of our thoughts, it's vital that we also begin to pay more attention to the quality of our environment and this topic will be covered in our next Planning Proverb.

Employ Quality Control Measures for Your Environment

"Do not be deceived: Evil company corrupts good habits" (1 Corinthians 15:33, NKJV). Evil corrupts good. So it's critical that you monitor your environment because a negative environment will often impact you before you can impact it.

We must seek to employ quality-control measures for our environment. In Psalm 101:3-4, King David says, "I will set nothing wicked before my eyes...I will not know wickedness." He also goes on to say that he refuses to endure "the one who has a haughty look and a proud heart" (Psalm 101:5, NKJV).

We must establish certain criteria, guidelines, and standards for our environment. We must vow to neither intentionally nor willingly expose ourselves to evil things, people, and circumstances. In short, we must establish effective environmental regulations.

Environmental Regulations

· ·

Create a Spiritually Uplifting Environment

I challenge you to create a spiritually uplifting environment for yourself. Post inspiring pictures, messages, and scriptures on your walls, mirrors, calendar, computer, daily planner, refrigerator, in your car, and in other places you frequent. Because we tend to spend an inordinate amount of time at work, it's particularly important that we incorporate positive affirmations into our own personal work environments.

Create a workspace that is spiritually edifying for you. If you are an employee, then by all means adhere to the guidelines set by your employer for changing the aesthetics of your work area. But if you do have some latitude in this area, then take time to enhance your work area in ways that affirm and uplift you.

Your workspace may be comprised of a simple computer and desk within a cubicle, or it might consist of a massive, luxurious corner office. The size of your work area doesn't matter. What matters is that your work area exudes positivity and is conducive to productivity. Design a space that is inviting and motivating for you. Create an environment that offers peace and tranquility. This doesn't necessarily require a major construction project. Sometimes, minor changes make a major difference.

In my office, I have a wooden plaque inscribed with the name "Jesus" that a dear friend gave me years ago. The plaque is intriguing because most people have to stare at it a few minutes before the script design of the word *Jesus* becomes apparent. You have to look in between the borders to see the name clearly, but once you see it, you can never look at the plaque again without being able to see it. Just describing this plaque is a sermon in and of itself, because sometimes in order for us to see the divine hand of Jesus in our lives, we have to look in between the borders of our problems and circumstances. Once we do this and begin to understand and witness the marvelous works of Jesus in our lives, we can never look back on those situations the same way again without seeing His divine influence.

My plaque was created by a retired gentleman who resided in Silver City, New Mexico, but has since gone to be with the Lord. He sold the plaques to raise proceeds for academic scholarships for Christian students. I often wonder if he realized just how many environments his plaques enhanced. I marvel by the number of lives he touched just by operating in what God called him to do.

I have given many of these Jesus plaques as gifts to business associates, friends, and family members. The plaques have proven to be a great tool for starting many interesting conversations with people on the topic of faith. I share this experience because when we enhance our environments with motivational items, positive affirmations, and scriptures, we not only lift our spirits, but we also sometimes brighten the days of others and have the opportunity to share our faith in the process.

Recognize and Avoid Negativity

You and I realize that we can't control everything that occurs in our environments during the course of every day. But we can certainly do our part in controlling some of it according to the guidelines God has established for us. The Bible says that evil company corrupts a good and positive environment (1 Corinthians 15:33). So we must be cognizant of and vigilant in recognizing and avoiding the various forms of evil and negativity.

Negativity in business operations manifests itself in ways that are both overt or obvious and covert or hidden and subtle. Negativity can take a myriad of forms, including gossiping coworkers, profanity-spewing associates, dishonest employees, condescending supervisors, pessimistic board members, offensive marketing tactics, substandard operations, and dishonorable accounting practices.

Another key to regulating your environment and avoiding negativity lies in the *choices* you make in being selective about what you expose yourself to. For instance:

- When you refuse to spend a great deal of time with co-workers who gossip, you are regulating your environment.

- When you refuse to join in with team members who are disparaging your boss, you are regulating your environment.

- When you refuse to join others in making slanderous remarks about your competitors, you are regulating your environment.

- When you refuse to spend inordinate amounts of time entertaining yourself with forms of media (e.g., television, music, radio, internet, books, and other publications) that are not spiritually edifying, you are regulating your environment.

The people with whom we associate play a major role in our environmental-regulation efforts in the business arena. We have to employ quality control measures for our environment by setting limitations on the amount of time we spend with certain individuals.

The majority of our time *should not* be spent in the company of people who are pessimistic, angry, insecure, vindictive, divisive, or harbor a victim mentality (Proverbs 22:24; Romans 16:17). The Bible says that we should not even associate ourselves with self-professed Christians who are immoral, rude, drunken, greedy, or extortionists (1 Corinthians 5:11-12). The scripture says we should not even eat with such people!

I believe one reason that the Word of God prohibits us from spending a lot of time with negative people is because doing so adversely impacts our thoughts, emotions, perspectives, environment, and our overall ways of behaving and operating. And ultimately, this makes it difficult for us to accomplish what God has called us to do.

It's critical that you make sure that you are *positively* impacting the people around you, or your target audience, and that they are not *negatively* impacting you and causing you to make compromises in your Christian beliefs and lifestyle. The Bible clearly states: "You must influence them; do not let them influence you" (Jeremiah 15:19, ESV; 1 Corinthians 15:33). I like the way minister Joyce Meyer captures this concept. She says to always make sure that you are *affecting* them and they are not *infecting* you. If you find yourself spending most of your time at work with negative people, it's time for you to take measures to regulate your environment in positive ways.

How Can I Operate as an Effective Ambassador for God If I Avoid Negative People?

Now, with all the talk about not even eating with evil or negative people, you might find yourself in a quandary wondering: How can I be an effective ambassador for God if I avoid negative people? Good question. You might also be thinking: Even Jesus associated with individuals of questionable character in order to bring them into the kingdom. Excellent observation.

As Christians, we walk a fine line. In the workplace and marketplace, we find ourselves associating with unbelievers and individuals of questionable ethics and integrity. These interactions offer prime opportunities for us to minister the Word of God to others in both word and deed. But they conversely offer the potential to negatively impact our spiritual walk with God.

The Bible relays many instances in which Jesus sought solitude to pray for God's guidance in various situations (Luke 9:18; Mark 1:35). Like Jesus, we also must seek private time to pray for God's wisdom and direction in working with negative people to ensure that we are positively influencing them without them adversely impacting us. God will let you know if He desires for you to spend more or less time with certain people. Just stay open to His promptings and follow Him.

Example: God may instruct you to continue to associate with certain individuals in order for you to lead them to salvation. On the contrary, He may direct you to distance yourself from them. Or, He may step in and divinely maneuver circumstances so that you become disassociated from them without any effort on your part. Regardless of the circumstance, as God's ambassadors in the business world, we must manage these situations by seeking guidance from Him and employing honesty, compassion, humility, and professionalism. Now, let's proceed to our final Planning Proverb for this chapter.

Operate in the Business World Without Being of the Business World

· ·

True Business Transformation

It's not sufficient to simply know God's principles. We must also demonstrate them in our operations. The Bible tells us that:

> We have received, not the spirit of the world, but the Spirit who is from God…not in words in which man's wisdom teaches but which the Holy Spirit teaches[because] we have the mind of Christ.
>
> 1 Corinthians 2:12-16 (NKJV)

Because we, as Christian business leaders, have been given the mind of Christ, we are the ones who should be setting Higher standards and raising the bar of excellence in the business world. We are the ones who are appointed by God to enhance business protocols and elevate operating standards. The rest of the business world should be benchmarking against us!

The Word of God tells us, "Do not love this world nor the things it offers you, for when you love the world, you do not have the love of the Father in you" (1 John 2:15, NLT). We are taught that "anyone who chooses to be a friend of the world becomes an enemy of God." (James 4:4, NIV) And we are instructed:

> Do not be conformed to this world, but be transformed
> by the renewing of your mind, that you may prove what is
> that good and acceptable and perfect will of God.

Romans 12:2 (NKJV)

As Christian business leaders, we are *in* the business world, but we must not be *of* the business world. This means that as God's disciples, we are to work and operate within the present free enterprise system, *not by conforming to it but by transforming it* through the power of God that resides within each one of us. This is the greatest and Highest form of business transformation. This is true business transformation.

Jesus says, "They are not of the world, just as I am not of the world" (John 17:16, NKJV). This means that, as business leaders, we are *not* to be conformed by the carnality of the business world. We are *not* to be molded and shaped by the commercial arena. But we are called to mold and shape the commercial arena by serving as effective living epistles of Christ.

Jesus tells us that "if you were of the world, the world would love its own...yet because *you are not of the world*, but I chose you *out of the world*, therefore the world hates you" (John 15:19, NKJV). Because God has set us apart and called us to operate at a Higher level, many of our colleagues will not understand us, and some may actually dislike or resent us for pursuing excellence. But that's all right, because Jesus tells us:

> He who has My commandments and keeps them, it is he
> who loves Me. And he who loves Me will be loved by My
> Father, and I will love him and manifest Myself to him.

John 14:21 (NKJV)

He also goes on to say that:

> If you keep My commandments, you will abide in My love
> just as I have kept My Father's commandments and abide
> in His love.

> John 15:10 (NKJV)

As long as you have the love of Jesus and God Almighty on your side, your colleagues' envy or hatred is their problem! You are called to adhere to operational directives and standards established by God, not just those endorsed by the business world. So don't be shocked or dismayed when the business world does not embrace your God-given operational mandates.

Our Ultimate Operational Mandate

The ways in which we operate in business are dictated by protocols and procedures endemic to companies and industries. But there is one operational mandate that God gives us as business leaders. This mandate transcends all types of commercial sectors, but ironically it's rarely associated with and mentioned in the workplace and marketplace. This mandate is simple in theory but complex in practice. This God-given mandate is for us to operate in love.

How God Defines Love

Before we get into the details of what love has to do with business operations, let's first consider how God defines love and a few dimensions of the concept. First and foremost, the Word of

God tells us that God is love. The Bible says that "he who does not love does not know God, for God is love" (1 John 4:8, NKJV). Whoever abides in love also abides in God, and God abides in Him (1 John 4:16). Whoever stands for love also stands for God and God stands for him.

The Bible paints a captivating picture of love for us in 1 Corinthians 13:4-13:

- Love is patient, love is kind. It does not envy; it does not boast; it is not proud.

- It is not rude; it is not self-seeking; it is not easily angered; it keeps no record of wrongs.

- Love does not delight in evil but rejoices with the truth. It always protects, always trusts, always hopes, and always perseveres.

- Love never fails.

- Of faith, hope, and love, the greatest of these is love.

God's love is perfected in us because He has given us His Spirit (1 John 4:12-13). His holy, all-encompassing love is referred to as agape (pronounced ah-gah-pey). Agape is generally defined as the love of God or Christ for humankind; the love of Christians for other persons, which corresponds to unselfish love of one person for another; or, brotherly love.

If we want our business practices and operations to be not only efficient and effective but also *reflective* of God's teachings, then they must exemplify the love of God that is within us.

God Loves You

There are numerous studies and books about how love is manifested within our personal relationships such as those with our parents, spouses, children, and friends. But how does God's agape love manifest itself in the commercial business arena? How does love relate to our business practices and operations?

In order to answer these questions, we have to consider the core of all businesses, which is a population of people. And we have to consider the core of this population of people which is *the individual.* Let's begin with *you* as an individual.

God loves you. Because of God's love for you and me, He sent His only Son into the world as Savior of the world so that we might have eternal life through Him (1 John 4:9). This is the ultimate everlasting love (Jeremiah 31:3). The Bible declares that *nothing*—no type of suffering, affliction, tribulation, calamity, or distress—shall separate us from the love of God which is in Christ Jesus our Lord (Romans 8:35-39):

> Neither death nor life, nor angels nor principalities nor powers, nor things present nor things to come, nor height nor depth, nor any other created thing, shall be able to separate us from the love of God which is in Christ Jesus our Lord.
>
> Romans 8:38-39 (NKJV)

Because God loves us so much, one would think that it would be natural for us to also love Him. But this is not always the case. God does not force us to love Him. Again, the choice is always ours.

We Are to Love God

For us as true Spirit-filled believers and recipients of God's grace daily, it would be difficult to not love Him! Nevertheless, when we profess to be believers, the Bible makes the requirements clear for us, including the fact that we are to:

> Fear the Lord your God, to walk in all His ways and to love Him, to serve the Lord your God with all your heart and with all your soul and to keep the commandments of the Lord and His statutes...
>
> Deuteronomy 10:12-13; 11:1 (NKJV)

When the scribes asked Jesus to name the first commandment of all, Jesus replied, "You shall love the Lord your God with all your heart, with all your soul, with all your mind, and with all your strength...this is the first commandment (Mark 12: 29-30, NKJV; Deuteronomy 6:5). In this way, Jesus encourages us to be "imitators of God as dear children" and "walk in love, as Christ also loved us and given Himself for us, an offering and a sacrifice to God..." (Ephesians 5:1-2, NKJV).

We Are to Love One Another

We know that God is love; He loves us, and we are to love Him. Now let's consider what the Bible teaches regarding our love for one another. In addition to the first commandment to love God, Jesus also told the scribes that the second commandment is that we are to love one another (John 15:12,17; Romans 12:9-10; 13:8; 1 Thessalonians 4:9). Jesus says, "A new commandment I give to you, that you love one another; as I have loved you, that you also love one another" (John 13:34, NKJV; 15:13). He declares,

"You shall love your neighbor as yourself. There is no other commandment greater than these" (Mark 12:31, NKJV).

The Word of God makes it clear that "he who loves God *must* love his brother also" (1 John 4:21, NKJV). One way for us to put this into perspective is to consider that if God loves us so much that He gave His only Son for us, then we should also reflect His love for us through our love for one another (1 John 4:11). For us, this means having brotherly love, care, and acceptance for our managers, colleagues, customers, clients, suppliers, and even competitors.

Jesus declared that if we have love for one another, we will know that we are one of His disciples (John 13:35). There are numerous references to love in the Bible, and they all have powerful implications for how we are to treat others and operate in business. Mahatma Gandhi eloquently stated, "We must be the change we want to see happen in the world." And this applies to the business world. Now that we are grounded in the importance of love, let's proceed in exploring how to manifest godly love in our daily operations.

Effectively Spiritual and Spiritually Effective

We are to display the love of God *at work*, literally and figuratively, in our daily lives. The Word of God says, "let's not merely say that we love each other; let us show the truth by our actions" (1 John 3:18, ESV). Let's not just talk about love, but let's make sure our actions toward our colleagues convey kindness, respect, and "brotherly love" (Romans 12:10, NKJV). As Mother Theresa profoundly stated, "Each person has been created to be love and to give love."

Why is the concept of love important to us in our day-to-day business operations? As God's ambassadors, we are called to operate our businesses in ways that are reflective of God's spiritual principles and teachings—which include the concept of love. We are called to Higher standards of operations that embody integrity and excellence. As Christian business leaders, we must ensure that our business operations are *effectively spiritual* and *spiritually effective*. Let's delineate these phrases.

When I say that our business operations should be *effectively spiritual*, I mean that they should be spiritual at the core. The way you run your business should emanate from and be grounded in the Spirit of God and His teachings. Example: Incorporating the importance of brotherly love and kindness into your business practices and protocols is effectively spiritual because it incorporates godly principles and His commandment to "let all *that* you *do* be done with love" (1 Corinthians 16:14, NKJV).

When I say that our operations should be *spiritually effective*, I mean that they should spiritually impact others in a positive way. Example: Demonstrating *operational excellence* is spiritually effective because it exposes others to God's grace and glory because He is a God of excellence (Romans 2:18; Philippians 1:10-11).

In Pursuit of Operational Excellence

We are called to be holy and display the virtues of God (1 Peter 1:13-16; 2:9). The Bible states that "as He who called you is holy, you also be holy in all your conduct…because it is written 'be holy for I am holy'" (1 Peter 1:15-16, NKJV; Proverbs 15:8-11).

The Word of God encourages us to approve and pursue excellence in our work (Philippians 1:10-11). But in order for us to operate within a realm of excellence, we must examine our ways of behaving to ensure that they glorify God (Lamentations 3:40; Haggai 1:5-7).

Whatever you are called to do, try to do your best to excel in it because excellence honors God and we serve a God of excellence. "Do you see a man who excels in his work? He will stand before kings; he will not stand before unknown men" (Proverbs 22:29, NKJV; Romans 2:18).

This pursuit of excellence also applies to the ways we conduct business and our commercial operations. The Bible says that we are to praise, magnify, and exalt God (Exodus 15:2; Psalm 34:3) and always strive to choose "a more excellent way" (1 Corinthians 12:31). This implies that the way you manage and operate your business should reflect and epitomize the fruit of the Spirit or whatever is true, worthy of reverence, honorable, pure, just, lovely, kind, gracious, praiseworthy, virtuous and excellent (Philippians 4:8).

The relentless pursuit of excellence is critical to our ability to raise the bar of operational standards, protocol, and ethics in business. We are called to surpass average levels of product and service quality. We are called to exceed customer and client expectations. Complacency and mediocrity are never options for us as His ambassadors. The pursuit of High operational standards is imperative for each of us regardless of our positions and roles within an organization. So make sure that your work embodies excellence in both content and execution. Be the consummate leader.

Check Your Operational Motivation

Don't love the praise of men more than the praise from God (John 12:43; Romans 2:29). We must understand and check, or monitor, our motives in business because they will affect the nature of our operations. Selfish motivations will invariably lead to selfish behavior and business practices, which consequently lead to corrupt operations. I challenge you to continually question, examine, and evaluate your motivations in business. Are you trying to please men or God? Are you trying to follow your own selfish desires or God's will?

God is not committed to sustaining businesses with operations that are contradictory to His teachings. Example: Companies with immoral leaders, discriminatory hiring practices, unethical accounting methods, and labor law violations do not glorify God. These types of organizations have virtually no spiritual viability and consequently will have limited commercial longevity.

As you pursue operational excellence, make sure that you are doing it for the purpose of glorifying God and facilitating His kingdom agenda and not just for selfish motivations such as job promotion and financial gain. Ironically, however, these are some of the rewards that we actually receive as a result of pursuing operational excellence based on God's principles!

We don't serve God to get something done for us; we serve Him for what He has *already* done for us. We are called to serve God because of Who He is, not for selfish gain. We are to commit all of our work to the Lord (Proverbs 16:3), and whatever we do, we are to do it heartily, as to the Lord and not to men, being obedient not "as men-pleasers, but in sincerity of heart, fearing God" (Colossians 3:22-24, NKJV).

Joshua challenges us, saying, "Choose for yourselves this day whom you will serve…but for me and my house, we will serve the Lord" (Joshua 24:15, NKJV). The Apostle Paul also explores this tendency of trying to please men, or the secular world in general, as opposed to seeking to serve and please God when he observes:

> All things are lawful for me, but all things are not help-
> ful. All things are lawful for me, but I will not be brought
> under the power of any.
>
> 1 Corinthians 6:12 (NKJV)

> Do I now persuade men, or God? Or, do I seek to please
> men? For if I still pleased men, I would not be a bondserv-
> ant of Christ.
>
> Galatians 1:10 (NKJV)

Motives that seek to satisfy the world and our flesh, or our human nature and selfish desires, lead to corrupt business practices and operations. And they will be revealed or brought to light in due time (1 Corinthians 4:5). We have witnessed this in many cases of corporate calamities involving major corporations such as Enron Corporation, Arthur Andersen, Tyco International, and WorldCom.

The Bible tells us that our God is a jealous God and that we should worship no other gods before Him (Exodus 20:5; 34:14). Undoubtedly, the unethical practices and illegal operations of many convicted executives stemmed from a desire to please both *flesh* and *man*. For instance, many of these individuals had an all-consuming desire to please:

- Flesh in the form of pride.

- Flesh in the form of greed.

- Man in the form of board members.

- Man in the form of Wall Street.

When we place our own desires and the desires of the world at the center of our operational motivations, we become disobedient to God. And this renders our testimonies ineffective to others and jeopardizes the longevity of our enterprises. Do away with pride and greed. Your approach to business operations will either seek to please people or seek to please God. The former approach will benefit you and your business for a season, but the latter approach will benefit you and your business for an eternity. Again, the choice is yours.

Operating Outside of the Crowd

When we are more loyal to the world's standards of operations than to God's standards, the Bible says that we become like double-minded people, unstable in all our ways (James 1:8). The Lord detests this type of behavior among Christians. He says, "I know all the things you do, that you are neither hot nor cold. I wish that you were one or the other!" (Revelation 3:15, ESV). In this scripture, Jesus is saying that He wishes we would commit to being either cold or hot. He then goes on to say that the fact that we are neither hot, nor cold, but are "lukewarm," makes Him want to vomit us from His mouth (Revelation 3:16-17, NKJV)!

Achieving operational excellence requires that we improve upon and excel beyond the world's standards of operations. But at times we may find that our crowd, or inner circle, group, or clique, of business associates, colleagues, and friends is made up of lukewarm Christians. Christians who don't want to reveal their Christianity. Christians who don't follow through on their word. Christians who find substandard and average levels of operations acceptable. Christians who operate in the realm of unprofessionalism.

As God's ambassadors, we simply cannot afford to be cold or lukewarm about the Lord and His standards for how we conduct business. When we find ourselves in the midst of a lukewarm crowd, we must operate outside of the crowd at a Higher level. We must be hot, fervent, zealous, and radically on fire for the Lord! We have to be passionate about strategically incorporating His principles into every aspect of our commercial initiatives.

In order to facilitate His divine operations plan, God will sometimes separate us from the lukewarm crowd. He will simply not allow us to fit in with this group. For instance, you might find that you don't fit in with the "popular" people at work or at school. You may not understand the reason, but somehow you know in your heart that you have been set apart. And this is often true. God has set you apart to operate outside of the crowd to set a new and Higher standard for them and others to follow.

The Bible says: "But know that the Lord has *set apart* for Himself him who is godly" (Psalm 4:3, NKJV). So if you feel somehow set apart from your colleagues or failing to fit in with the popular "in" group, then know that this is *a good thing*. It is *a God thing*. We are set apart and called to stand out in the world in a positive and powerful way. Recently, I was watching a television documentary about the Oprah Winfrey Leadership Academy for Girls: South Africa. One of the girls featured on the show captured this idea of being set apart and standing out in such an eloquent and intriguing way. She said, "Don't blend in. Blend out!"

Remember, Jesus said that we are the salt of the earth. Just as salt is used as a preservative and seasoning, we are called to preserve God's principles and season the commercial arena with His Spirit. We should not attempt to blend into the average standards of the business world, but we should blend out of them by setting Higher operational standards for the business world to follow. Out is the "new in"!

We Don't Operate in Excellence to Get Saved; We Operate in Excellence Because We Are Saved

The Bible says we were created in the image of God to do good works (Genesis 1:27; Ephesians 2:8-10).

> God saved you by His grace when you believed. And you can't take credit for this; it is a gift from God. Salvation is not a reward for the good things we have done, so none of us can boast about it.
>
> Ephesians 2:8-9 (NLT)

In other words, we're saved not by what we do but by what Christ has already done. We don't operate in excellence to get saved; we operate in excellence because we are saved. It would be impossible for us as human beings to do enough good works to win the blessing of salvation. This is the reason God sent His Son, Jesus Christ, to save us in all of our imperfect ways.

Spiritual salvation is a critical factor not only in how you operate or what you do but also in *who you are* as an individual, *your character*. What you *do* is a result of who you *are* as a person. One of the ways in which we honor the Lord and show our gratitude to Him for the life He has given us is by applying His principles, reflecting His character, and magnifying His Spirit.

Understanding Secular Versus
Spiritual Operating Principles

We know that we are called to be the light in an otherwise dark business world. Practically speaking, this means that we are to adhere to godly, spiritual, biblical-based operating principles while competing in a commercial business world that adheres to profit-based, ego-centric, people-pleasing, data-driven, secular operating principles. This may seem difficult to accomplish, but it can be done. It is God's will for it to be done.

We must continue to challenge the conventional operating principles of the business world in order to raise them to a Higher level of excellence. This takes constant vigilance on our part, and it is certainly a challenge at times, but we know that nothing is impossible with God. Following is a contrast and comparison of secular versus spiritual operating principles:

Secular Operating Principles:	Spiritual Operating Principles:
"Self-reliance" mentality:	"God-reliance" mentality:
We rely on ourselves to get what we need i.e., every woman for herself and every man for himself.	We rely on God to get what we need. We rely on Him for everything (2 Chronicles 16:8; Zechariah 4:6).
"Me first" mentality:	"You first" mentality:
The priority is me first and you second.	The priority is you first and me second. We are to esteem others more highly than ourselves (Philippians 2:3; Romans 15:1; 1 Corinthians 10:24).
"Get to Give" mentality:	"Give to Get" mentality:
It's better to receive than to give.	It is better and more blessed to give than to receive (Acts 20:35).
We have to first get the new job, business, or lucrative account in order to be in a position to give our time, talents, and resources to others such as family, coworkers, church, and the community.	We must first give our time, talents, and resources to others such as family, coworkers, church, and the community in order for us to get the blessings that God has for us such as a new job, business, or lucrative account. We reap what we sow, so we must not grow tired of doing good, because in due season we'll reap if we don't grow weary (Galatians 6:7-9).

Secular Operating Principles:	Spiritual Operating Principles:
Get all you can out of the business arena. Focus on getting your just rewards.	Give all you can to the business arena for God and it will be given back to you in abundance (Luke 6:38; Proverbs 11:24-25) Focus on serving others.
"Seeing is believing" mentality:	"Believing is seeing" mentality:
You have to first see it to believe it.	You have to first believe it to see it.
You must first see the new business, job, or multi-million dollar account in order to believe it.	You must first believe God for the new business, job, or multi-million dollar account in order to see it manifested. We walk by faith, not by sight (Matthew 21:22; Mark 11:24; Romans 4:17; 8:24-25; John 7:24).
Victory precedes praise:	Praise precedes victory:
We celebrate after the victory of a job promotion or lucrative deal.	We celebrate and praise God before the victory of a job promotion or lucrative deal. We praise God for what He has already done in the spiritual realm before it is even manifested in the commercial realm (Hebrews 11:30; Isaiah 25:1; 55:1; Psalm 52:9).

Secular Operating Principles:	Spiritual Operating Principles:
We can only experience victory after the battle in the marketplace.	We have victory before the battle in the marketplace even begins (1 Corinthians 15:57; 1 John 5:4)!
"Ego-centric" success strategies: You have to be egotistical, i.e., full of yourself, to succeed. My success is based on my skills, talents, knowledge, experience, credentials, and professional contacts. The best way to get promoted is to advance up by gaining more education, credentials, and professional contacts. To climb the corporate ladder and get to the top, you have to step on or over people. Help only those who can help or repay you i.e., you scratch my back, I'll scratch yours. Professional success will help supply your needs.	"God-centric" success strategies: You have to be humble, i.e., empty yourself like Jesus did in order to succeed (Philippians 2:7). My success is based on my ability to do all things through Christ who strengthens me (Philippians 4:13). The best way to get promoted is to bow down by honoring God's plan through humility and service to others (Genesis 12:1-4; Proverbs 19:21; 1 Peter 4:10). To climb the corporate ladder and get to the top, you have to serve people (1 Peter 4:10). God will repay all people as their actions deserve (Proverbs 24: 12) Help those who cannot help or repay you and you will be blessed. (Luke 6:32-35; 14:12-14).

Secular Operating Principles:	Spiritual Operating Principles:
Professional success will help supply your needs.	God will supply all your needs according to His riches in glory through Christ Jesus (Philippians 4:19).
You can't be humble and still operate in authority.	You can, and must be, humble in order to operate in God-given authority (2 Samuel 22:28; 2 Corinthians 10:8).
In order to be influential, you must first and foremost be aggressive.	In order to be influential, you must first and foremost be humble (Psalm 25:9; 147:6; Proverbs 3:34).
Retaliate against your enemies and those who hurt and deceive you; overcome ruthless tactics with ruthless tactics.	Love your enemies and treat them well. Overcome evil with good and God will vindicate you (Proverbs 20:22; 25:21-22; Matthew 5:44; Romans 12:17-21).
Always be proactive with a hands-on approach.	Sometimes, we must be still and know that He is God and allow Him to take control of the situation (Psalm 46:10; 4:4).

Secular Operating Principles:	Spiritual Operating Principles:
"First facts, then faith" approach:	"First faith, then facts" approach:
First operate in facts, data, and research that we can see and interpret.	First operate in faith, being led by the Spirit of God and not by sight (2 Corinthians 5:7; Galatians 5:16; Hebrews 12:2).
Secondarily have faith to support our business goals and objectives.	Secondarily utilize research data and tools to support our God-given business goals and objectives.
To judge, criticize, and condemn our business associates is perfectly acceptable.	To judge, criticize, and condemn our business associates is unacceptable. We are not to judge, criticize, or condemn others, so that we won't be judged, criticized, or condemned ourselves (Matthew 7:1-5; James 2: 12-13).
"The first to market will lead" principle:	"The last to market will lead" principle:
The first to market will lead the category in the marketplace.	The last to market will lead the category in the marketplace (Matthew 19:30; 20:16; Mark 10:31; Luke 13:30).

Operationalizing God's Principles in the Commercial Arena

I'll begin this section by acknowledging that I believe most mature Christians understand the underlying principles and fundamental differences between right and wrong. However, the question of whether or not we adhere to these principles in the workplace and marketplace is debatable. As observed by the former chairman and CEO of PepsiCo, Inc., Steven S. Reinemund, it is important to provide "the logic and the tools for building a sound bridge connecting individual faith and workplace conduct."[26]

While many of the principles raised in this section may appear to be basic codes of conduct and common courtesies that we have been taught throughout our careers, they are broken virtually every hour in the workplace. I won't attempt to take you through a litany of examples of ethical versus unethical behavior, or a myriad of illustrations of legal versus illegal business practices, and the gray areas of gender, cultural, social, racial, political, and economic ramification and implications therein. But I will point out a few pragmatic, powerful, biblically based principles that will undoubtedly strengthen your operational efficiency and effectiveness in the workplace and marketplace.

The Bible imparts volumes of information regarding how we should behave and operate in business. We know, for instance, that in Exodus 20 the Bible delineates the Ten Commandments, which include directives against stealing and bearing false witness. These commandments may be aptly applied to the commercial arena. The books of Psalms and Proverbs also offer a wealth of wisdom and practical advice that may be applied to business practices and protocols.

In the following list, I highlight a few general commandments and practical principles that I believe are especially relevant to us in the workplace and marketplace. This is by no means an exhaustive list, but it includes a few reminders of some of God's expectations of us when it comes to our professional behavior and commercial operations:

- Serve and obey God (Joshua 24:15; Psalm 2:11; John 2:5; 1 Peter 1:14).

- Seek and accept wise counsel and advice (Proverbs 11:14; 12:1,15; 13:20; 19:20; 20:18; James 1:5).

- Behave and operate in wisdom and integrity (Psalm 101:2; Proverbs 10:9; 11:1-3; 13:6; 26:4; Micah 6:8; Matthew 7:21-23; 26:41; 2 Corinthians 4:2; Ephesians 5:15-17; 1 Thessalonians 5:22; Titus 2:7).

- Pursue peace and harmony with others (Matthew 5:9; Romans 12:18; 14:19; Philippians 4: 5; Hebrews 12:14).

- Pursue excellence in your profession (Proverbs 10:4; John 15:8,16; Romans 12:11).

- Submit to your employer or superiors (Proverbs 27:18; Colossians 3:22; 1 Peter 2:18).

- Treat your employees well and compensate them fairly (Deuteronomy 1:16-17; 24: 14-15; Colossians 4:1).

- Don't gossip or reveal confidences and company trade secrets (Proverbs 11:13; 16:28; Leviticus 19:16).

- Love and respect others and treat them as you would want them to treat you (Proverbs 3:27; Matthew 7:12; John 13:35; Romans 12:10; Galatians 6:7-10; Philippians 3:14; 1Thessalonians 4:9; Hebrews 10:24; James 5:16; 1 John 4:7).

- Support one another in words and deeds (Romans 14:19; 1 Corinthians 14:20; Ephesians 4:29; 1 Thessalonians 5:11; James 3:1-10; 1 Peter 2:1-2).

- Be patient and forgive one another (2 Timothy 2:24; Hebrews 10:36; James 5:7-8; Leviticus 19:18; Mark 11:25-26; Luke 6:37; Ephesians 4:32; 2 Corinthians 2:10; Colossians 3: 12-13).

- Don't seek revenge or slander your colleagues (Proverbs 24:29: 30:10; Romans 12:19; 1 Thessalonians 5:15; 1 Peter 3:8-9).

- Refrain from arguing and complaining (Proverbs 15:18; 2 Timothy 2:23; Titus 3:9; Philippians 2:14; Ecclesiastes 7:9).

- Never accept bribes (Deuteronomy 16:19).

- Don't harbor pride, arrogance, anger, or bitterness (Proverbs 8:13; 15:1; 16:24; 22:4; Isaiah 2:17; 13:11; Romans 12:16; 1 Corinthians 13:5; Ephesians 4:29-31; Colossians 3:8-10).

Incorporating Godly Communication and Confrontation Techniques

Communication is such an integral and vital aspect of business management and operations that I believe it's important for us to review a few scriptures pertaining specifically to the discipline of effective communication.

We communicate both verbally and nonverbally with a multitude of people every day, including our managers, employees, coworkers, customers, clients, suppliers, and members of the media. As Christian business leaders, we must make every effort to ensure that our communication content, style, and technique are reflective of God's principles and teachings.

Following are a few biblically based instructions for following godly communication protocol and procedures. Again, this is not meant to be an exhaustive list, but it does include a number of scriptures to guide us in achieving efficient and effective communications in business:

- Speak the truth in love (Ephesians 4:15; Colossians 3:9).

- Speak the wisdom of God and encourage one another (1 Corinthians 2:7; 1 Timothy 4:13).

- Be quick to listen, slow to speak, and slow to anger (Proverbs 14:29; James 1:19).

- Be careful of what you say and how you speak to others (Proverbs 10:6-21; 13:3; 15:4; 18:21; 15:4; 21:23; Matthew 15:11).

- Do not use profanity or other forms of foul language (Ephesians 4:29; Colossians 3:8-10; 2 Timothy 2:16).

- If you must confront or correct individuals, then do it privately and with respect and humility (Mathew 18:15; 2 Timothy 2:25).

Based on many years of experience in corporate America, I would be remiss if I did not comment on the pervasive use of offensive language. Profanity has unfortunately become commonplace in the business world. The Bible makes it clear that we are to abstain from corrupt words and foul language (Ephesians 4:29; Colossians 3:8; 2 Timothy 2:16). Yet, it never ceases to amaze me how otherwise intelligent professionals will use vulgarity in the workplace and marketplace as if it was socially acceptable to everyone!

Not everyone uses foul language. Not everyone appreciates hearing it—regardless of whether it's used in anger or in humor or jest. I've always believed that the use of profanity is a sign of inarticulateness, mental and verbal laziness, and a lack of intelligence, grace, refinement, and class. Please do not perpetuate the use of foul language. It is a crutch that poorly reflects on you as an individual, and it is ultimately an insult to God.

It's amazing that, particularly in Western society, people avoid mentioning God for fear that someone might be offended, yet they have no problem with the use of vulgar and obscene language! In many major U.S. corporations, employees are allowed to splutter expletives, but they're discouraged from uttering the sovereign name of Jesus Christ! And progress in corporate America marches on...

For us as Christian business leaders, we need to adhere to God's communication guidelines and set a Higher standard of professionalism in the business arena. If you are guilty of using profanity, and especially if you profess to be a Christian, then you are not exemplifying the Spirit of God. You are rendering your testimony ineffective. It's time for you to repent to God, ask for His forgiveness, and begin today to enhance the overall content and quality of your language.

Leveraging the Three-Step Confrontation Process of Jesus

Miscommunication occurs daily, if not hourly, in the workplace and marketplace. Lack of clear and concise communication leads to miscommunications and misunderstandings, which can ultimately lead to confrontations. Being a humble servant of God does not mean that you can't be confrontational. The key is in the way in which you manage the situation and communication with the people with whom God leads you to confront. Notice that I emphasize here that we should be *led by God* in our confrontations with others as opposed to just being led by our personal agenda, anger, frustration, or other selfish inclinations of the flesh. If God desires for you to confront someone, He will send the Holy Spirit to encourage and guide you. And He will provide the appropriate opportunity and setting.

When we are led by God to confront someone, it's critical that we approach confrontations in a respectful manner regardless of whether we are dealing with a person who is a colleague, a superior, or a subordinate. Galatians 6:1-10 encourages us to always seek to do good for one another and to confront or restore others with a spirit of gentleness.

Let's consider our professional coach and role model, Jesus, as an example. Jesus was confrontational. The Bible describes numerous incidents in which Jesus confronted others, but He was confrontational in a respectful way that conveyed kindness, wisdom, and compassion. For instance, when Jesus corrected Martha in Luke 10:38-42, He did so in a kind and respectful manner, saying:

> Martha, Martha, you are worried and troubled about many things. But one thing is needed, and Mary has chosen that good part, which will not be taken away from her.
>
> Luke 10:41-42 (NKJV)

In this passage, Jesus employs a three-step process when He confronts Martha by:

1. Acknowledging her feelings and concerns (e.g., "you are worried and troubled").

2. Sharing godly wisdom and advice with her (e.g., "only one thing is needed").

3. Offering practical suggestions and examples to help her learn (e.g., "Mary has chosen that good part").

Another example of the confrontation methods of Jesus involves times when He healed individuals who were blind and mute and cast demons out of others. The Pharisees had the audacity to question His ability to cast out demons without the help of a demon (Matthew 12:22-30; Mark 3: 20-27)! In this particular case, Jesus used the same approach He used with Martha in confronting the Pharisees to help them understand how preposterous their questions and comments were.

In confronting the Pharisees, Jesus, 1) acknowledges their feelings and concerns by asking them a number of thought-provoking questions such as, "How can Satan cast out Satan?"(Mark 3:23, NKJV). He then, 2) shares godly wisdom with them regarding the fact that "if Satan casts out Satan, he is divided against himself. How then will his kingdom stand? But if I cast out demons by the Spirit of God, surely the kingdom of God has come upon you" (Matthew 12:25-28, NKJV). And Jesus, 3) offers practical suggestions to the Pharisees by clearly affirming truth and encouraging them to be with Him and not against Him, because this is the only way to achieve forgiveness and eternal salvation (Matthew 12:30-32).

Jesus is a living testament of the effectiveness of following God's communication guidelines and confronting others in truth, peace, and wisdom. His three-step confrontation process of acknowledging feelings, sharing wisdom, and offering practical suggestions worked for Him, and it will work for you. It is a wise, straightforward, and powerful approach that you can use during those times when God leads you to confront others.

Providing Excellent Customer and Client Service

Consumers, customers, and clients are integral to any business. But I have noticed a significant decline in customer service standards across virtually every industry. I've had countless conversations with others who are also concerned about the lack of excellence in customer and client service.

The American Customer Satisfaction Index (ACSI), a national economic indicator of customer evaluations of the quality of products and services available to household consumers in the U.S., reports that customer satisfaction continues to decline in many sectors. This issue has become so prevalent that I've gotten to the point to which I am actually astounded when I receive outstanding customer service or encounter a representative who is proactive and willing to put forth the effort and go the extra mile to not only win my business but also ensure that I am delighted to the point that I will recommend others to the company.

I am not sure of the root cause of declining customer care and client service. Perhaps people are too busy, overworked, or distracted. Maybe there's a lack of proper performance management and training techniques. I can't begin to tell you the number of times that I have made requests, as a customer, and have had salespersons immediately give an excuse for why something *can't* be done before they even consider and investigate all the options. It is as if their first response is "No" with the thought being "How can I get out of doing extra work?" as opposed to "I'm not sure, but let me check into that for you." My requests have been as simple as asking to supplement an existing order with additional items *I'd like to purchase*, which clearly benefits the bottom line of the company!

I make it a point of sending letters of commendation to the managers of individuals who have provided me with exceptional customer service because this level of service is unfortunately uncommon. For us as Christian business leaders, we must not only ensure that our work, as individuals, is excellent. But we must also ensure that our employees and work teams are appropriately trained to operate in a mode of providing the Highest possible level of customer care and client service.

Honoring Your Commitments to Others

As Christians, our reputation is tied to God's reputation. A great part of achieving operational excellence and providing outstanding service involves simply honoring your vows to God and your commitments and promises to others. The Bible tells us that when we vow to do something for God, then we should follow through on it and do it. God does not take pleasure in our disingenuous promises, and He is not interested in our excuses.

If you say you're going to do something for someone, then do it. When you as a Christian constantly fail to keep your promises, then you give others a reason not to believe anything you say. And consequently, they will have little interest in, and respect for, hearing about God from you. Your testimony has been rendered ineffective because of your lack of integrity. The Bible tells us that it is better to *not* commit in the first place than to commit and fail to follow through on your promise (Ecclesiastes 5:1-7). As Jesus says, you are to: "Let your 'Yes' be 'Yes,' and your

'No,' 'No.' For whatever is more than these is from the evil one" (Matthew 5:37, NKJV).

In business, we must do our best to keep our promises to others even in the simplest ways. When you give your word in agreement to a commitment, you should honor it, because your word and actions make up the bond that cements your reputation. An excellent reputation is invaluable, so, as the Bible tells us, "choose a good reputation over great riches" (Proverbs 22:1, NLT; Ecclesiastes 7:1; Deuteronomy 23:21-23). People can tell your character by the words you speak and the promises you keep. Your name is only as good as your word or reputation. Your word is your bond.

Never commit to anything that you have no intention of doing. It reflects badly on you and is disrespectful and an inconvenience to others. Try not to break your promises. Of course, there will always be factors beyond your control and extenuating circumstances that may prevent you from keeping your word. But when these occur, it's important for you to reach out to the appropriate persons and apprise them of the situation immediately. This may sound like such a rudimentary concern, but it warrants acknowledgement because these infractions occur all the time. And the repercussions to our reputations can sometimes be irreparable.

Sometimes we fail to honor our promises to others. And at times others fail to honor their commitments to us. Both of these situations have the potential to place us in a predicament with our business operations and reputations. Example: Imagine if one of your customer service representatives promises a residential customer that he will call the customer in advance to confirm the date and time of a delivery. But he fails to call the customer and proceeds to schedule delivery without confirming with the customer. The delivery is attempted at a time when the customer is not home. Hence, the process has to start all over because of an employee not keeping his word. This costs your organization time and money. It inconveniences and probably infuriates the customer. And as a result, the customer now has a negative perception of your company. What are the chances that they will highly recommend your company to others? Unlikely indeed.

Let's consider another example: If you commit to participating in a meeting, don't attend the meeting and then stay on your PDA, laptop, or cell phone the entire time! If you committed to participating in the meeting, then engage in it or don't attend at all if you can't be 100 percent present in mind and body. I'll never forget the time I was interviewed for a corporate position by a VP who proceeded to send e-mails on his PDA while he interviewed me! It's just an example of how some people can gain position but lack perspicacity. When this occurs, they will often find themselves demoted.

The Bottom Line Benefits of Godly Operations

Godly operating principles and practices are pursued by those of us who have a heart for God. As Christian business leaders, we should always seek to take a God-centric and Christ-centered approach to our commercial endeavors, for as a person "thinks in his heart, so is he" (Proverbs 23:7, NKJV). When we choose to follow God's divine plan for our operations, we'll be wonderfully surprised by the brilliant and innovative ideas He gives us to increase our organizational efficiency, effectiveness, and drive overall performance and profitability. Following are five key benefits of infusing spiritual principles into commercial operations:

1.   Improved employee job satisfaction

In the book *A Spiritual Audit of Corporate America: A Hard Look at Spirituality, Religion, and Values in the Workplace,*[27] the authors, Ian I. Mitroff and Elizabeth A. Denton, found that employees who work for organizations where company values and spiritual values coalesce, are less fearful, less likely to compromise their values, and more able to immerse themselves into their jobs. And improved employee job satisfaction often leads to increased productivity, decreased absenteeism, and reduced turnover rates, or the rate at which an employer gains or losses staff.

2.   Increased employee productivity

A number of successful companies have already begun incorporating spirituality into their operations, particularly within the realm of employee support services. Leading corporations such as AT&T, Ford Motor Company, Toyota, American Airlines, The Coca-Cola Company, Continental Airlines, Intel, Texas Instruments, and Sears have begun supporting their employees by providing conference rooms and other facilities for employees to conduct on-site Bible studies and prayer sessions during lunchtime and other break times.

The *Business Week* cover story, "Religion in the Workplace: The Growing Presence of Spirituality in Corporate America,"[28] reports that several companies, including Taco Bell, Pizza Hut, and subsidiaries of Wal-Mart, have hired Army-style chaplains representing several denominations. These chaplains, who are often on call for twenty-four hours, seven days a week, offer a variety of support services from visiting employees who are hospitalized to providing a variety of counseling services.

3.   Reduced employee turnover rates

The *Business Week* article on "Religion in the Workplace" also reports that there is mounting evidence that spirituality-centric programs in the workplace not only soothe employees' psyches but also help to improve employee productivity, which helps reduce employee turnover rates and improve employee retention. Example: A study conducted by McKinsey & Co. Australia in the late nineties found that when companies offer employee assistance programs that include spiritual elements, employee productivity improves and turnover rates are significantly reduced.

4. Stronger civic and community outreach efforts

Companies that incorporate spiritual values into their commercial operations also benefit from stronger civic and community outreach efforts. Example: The Coca-Cola Christian Fellowship was formed in 2002 with a mission to bring together a community of Christians to support each other and The Coca-Cola Company's values and goals, and to achieve balance by integrating their Christian faith at work. The members of this corporate fellowship group, which holds weekly prayer meetings and Bible studies, perform various civic and social initiatives.

In 2004, after Jamaica was struck by a devastating hurricane, the Coca-Cola Christian Fellowship group convened, coordinated, and distributed over ninety boxes of clothing to the country to aid victims with shipping costs being covered by The Coca-Cola Company.

5. Enhanced public perception of the company

Companies that incorporate philanthropic initiatives and spiritual values into their operations, will find that the perception of the company is enhanced in the eyes of their *current* employees as well as *prospective* employees and the general public. For instance, Ray Berryman, former chairman and CEO of Berryman & Henigar Enterprises, shares the following:

> People know I'm a Christian, and that's good...
> potential hires will often mention that the reason

they want to join our firm is because they've heard we practice Christian principles. Many executives have Bibles on their desks...we open our business meetings with prayer. If someone protests any of these practices, I simply, lovingly, explain that we have the right to do this.[29]

Real-Life Examples of the Divine Operations Plan

Auntie Anne's Pretzels

There are a number of practical ways to ensure that God's principles of excellence are incorporated into your operations. Auntie Anne's Pretzels offers spiritual and religious support to their employees. The founder of Auntie Anne's Pretzels, Anne Beiler, also shares some insights about the spiritual aspects of their operations:

> We have prayer at many of our meetings. When I'm present, I share something that God has done for me lately. I've never had anyone express unhappiness about this. At our annual conventions I always share with our franchisees the ways God has been faithful to us as a company. I give Him all the glory.[30]

ServiceMaster Company

In *The Soul of the Firm*,[31] former chairman of the ServiceMaster Company, C. William Pollard, describes a program called "We Serve," which reinforces their business ethics and operations as well as godly principles.

The program requires that every employee spend at least one day per year working in the field, supporting a customer. One of the benefits of "We Serve" is that it gives senior managers experience and a renewed respect for some of the operational challenges faced by their frontline employees. Pollard states: "The opportunity to serve a customer is for everybody, including those we recruit into the business as senior officers and those who have been around a long time."[32]

Wendy's

The founder of Wendy's, the late Dave Thomas, encouraged excellence in product quality and customer service. His biography on the corporate website states that he believed that everybody at Wendy's should have an MBA—a "Mop Bucket Attitude"—and should treat every customer as if their jobs depended on it because they do!

Johnson & Johnson

With regards to operating in faith and taking risks, one of the three brothers who founded Johnson & Johnson, the late Robert Wood Johnson, reportedly encouraged his employees to make mistakes and take risks. He explained that mistakes mean that they are taking risks, and the company would not grow unless they took risks. This philosophy became an integral part of the company's guiding principles.

The Ritz-Carlton

The Ritz-Carlton is a leader in excellent service and operations. One of the ways that they have done this is by empowering their frontline associates. In the book, *The Servant Leader: Transforming Your Heart, Head, Hands & Habits*, Ken Blanchard and Phil Hodges highlight the fact that in the past, the Ritz Carlton has given certain frontline employees "a $2,000 discretionary fund that they could use to solve customer problems without consulting with anybody."[33] In this way, the company puts money behind their motto, "We are Ladies and Gentlemen serving Ladies and Gentlemen," by empowering their employees to both anticipate customer needs and address them.

As Christian business leaders, let's strive to enhance our operations in such a way that everyone who comes in contact with our business is in some way blessed by virtue of the encounter. Following are a few practical recommendations to achieve this.

Directives for Executing the Divine Operations Plan

Following are six suggestions for implementing the divine operations plan for your business:

1. Pray for God's wisdom and guidance in ensuring that your operations glorify Him.

    Every commercial enterprise is different and faces its own unique set of operational standards and challenges. Most companies have formal manuals for operations and procedures. But these guides *are not* meant to be *stagnate*. Make sure that your guidelines are updated to reflect major social, demographic, technological, political, industrial, and economic trends impacting your operations.

    Pray for spiritual discernment of what God would have you to focus on in your operations, and make the necessary changes as He prompts you. Remember operations start in the mind of the individual. Meditate on Psalm 19:14 and Romans 8:1-39 to make sure you are in the right spiritual mind-set for strengthening your operations.

2. Develop contingency plans.

Contingency plans are typically created as a proactive response to potential *threats* or *failings* or for disaster recovery purposes (e.g., unforeseen emergencies, accidents, network failures, natural disasters, and terrorist threats). However, it's also important that you to develop contingency plans for *unparalleled success* because if you are following the will of God for your life and business, then success is imminent and often remarkable. Plan for success!

Develop contingency plans to ensure that your team has the capacity and capability to operate during times of downturn in business but also during times of extraordinary growth and overwhelming success (Genesis 39:3; Joshua 1:7-8).

3. Create a spiritually supportive environment.

Take a lesson from some of the innovative companies featured in this chapter by creating a spiritually supportive environment for yourself and your employees that includes provisions such as on-site chaplains and the use of company facilities for lunchtime prayer and Bible studies. Believe me, if you acknowledge and support your employees' faith, they will have tremendous respect and appreciation for you and the company. And *everyone* will benefit both spiritually and operationally (1 Corinthians 15:44).

4. Adhere to laws against religious discrimination.

Be aware of the laws regarding religion in the workplace and marketplace as they pertain to your country, and honor them (1 Peter 2:13-15). Example: The United States Civil Rights Act of 1964 prohibits religious discrimination by employers with fifteen or more workers. Title VII of the

act outlines the specific guidelines. If your workplace prohibits formalized faith-based initiatives, remember you
can always exemplify godly excellence in your work and
pray silently throughout your workday (Philippians 1:10-
11; 1 Thessalonians 5:17; Matthew 5:11).

5. Examples of biblical coaches who followed a divine operations plan include a number of disciples such as Jesus,
Moses (book of Exodus), and David (books of 1 Samuel
and 2 Samuel).

6. Praise God for revealing His divine principles of operations and showing you how to incorporate them into your
commercial endeavors (Psalm 145:1-7; Luke 19:37)!

As we conclude this chapter, I hope you come away with a
sense of the critical linkages and interdependencies between our
thoughts, environment, and operations:

Your thoughts impact your environment; and your environment impacts your operations. And God's principles
can help guide you through all of them.

In the next chapter, we'll explore strategies for building a spiritually strong and commercially viable management and organization structure. But before proceeding, we'll close this chapter
with a quote by the late Peter Drucker, who is widely known as
the father of modern management.

Efficiency is doing things right; effectiveness is doing the
right things.[34]

—Peter Drucker

VI

The Divine Management and Organization Plan

> Everyone must submit himself to the governing authorities, for there is no authority except that which God has established. The authorities that exist have been established by God. Consequently, he who rebels against the authority is rebelling against what God has instituted, and those who do so will bring judgment on themselves.
>
> Romans 13:1-2 (NIV)

How do you manage your business? What is your organizational plan? Who do you really work for? The management and organization section of your business plan focuses on one of the most critical aspects of any business: people.

A management and organization plan addresses: 1) the person or people running the business, and 2) the individuals who make up the remainder of the organizational structure. This section of your business plan includes topics such as the business owners or principals, management structure and style, chart of authority, boards of directors, advisory committees, and professional consultants.

Three Planning Proverbs for the Divine Management and Organization Plan

The management and organization plan of your business must be based on God's principles. His guidelines are appropriate and applicable regardless of whether you are an employer or employee. Most of us are familiar with organizational charts, layers of management, and hierarchical authority within a corporate environment. But what does the Word of God say about how we should approach our management and organization plans? We'll explore many aspects of this question and others as we explore the divine management and organization plan and the three Planning Proverbs of this chapter, which are as follows:

1.   Remember Who you work for.

2.   Establish a Top-Down management and organization plan.

3.   Realize that you are on divine assignment.

Let's proceed with the first Planning Proverb:

Remember Who You Work For

Who do you work for? In responding to this question, many of us would readily offer the name of a particular *institution or individual.* Some of us might even answer by saying, "I work for myself," "a small business," or even "the government." All of these answers may be true to a certain degree. But as God's ambassadors in the business world, it's important that we remember that, first and foremost you and I work *for God* (Acts 5:29).

"Now look, God Himself is with us as *our* head" (2 Chronicles 13:12, NKJV). There is only one kingdom and one King (Ezekiel 37:15-28; Colossians 3:24). God is the Head and Leader of all of our organizations. As Christians, we are members of God's universal kingdom and family. His divine organization. His sovereign corporation. So we ultimately work for and report to God. Your professional position is primarily within His kingdom and secondarily within an organization.

The Bible reminds us that each of us has distinct value and purpose as servants of God regardless of our respective positions (1 Corinthians 12:12-27; Ephesians 4:11-16). Example: "He Himself gave some *to be* Apostles, some prophets, some evangelists, and some pastors and teachers, for the equipping of the saints for the work of ministry, for the edifying of the body of Christ" (Ephesians 4:11-12, NKJV). So we all have different titles, functions, roles, and responsibilities that are equally important to advancing God's kingdom agenda in the marketplace.

Because we were created by God to serve and glorify Him, we are also accountable to Him. Therefore, we must not be overly preoccupied with corporate hierarchy and reporting structure. You are to serve Him first and then your family, church, government, employer, employees, and customers. Your job is not your provider. Your manager is not your provider. God is your Provider. He is The Source of our security. Everything else is simply a resource. God is our Ultimate Superior. We report to Him. We work for Him.

Servant Leadership

At its core, business entails serving others and creating value through products and services. Most of us have heard of the concept of servant leadership. But while you might think of yourself as a professional and a leader in business, have you really considered yourself to be a servant?

We tend to have negative connotations of the concept of a "servant" because of the propensity to equate it with the idea of being weak, unskilled, menial, ancillary, and low in status. But being a servant is honorable in God's eyes. We are to serve the living God now, and we will serve Him in eternity (Hebrews 9:14; Revelation 22:3). As Jesus tells us:

> Anyone who wants to be my disciple must follow me, because my servants must be where I am. And the Father will honor anyone who serves me.
>
> John 12:26 (NLT)

> The greatest among you must be a servant. But those who exalt themselves will be humbled, and those who humble themselves will be exalted.
>
> Matthew 23:11-12 (NLT)

The concept of servant leadership was broadly introduced to the world initially through the work of the late Robert K. Greenleaf who spent most of his career working for AT&T. After retirement, he wrote essays and books on the subject of servant leadership, and today the Greenleaf Center for Servant-Leadership, which was founded in 1964, continues his legacy.

On their website, the Greenleaf Center defines servant leadership by referencing the essay, "The Servant as Leader," which Greenleaf first published in 1970. In that essay, he says:

> The servant-leader is servant first… It begins with the natural feeling that one wants to serve, to serve first. Then conscious choice brings one to aspire to lead. That person is sharply different from one who is leader first, perhaps because of the need to assuage an unusual power drive or to acquire material possessions…The leader-first and the servant-first are two extreme types. Between them there are shadings and blends that are part of the infinite variety of human nature.
>
> The difference manifests itself in the care taken by the servant-first to make sure that other people's highest priority needs are being served. The best test, and difficult to administer, is: Do those served grow as persons? Do they, while being served, become healthier, wiser, freer, more autonomous, more likely themselves to become servants? And what is the effect on the least privileged in society? Will they benefit or at least not be further deprived?

Servant leadership focuses on the importance of first serving and then leading when it comes to organizational management. Are you more focused on serving or leading others? Are you more focused on serving yourself or serving others?

God calls us to be servant leaders in the business world. Galatians 5:13 tells us that we have been called to serve one another, as opposed to being self-serving. The Word of God encourages us to care for the flock that God has given us (1 Peter 5:2; 1 Timothy 4:13). Your "flock" may be your team, department, division, or an entire corporation. Or, your "flock" may consist of your customers or suppliers. Regardless of whether you hold a formally appointed management position, you are still one of God's appointed leaders. And if you will be a servant leader to the people with whom God has entrusted you, the Bible says that they will serve you forever (1 Kings 12:7). You will be blessed and God will be glorified.

There is honor in serving. Jesus describes Himself as a servant when He states: "For even the Son of Man did not come to be served, but to serve, and to give His life a ransom for many" (Mark 10:45, NKJV).

Moses is referred to as a "servant of the Lord" (Joshua 14:7, NKJV; 18:7; 22:2-5). Joshua, the successor of Moses, was also an excellent example of a servant leader, and by the time of his death, he was widely known as "the servant of the Lord" (Judges 2:7-8, NKJV). Like these disciples, you too are a servant of the Lord in both the workplace and the marketplace.

Are You Modeling a Servant Spirit?

In Isaiah 42: 1-3 (NLT), God describes the spirit of one of His chosen servants as follows:

> Look at my servant, whom I strengthen. He is my chosen one, who pleases me. I have put my Spirit upon him. He will bring justice to the nations. He will not shout or raise his voice in public. He will not crush the weakest reed or put out a flickering candle. He will bring justice to all who have been wronged.

Recently, I was reading one of the *In Touch* magazines produced by Dr. Charles Stanley's church, First Baptist Atlanta. The magazine featured an article titled: "Dan Cathy: Leading the Next Generation at Chick-fil-A." The article mentioned that Dan "spends most of his time traveling, helping with grand openings for new franchises, staying attuned to customers' needs, and modeling a servant spirit for the employees."

The fact that Chick-fil-A includes "modeling a servant spirit for employees" as one of their most critical business imperatives speaks volumes for their focus on servant leadership. In the article, Dan states:

> God wants to use the local church to make a difference. There are so many negative forces going on in our society. This is a fallen culture that we live in…but if we'll acknowledge God in all our ways, then not only for us as a family and as a business but even for us all as a nation, God will continue to direct our paths.[35]

I had the unique opportunity to experience Dan Cathy's humble attitude and servant leadership approach in person when I recently had the pleasure of meeting and chatting with him at a Dallas Regional Chamber of Commerce luncheon where he was the keynote speaker. During his powerful presentation, he shared a number of interesting items and artifacts and explained how each symbolized specific leadership principles. One of these articles was a shoe brush. Dan explained how it was used for brushing and shining shoes, but, for him, it also represented the importance of remaining a humble servant and reminded him of how Jesus washed the feet of His disciples.

Well, after explaining this, Dan asked a gentleman from the audience to come and stand beside him. And to our utter amazement, Dan got on his knees and actually rolled up the cuffs of the man's trousers and brushed and shined his shoes! When he finished, he pulled the cuffs back down, stood up, and gave the man a hug! Dan explained that this is the type of servant attitude that he tries to impart to his employees. Dan's actions transcended his words in an extraordinary way and left an affirmative, indelible impression that I will never forget.

In order for us to have the heart of one of God's servants and exemplify servant leadership, the Bible states that because "He who called you is holy, then you also be holy in all *your* conduct, because it is written, 'Be holy for I am holy'" (1 Peter 1: 14-16, NKJV). In order to do this, we must fervently seek God. For instance, in 1 Kings 3:9 (NIV), King Solomon implores God:

> So give your servant a discerning heart to govern your people and to distinguish between right and wrong. For who is able to govern this great people of yours?

God Holds You Accountable for Your Leadership and Management Methods

We must always pray for spiritual discernment in doing what is right as we manage and lead others, because we are ultimately accountable to God. He holds us accountable for how we treat others. If you are a business owner or corporate executive who is responsible for managing others, then God has obviously appointed you in a leadership position, and He will hold you responsible for the employees who are under your authority and individuals within your realm of influence. You are not just accountable to your superiors in the corporate hierarchy. You are accountable to the Highest standard of power and authority: Almighty God.

The Lord tells us that we will have to give an account of our management or else we will no longer be allowed to serve as a manager (Luke 16:2). Remember, to whom much is given, much is required (Luke 12:48). If we don't honor God's principles for servant leadership, He has a way of bringing down those who "dwell on high" (Isaiah 26:5, NKJV), or who have an attitude of arrogance and superiority.

You should be so much of a positive influence on others that their lives should be *enhanced* as a result of being under your leadership and authority. I believe the definition of an exceptional leader is one who serves and enhances the lives of others by moving them closer to God and the achievement of their spiritual calling and purpose. In the following sections, we'll consider four critical requirements and characteristics of having the heart of one of God's servants:

1. Have a humble attitude.

   The Bible teaches us that, as servants, we are to be humble, not selfish, and to have a mind and a heart like God (Philippians 2:1-5). Jesus reinforces this when He declares: "he who is greatest among you, let him be as the younger, and he who governs as he who serves" (Luke 22:26, NKJV). When applied to the business arena, this means that a senior level executive with many years of experience should be humble just like a junior level manager whose career is just beginning.

   Never allow your leadership position to keep you from having a humble and compassionate attitude toward others. "Remember also those being mistreated, as if you felt their pain in your own bodies" (Hebrews 13:3, NLT). Never think of yourself as too good to associate with people who may be not be as accomplished as you are or who may fall on lower socioeconomic strata. We can all learn something from everyone. Be humble and friendly toward people on every level of corporate hierarchy—from the maintenance and cleaning crew to the executive leadership team.

2. Don't be arrogant.

While this section supports the sentiments expressed in the previous section, I've purposely chosen to highlight the character trait of arrogance because it is unfortunately so prevalent in the business world and it runs completely contradictory to the principles of God.

The Word of God says that we should not be haughty or arrogant, boastful, and prideful (1 Timothy 6: 17). God despises arrogance, and He makes it clear that pride results in destruction (Proverbs 16:5,18; 29:23; Psalm 32:23). Furthermore, God tells us that He will break our prideful spirit to the point that all our work will be in vain (Leviticus 26:19-20).

1 Timothy 6:17-19 (NIV) explicitly says:

> Command those who are rich in this present world not to be arrogant… Command them to do good, to be rich in good deeds, and to be generous and willing to share. In this way they will lay up treasure for themselves as a firm foundation for the coming age, so that they may take hold of the life that is truly life.

Jesus makes it clear that those who exalt themselves will be humbled and those who humble themselves will be exalted (Matthew 23:11-12). Keep in mind that I'm not confusing confidence with arrogance. The Word of God says that the Lord shall be our confidence and we are to boldly draw near to Him (Proverbs 3:26; Hebrews 4:16; 13:6). A confident attitude is good as long as it doesn't plummet into the negative sphere of arrogance and pretentiousness. In this section, I'm specifically referring to attitudes of superiority, egotism, and overbearing pride that boast oneself while degrading others. As Jesus says: "It's not what goes into your mouth that defiles you; you are defiled by the words that come out of your mouth" (Matthew 15:11, NLT).

Many of us are highly educated, credentialed, experienced, and skilled business professionals with a wealth of knowledge. But the Bible says that:

> We know that we all possess knowledge. Knowledge puffs up, but love builds up. The man who thinks he knows something does not yet know as he ought to know. But the man who loves God is known by God.
>
> 1 Corinthians 8:1-3 (NIV)

This scripture tells us that sometimes our professional expertise and knowledge will cause us to "puff up" or to think loftily of ourselves and become proud and boastful (i.e., arrogant and pretentious). But it is love, goodwill, and benevolence that edifies and encourages us to grow as individuals and be recognized by God as one of His humble, faithful servants.

As God's servant leaders in the business world, we are instructed to live in harmony with one another and not be prideful, boastful, pretentious, or conceited (Romans 12:14-21; Jeremiah 9:23-24). Don't be unkind, unappreciative, and unwilling to listen to your employees. And never demean or humiliate them. You can supervise your team faithfully with loving kindness, humility, respect, and encouragement and still be a firm, diligent, responsible, and successful manager.

The Bible is full of information and inspiration to help you counteract the spirit of pride and arrogance. Let's be humble. Let's embrace and embody the spirit of humility. If the Son of the Creator of the universe was humble, then who are we not to be?

3. Pursue what is good for yourself and for others.

In 1 Thessalonians 5:15 (NKJV), the Word of God advises that "no one renders evil for evil to anyone, but always pursue what is good both for yourselves and for all." This scripture alludes to what's commonly referred to as the "win-win" scenario or one in which decisions that are made actually benefit all parties involved.

If you are truly one of God's ambassadors, then you will not have a sense of peace about a decision you make that is good for you but bad for your constituents (e.g., your investors, employees, customers, or suppliers). Likewise, you won't feel at peace about a decision that is good for your constituents but bad for you. Now, believe me, I know that in today's competitive and challenging marketplace it's very difficult to make decisions that are genuinely in the best interest of all parties or are mutually beneficial. But it is not impossible. And the Word of God calls us to strive to this level of excellence in management and leadership.

4.   Don't practice respect based on hierarchy.

The Word of God makes it clear that God does not show favoritism (Galatians 3:26-28; Acts 10:34). It makes no difference who you are or where you're from; God doesn't play favorites and neither should we. In business, we shouldn't esteem some individuals more highly than others or offer preferential treatment to some people over others. I can't tell you how many times I have seen this played out within the walls of corporate America.

Example: A colleague, walking down the hall, comes in contact with a janitor and completely ignores him. No smile. No verbal greeting. Minimal eye contact. Nothing. But moments later, this same colleague is walking down the hall and comes in contact with a senior executive and almost falls over himself beaming at the executive, smiling with a friendly, verbal greeting and clever anecdotes!

Ridiculous. Why do we behave this way? Why is a senior-level executive treated with more respect than a maintenance crew member? I believe the answers to these questions lie within our propensity to esteem some individuals more highly than others, particularly when it comes to position, rank, and title in the workplace and marketplace. We tend to offer more courtesies to individuals who are at the highest socioeconomic levels in society or on the "corporate ladder" of an organization. This is what I call *respect based on hierarchy*. And I believe its primary root cause is a nasty parasite called insecurity.

Insecurity Breeds Respect Based on Hierarchy

Examine yourself. Pay attention to your behavior. In the evening, as you're leaving the office and riding the elevator down to the parking lot, do you acknowledge and speak to the executive on the elevator but ignore the maintenance worker who is also on the elevator? Are you more courteous toward your team members during those times when your supervisor is actually present and sitting in on your team meeting?

The Apostle Paul alludes to these scenarios and the issue of respect based on hierarchy in his speech to the Galatians when he states: "It is good to be zealous in a good thing *always*, and not only *when I am present with you*" (Galatians 4:18, NKJV). Essentially, he's saying that we should behave in a positive and respectful manner always—not just toward the leader and not just when the leader is around.

We know that behavioral dynamics and personality conflicts will always come into play given the myriad personalities in the workplace and marketplace. But I believe that people who practice respect based on hierarchy are operating out of a place of insecurity. They play the games of corporate politics and posturing and try to ingratiate and disingenuously position themselves with those who they believe have the power to advance their careers. As a result, they have relegated their faith to ridiculous power plays and positioning tactics as opposed to placing their faith in the power of God.

As sons and daughters of the Most High God, we must rise above such irreverent behavior. We should already know our true brand value and who we are in Him. So we can rest secure *in Him* knowing that He's in control of everything. The Word of God says, "*Let* nothing *be done* through selfish ambition or conceit, but in lowliness of mind let each esteem others better than himself" (Philippians 2:3, NKJV). We should respect and honor *all people* (1 Peter 2:17)—not just the ones who are in a position to hire, fire, or promote us.

I love the way the Apostle James challenges us:

> My dear brothers and sisters, how can you claim to have faith in our glorious Lord Jesus Christ if you favor some people over others?
>
> For example, suppose someone comes into your meeting dressed in fancy clothes and expensive jewelry, and another comes in who is poor and dressed in dirty clothes. If you give special attention and a good seat to the rich person, but you say to the poor one, 'You can stand over there, or else sit on the floor'—well, doesn't this discrimination show that your judgments are guided by evil motives?
>
> James 2:1-4 (NLT)

We must commit to Higher standards in executing our management and organizational plans. Treat everyone with dignity and respect regardless of their position or lot in life. A married executive with children has the potential to support your business just as effectively as an unmarried executive with no children. Your front-line salespeople and your corporate board of directors are equally critical to the success of your business.

Both your superiors and subordinates should be highly esteemed. Never offer more respect to one person over another, one client over another, one supplier over another, a management employee over a non-management employee, a highly compensated worker over a minimum-wage worker, a white-collar professional over a blue-collar professional, one ethnicity over another, or one gender over the other. We are all human beings. We are all God's children.

The Consequences of Practicing Respect Based on Hierarchy

The Bible recounts a compelling example of the importance of respecting others regardless of their position. It involves Naaman, who was "commander of the army of the King of Syria" and who "was a great and honorable man in the eyes of his master because by him the Lord had given victory to Syria" (2 Kings 5:1, NKJV). The Bible also explains that "he was a mighty man of valor, but a leper," (2 Kings 5:1, NKJV), which meant he was inflicted with leprosy, a life-threatening disease.

Naaman wanted so badly to be healed from his infirmity that he made arrangements to meet Elisha, a man of God and prophet known for healing people. When Naaman arrived at Elisha's door, instead of Elisha meeting him, Elisha *actually sent a servant* to meet Naaman and give him the message for how to be healed, which was: "Go, wash yourself seven times in the Jordan, and your flesh will be restored and you will be cleansed" (2 Kings 5:10, NIV).

Naaman was furious that Elisha hadn't taken the time to meet with him personally. Naaman left in a rage, complaining, "I thought that he would surely come out to me and stand and call on the name of the Lord his God, wave his hand over the spot and cure me of my leprosy" (2 Kings 5:11-12, NIV)!

Naaman's servants caught up with him and encouraged him to follow the instructions for healing as relayed by Elisha's servant (2 Kings 5:13). His servants stressed the fact that although the information was given to them by Elisha's *servant*, the information still originated from Elisha, the prophet, so it was *still valid*.

Naaman conceded and "so he went down and dipped himself in the Jordan seven times, as the man of God had told him, and his flesh was restored and became clean like that of a young boy" (2 Kings 5:14, NIV). Naaman was extremely grateful to finally be healed!

I love this story because it shows us how this powerful man was healed and his life transformed by the influence of *his servants*, who encouraged him to follow Elisha's instructions for healing (2 Kings 5:1-27) as relayed through *Elisha's servant*. If Naaman had not listened to these servants, he might not have ever been healed.

The moral of this story is twofold: 1) One of the main consequences of practicing respect based on hierarchy is that we can miss out on blessings from God because we are behaving in a way that is contrary to His Word; and 2) No matter where we are on the organizational ladder, we should never view subordinate positions as being insignificant.

The Cost of Bad Leadership and Management

I had an unfortunate incident happen during my tenure with a major company. After years of serving under extremely competent, knowledgeable, kind, and supportive leaders, I joined a small, newly instituted division of the company. The person I reported to was a fairly good manager who, in turn, reported to the division leader—who was a different story.

Although the division leader was extremely bright and had a wealth of industry experience, this person was also extremely insecure, unfriendly, negative, verbally abrasive, and lacking in strong leadership skills. Everyone was constantly complaining about how our division leader never really stood up for us, nor represented us well among other internal groups and executive leadership.

Because I had been with the company for many years and had always had a positive experience during my tenure, I knew that the dysfunctional dynamics of this particular division and the lack of genuine amicability, support, and guidance by the primary leader were not indicative of the company's leadership team as a whole. But what was truly unfortunate about the situation was that we had so many employees on the team who were new to the company and for whom this was their *first experience* as employees with this company.

I, along with several other long-tenured employees, found myself constantly trying to convince my new team members: "This is really not how the whole company operates!" "Not all of our divisions are like this!" "We really do have some excellent leaders!" Yet, this was the only experience from which our new team members had to judge the overall company.

Many of our new colleagues heard what we were saying *in theory*, but what they saw from our pseudo-leader *in practice* was a constant contradiction. It was virtually impossible for our words to combat the bad leadership and management they observed on a daily basis. Sadly, after a few months, a number of them left the company as a result of that experience.

This was a regrettable situation for the new employees because they never had a chance to experience so many of the positive facets of leadership that the company had to offer. This was also unfortunate for the company because, financially, it had invested significantly in hiring these talented individuals, but it never fully reaped the return on this investment. And presumably many of these former employees may not speak highly of the company to others.

As Christian business leaders, we must remember that even though we may have been with our current company for decades, we still serve as the introductory face and culture of the company for new employees as well as for potentially new customers, consumers, suppliers, investors, and strategic partners. To this point, I will end this Planning Proverb the way we started with a simple reminder: Remember Who you work for.

Establish a Top-Down Management and Organization Plan

· ·

Submission = Under the Mission of Another

What exactly is submission, and how do we incorporate godly principles of submission into our management and organization plans? The term *submission* is generally defined as the act of yielding to the power, control, or authority of another. But let's dissect the word *submission* into its two core components: the prefix "sub" and the word *mission.*

"Sub" is a prefix of Latin origin meaning "*to be under, below, or beneath.*" In the divine mission and vision chapter, we defined the word *mission* as one's business or calling. So we might conclude that the term *submission* means to be under the business or calling of another.

Being under the business or calling of another applies to all types of authority whether it's the authority of an *individual,* such as a supervisor or company president, or the authority of an *organization,* such as a board of directors or a local government entity.

God Ordained Submission

God ordained order, authority, and submission for mankind. He instructs us to "let all things be done decently and in order" (1 Corinthians 14:40, NKJV). So He designed a divine hierarchy for the world, governments, churches, businesses, and families. And these hierarchies are clearly delineated in the Bible. Romans 13:1-2 (NIV) states:

> Everyone must submit himself to the governing authorities, for there is no authority except that which God has established. The authorities that exist have been established by God. Consequently, he who rebels against the authority is rebelling against what God has instituted, and those who do so will bring judgment on themselves.

We all submit to some type and level of authority, but ultimately we are all called to submit to God. There is only "one God and Father, who is over all and in all and living through all" (Ephesians

4:6, ESV; Psalm 22:28; 103:19; Daniel 4:32). This is how the body of Christ is organized. So when I recommend that you establish a top-down management and organization plan, I'm advocating that you place God at the top. Make Him the Ultimate Authority for your organizational design and makeup. Allow Him to lead you in creating the right organizational chart and incorporating the appropriate human resources for your business.

We Submit to Jesus and Jesus Submits to God

1 Corinthians 3:23 (ESV) states: "You belong to Christ, and Christ belongs to God." According to God's divine order, we are to submit to Jesus and Jesus submits to God. The way we submit to God is through our belief in and commitment to His Son, Jesus Christ (Colossians 3: 24; Ephesians 5:23; 6:7; Psalm 100:2). Jesus is under the authority of God, and we, along with all world systems, governments, and churches, are under the authority of Jesus. Scripture states:

> For unto us a child is born, unto us a son is given; *and the government shall be upon his shoulder.* And his name shall be called Wonderful, Counselor, the Mighty God, the everlasting Father, the Prince of Peace.
>
> Isaiah 9:6 (NKJV)

Jesus further explains: "All things that the Father has are Mine. Therefore I said that He will take of Mine and declare it to you" (John 16:15, NKJV).

Jesus serves as the ultimate example of submission. He was so fully submitted to God and to the Holy Spirit that, during His baptism, God's voice came from heaven and said, "You are

My beloved Son; in You I am well pleased" (Luke 3:22, NKJV). The Bible tells us that we are to pray for and submit ourselves "to every ordinance of man for the Lord's sake, whether to the king as supreme, or to governors..." (1 Peter 2:13-14, NKJV; 1 Timothy 2:1-2). Let's consider the following list, which highlights some of the authority figures to whom the Word of God says we are to submit:

- God (James 4:7; 1 Peter 5: 5-11; Job 22:21)

- Jesus (Colossians 3: 24; Ephesians 6:7)

- Elders (1 Peter 5:5)

- Parents (Deuteronomy 5:16; Leviticus 19:3; Colossians 3:20)

- Government (1 Peter 2: 13-15)

- Church Leadership (Hebrews 13:17)

- Employers (1 Peter 2:18; Colossians 3:22; Ephesians 6:5-9)

- Spouses (1 Peter 3:1; Ephesians 5:22; Colossians3:18-19)

Obedience to authority must be a lifestyle for us as Christians in general and a practice for us as Christians in business. We are called to follow God's spiritual guidelines for submission and obedience within our commercial organizations simply because: 1) We love Him and 2) He commands it. As Jesus observes, if we love Him, then we will keep His commandments (John 14:15).

We must always be obedient to those who God has placed in authority over us. Jesus says: "Most assuredly, I say to you, a servant is not greater than his master; nor is he who is sent greater than he who sent him" (John 13:16, NKJV).

Employees don't give orders to their employers. Employees must respect their superiors, or individuals of higher ranking and authority, in the workplace and marketplace. The Bible says that we are to honor our employers (Proverbs 27:18). So adherence to leadership hierarchy and organizational protocol should be done with proper order, respect, and decency.

The Benefits of Submission in Business

In business, each of us has a certain degree of personal responsibility and accountability. But each of us must also submit to those who God has placed in authority over us. And for this we should be eternally grateful.

It is a blessing and a privilege to be in a position to submit to God-ordained authorities, because it takes the weight and stress of *total* responsibility and accountability off us as business practitioners. Being under submission to others allows us to relax and lay down our burdens (Matthew 11: 28:30).

There is peace and comfort in knowing that God has ordained the authority that is over you according to His good and perfect will (Romans 12:2). What a relief it is to be provided with graduated levels of authority. What a blessing it is to not have to shoulder total responsibility in business. We can rest in the realization, comfort, and assurance that God is in complete control and He has ultimate responsibility.

What If I Have to Submit to Someone I Don't Respect?

Oftentimes we may not necessarily like, or agree with, the people who God has placed in authority over us. Yet, God still calls us to serve them. He commands that we respect and submit to them, not necessarily because they deserve it, but because their position or office of authority commands it. And because God ordains it (Ecclesiastes 8: 1-9).

God may instruct you to submit to a manager who has a vision that may not make sense to you. You might not see the big picture. You may be wondering how the organization will profit or how you'll benefit from the work you're doing. But rest assured that you do not have to understand the ultimate goal, or the big picture, in order to submit to authority. God knows the big picture. Your manager may actually know it. Your job is to simply flow with it.

Support and pursue your manager's plan even if you're not completely convinced of it. Commit to respecting authority and trust that everything will work out just fine. Be obedient and follow God's commandments for submission, knowing that He'll make everything clear and "He has made everything beautiful in its time" (Ecclesiastes 3:11, NKJV). When we obey God and submit to His will and to those who are in authority over us, blessings will overtake us (Deuteronomy 28:2).

But what if your authority figure (e.g., manager, CEO, or board of directors) requests you do something that goes against God's principles? This is a very awkward and difficult predicament, as acknowledged in Proverbs 29:2 (NKJV): "When the righteous are in authority, the people rejoice; but when a wicked *man* rules, the people groan," and, "Wise and knowledgeable leaders bring stability" (Proverbs 28:2, NLT).

According to the Bible, we are to submit ourselves one to another *in the fear of God* (Ephesians 5:21). Many leaders mistreat others because they *do not* have the fear of God within them (Nehemiah 5:15; 2 Corinthians 7:1). But God protects and guides us, even in these situations, when He says: "Therefore you shall keep My commandments, and perform them: I am the Lord (Leviticus 22:31, NKJV).

As Christian business professionals, we are to submit to our superiors as long as they are not asking us to compromise our spiritual values, integrity, ethics, and morals by violating godly principles and commandments. This is where we draw the line. If you are asked to perform any tasks that are immoral, unethical, or illegal, you must respectfully state your position and rationale for refusing to comply. If necessary, you might consider changing job assignments or seeking employment elsewhere.

Your peace of mind, character, integrity, reputation, and ultimate salvation are more important than any job, professional title, or compensation package. Stand firm for God, and He will stand firm for you (1 Samuel 2:30; Matthew 10:32). If by standing firm in your conviction for God, you end up losing your job, then rest assured that this is for your good (Romans 8:28). God will place the proper individuals and resources in your life to sustain you during this transition period. And He will bless you with more career opportunities and in more wonderful ways than you could have ever imagined.

Equally Yoked Business Partnerships

In an effort to expand or gain scale and relevance in the marketplace, we often partner with other individuals and entities. But we must be judicious when forming business partnerships. Your business partnership may have a commercial veneer, but at its core it is a spiritual venture. Remember, we are all spirits having a temporary human experience.

By "business partnerships," I'm referring to long-term, formal, or contractual strategic partnerships that include joint ventures, mergers, and acquisitions as well as short-term, informal "hand-shake" alliances. I'm referring to any type of commercial partnership in which two or more individuals or entities enter for the pursuit of common goals. These partnerships include alliances with *individuals* (e.g., contract employees and consultants) as well as cobranded deals and alliances with other *organizations* (e.g., other commercial enterprises, industry suppliers, philanthropic groups, academic institutions, and churches).

Regardless of the *type* of business partnership, the *nature* of these alliances should be rooted in spiritual accord, or spiritual agreement, sharing common spiritual, moral, and religious beliefs. Now, I realize that some potential partnerships are easier to control than others. Example: It's easier for a sole proprietor to be more discerning about her partnerships as opposed to a director of a publicly held company who may not have any input into the partnerships approved by the corporate board of directors. Nevertheless, as one of God's ambassadors, you must be mindful of His guidelines whether you are the person making the decision about a potential business partnership or the person *praying for* the people who are making the decisions.

We often rush into business relationships without knowing whether or not they are ordained by God. If they are *not* blessed by Him, they'll contaminate our environment, become problematic, unproductive, and short-lived. Let God orchestrate and oversee your professional partnerships and create divinely ordained and inextricable connections.

A Threefold Cord

Two people are better off than one, for they can help each other succeed (Ecclesiastes 4:9). But you and your partner in business should "be of one mind, united in thought and purpose" (1 Corinthians 1:10, NLT). You both should have common spiritual beliefs and values and be on one accord with God. You and your partner are accountable to each other and ultimately to God. So your partnership should be grounded in a spiritual threefold cord consisting of you, your partner, and God, because this type of "a threefold cord is not quickly broken" (Ecclesiastes 4:12, NKJV; Philippians 2:2).

The Bible provides great insights on the importance of alliances that are based on common spiritual beliefs. Jesus says:

> I also tell you this: If two of you agree here on earth concerning anything you ask, my Father in heaven will do it for you. For where two or three are gathered together in My name, I am there in the midst of them.
>
> Matthew 18:19-20 (NLT)

This scripture is commonly referenced within the context of believers "coming together" as a church congregation or a prayer group, but it also offers wisdom and guidance for Christian business leaders who are contemplating "coming together" in commercial partnerships.

In Amos 3:3, the Word of God poses the question: *How can two walk together unless they agree?* Scripture goes on to declare:

> Do not be unequally yoked together with unbelievers. For
> what fellowship has righteousness with lawlessness? And
> what communion has light with darkness.
>
> 2 Corinthians 6:14 (NKJV)

And Jesus declares, "What God has joined together, let not man separate" (Mark 10:9, NKJV; Matthew 19:6).

These scriptures are usually referenced within the context of individuals who are contemplating a traditional marriage partnership, but they also offer divine revelation with regards to commercial business partnerships. Just like during biblical times when the people of Israel faced the judgment of God when they entered into relationships with immoral and idolatrous individuals, the Lord *will not* bless business partnerships that go against His teachings (Isaiah 2:6-9).

How to Make Sure Your Partnerships Are Equally Yoked

In many cultures, a traditional marriage between a man and a woman represents a covenant with God. Similarly, for us as Christians, a business alliance should also be ordained by God and represent a covenant with Him. Like a marriage, a business partnership is also formed by individuals who are committed to one another and believe in the institution—whether it involves the institution of marriage or business.

A traditional marriage and a business partnership have many similarities. Both are established based on "equally yoked" or common spiritual values, beliefs, interests, and goals. Both types of unions may last for a season or for a lifetime. And both have the potential to impact your environment and your life in profound ways—positively and negatively.

How do we make sure our partnerships are equally yoked and joined together by God? How do we connect with the right types of business partners? The recommended approach is similar to the traditional matrimonial dating process in Western society, in which individuals meet and date or get to know each other for a period of time before deciding to formalize the partnership as an engagement or in matrimony. Likewise, a business relationship also requires time for the potential partners to get acquainted. Even if the partners have known each other for years, it's still important to take time to *hear from God* and spiritually discern His desires and plans about their potential alliance.

Never rush into a strategic business partnership, regardless of how promising they appear or how lucrative the potential. Take the time to get to know your potential partners—not just socially and professionally but *spiritually*. Seek to understand their religious, moral, and ethical beliefs. Learn about their background, lifestyle, and family. Consider their behavioral track record, because all of this will affect the ways in which they plan, manage, and execute commercial initiatives.

In an interview with the *Atlanta Journal Constitution*, Truett Cathy explained that the key to customer service for Chick-fil-A is finding the right employees, partners, and franchise operators:

> We're seeking people with character rather than experience. If you can't manage your own life, how do you expect to manage a business?[36]

Before entering into any professional alliance, whether it involves selecting a business partner, voting in a new corporate board member, or hiring another employee or consultant, take the time to pray for spiritual discernment and wisdom from God. If you're already in a partnership, then pray for God's guidance in achieving His will for it and follow His instructions even if it requires dissolution of the alliance. I like the way Proverbs 11:15 (MSG) warns us: "Whoever makes deals with strangers is sure to get burned; if you keep a cool head, you'll avoid rash bargains."

Another example of taking a spiritual approach to a potential commercial alliance is relayed by the president of Hearst Magazines, Cathie Black. In her book, *Basic Black: The Essential Guide for Getting Ahead at Work (and in Life)*,[37] she recounts the presentation she and her team made to media mogul Oprah Winfrey. When Cathie and her team first pitched Oprah on the idea of publishing her own magazine by forming an alliance with Hearst Magazines, Oprah did not make an immediate decision. Instead, Oprah simply said she wanted to *pray* about it. A wise move indeed.

Do you have any idea how strong and successful a professional partnership can be when the individuals are in agreement and alignment with the will of God? *Remarkably powerful.* Pray and ask God to show you the *true character* of your potential partners, and then be patient and wait for Him to reveal it to you. Commit to only entering into strategic partnerships that you know in your heart are divinely ordained by God.

Signs of a God-Ordained Partnership

There are two critical signs or indicators as to whether or not a business partnership is ordained and blessed by God: 1) You will know divinely ordained partners by their fruit, and 2) the partnership will be divinely orchestrated. Let's begin by exploring the first sign.

You Will Know Divine Partners by Their Fruit

The term fruition is derived from the root word fruit. It's important that you evaluate potential partners to see what they are bringing to fruition, not merely what they say they want to accomplish.

Jesus tells us that "a good tree does not bear bad fruit, nor does a bad tree bear good fruit" (Luke 6:43, NKJV). He goes on to say that:

> Every tree is known by its own fruit…a good man out of the good treasure of his heart brings forth good…and an evil man out of the evil treasure of his heart brings forth evil.
>
> Luke 6:44-45 (NKJV); Matthew 12:35

When Jesus warned His disciples about false prophets who might try to influence them, He said that you would know them by their fruit. "Yes, just as you can identify a tree by its fruit, so you can identify people by their actions" (Matthew 7:20, NLT). In a similar fashion, and from a business perspective, He is encouraging us to consider the demeanor, behavior, reputation, and previous contributions of potential business partners. We will be able to discern appropriate business partners based on their fruit, or their godly conduct and results.

Wait to discern if the individual or organization is indeed performing good works and bearing the fruit of the Spirit such as godly wisdom, love, joy, peace, patience, kindness, goodness, faithfulness, gentleness, and self-control (Galatians 5:22-23). Example: Some potential partners might initially appear to be strong candidates for alliances because of their commercial success or monetary wealth. But how are they leveraging their success and wealth? Are they blessing others with charitable programs? Are they following God's principles of financial management and stewardship? What are their legacy building initiatives?

In order to accomplish all that God has ordained for you and for your business and to be sure that you bear lasting fruit (John 15:16), you must be discerning about the individuals with whom, and entities with which, you enter into partnerships. Allow God to guide you in the decision-making process. He knows about everyone everywhere (Hebrews 4:13). He knows which prospects aren't doing as well as they appear to be on paper. And He knows if they don't genuinely share your strategic mission and vision for the venture. If a potential partner is not appropriate for you, God will surely let you know because He declares that we are to "have nothing to do with the fruitless deeds of darkness" (Ephesians 5:11, NIV). Don't show me the money. Show me the fruit!

The Partnership Will Be Divinely Orchestrated

God will divinely introduce you to and connect you with individuals with whom He desires for you to partner for His kingdom-building purposes. Sometimes He does this at a time when a commercial partnership is the furthest thing from your mind. You might not even realize you need one! But He brings it to your attention and then miraculously the perfect opportunity with a fellow ambassador for God presents itself.

God will sometimes confirm His desires for you to enter into the partnership by giving you an undeniable and indescribable sense of peace about the entire situation. You know the alliance is right and the logistics just seems to flow effortlessly by the grace of God. The potential partners, commercial philosophy, organizational charter, and operations all reinforce godly principles.

And the alliance serves as a blessing, not only for the partners but also for the employees and virtually everyone who comes in contact with the venture.

Keep in mind, however, that sometimes even when we feel our partnerships have been divinely orchestrated, they'll sometimes fail or fall apart. Just like in a traditional marriage, and in any other type of relationship, things change. People grow apart. Common goals disappear. Communication ceases. Trust becomes jeopardized. Tragedies occur. Seasons and circumstances change. But we must continue to trust God and seek His guidance and wisdom. These are just a few ways in which we can seek God's guidance in making wise choices around business partnerships that will ultimately position us for success and significance in the marketplace. Now, let's move on to our final Planning Proverb for this chapter.

Realize that You Are on Divine Assignment

Most of us have heard the rally cry of American voters, who have sent their elected officials to DC to serve on their behalf, exclaiming, "Remember who sent you there!" Well, in the workplace and marketplace, as Christian business leaders, we too must remember Who sent us there. Wherever we may be within a company or organization, we are actually planted there by God to accomplish the unique and special assignments He has given us for that particular time or season in our lives. For purposes of Divine Business Planning, I'll refer to this "special assignment" as a divine assignment.

Godly people serve in wordly places, and you are on divine assignment from God. It's critical that we understand the power and anointing of our assignments and roles within the commercial sector.

Strategically Planted by God

Our professional positions are a blessing and a privilege, and we should be thankful for them (Ephesians 5:20). You have been strategically planted or placed in your job assignment by God to facilitate His kingdom agenda and plan. Your career is just another vehicle for serving Him. And you have a purpose and an assignment right where you are planted.

Regardless of your position, title, role, or responsibility within an organization, you have been appointed and anointed by God to accomplish what He has called you to do during your time with the organization. Your current job, manager, coworkers, clients, customers, and associates are all integral aspects of your divine assignment for this season of your life.

Consider your current professional position or job assignment from a Higher perspective. Example: In the *natural realm*, you may be an intern or an entry-level manager, but in the *spiritual realm* you are an ambassador, a king, and a priest of the kingdom (Revelation1:6; 5:10). It's important to note here that the terms *king* and *priest* are not gender specific. They refer to both males and females as they are kingdom-based titles and brand names that God gives His children.

The sooner you realize and embrace the fact that God has you on a divine assignment right now within your organization, the sooner you will be emancipated and liberated from the common workplace and marketplace trials and challenges that we complain about daily. One way to approach your assignment is by prayerfully asking God to reveal:

1. His will for you while you are in the assignment.

2. What He desires for you to accomplish during your assignment.

Afterward, relax and allow the Holy Spirit to speak to you and guide you in completing your divine assignment with a positive attitude. Embrace your current position, roles, and responsibilities because oftentimes God will not allow you to proceed to the next new season of position and promotion until you have successfully achieved what He has called you to accomplish in your current one. In the next sections, we'll explore some of God's purposes for planting you in your divine assignment.

Planted for Your Growth

Many of us complain about working with annoying coworkers and ruthless business associates. Sometimes we find ourselves in departments full of people who neither share nor appreciate our reverence for God and our Christian lifestyle. We tend to believe that our compassionate and loving God would never place us in such difficult environments, so surely this must be the work of Satan. But this may not necessarily be the case.

Sometimes God plants us in extremely challenging organizations and with incredibly annoying people so that we might mature and develop as individuals from the experience. He is able to use the most horrendous of circumstances to strengthen our character so that we can be more like Him. Your experiences, both positive and negative, in your divine assignment just might be necessary in order for you to achieve your personal mission and vision.

So instead of praying, *Lord get me out of this situation*, commit to praying, *Lord, what would you have me get out of, or learn from, this situation? Lord, what would you have me to impart to others during my divine assignment? Lord, how can I best glorify you in this situation?*

God gives us the grace we need to fulfill His will even in the most dreadful circumstances "for it *is* better, if it is the will of God, to suffer for doing good than for doing evil" (1 Peter 3:17, NKJV; Hebrews 4:16). So try not to get discouraged when your divine assignment gets difficult. Refuse to give up and never compromise your God-given principles (2 Peter 3:17). Keep pressing on to serve God and learn the lesson in the midst of the journey.

Planted for the Growth of Others

Another reason God will sometimes plant us in a particular assignment, and one that's easy to miss when we're so focused on ourselves, is this: Your presence within a particular organization may be ordained by God to help facilitate His plan for another person's life or business. He may be using you as an agent for positive change.

God will place us on a team with people who are struggling in one area or another so that we might help support them and grow the business. He plants us where Christian ambassadors are desperately needed. Remember, you are God's ambassador, the light of the business world, salt of the earth, and a fisher of men. When business is declining and employees are at their lowest points, this is when we as Christians shine brightest with our faith and have the opportunity to illuminate a gloomy environment.

Example: Let's say you work for a small, privately owned firm that is faltering and struggling to stay open. Perhaps some of your coworkers are unsaved and quite nervous about losing their jobs. God may have planted you there in order to help the owner increase revenue and expand the business. He might also be using you as a vehicle for sharing His principles in words and deeds with your fellow coworkers who need extra support and encouragement during this trying time.

You and I know that our thoughts and ways are not like His (Isaiah 55:8). God operates at the Highest level. So be open to whatever He is orchestrating in your life and business even if you don't fully understand everything He's doing, because many times you won't.

Influencing Up

Most of us realize the considerable influence we can have on our subordinates, or people in lower-level positions and those reporting to us in the workplace. But we fail to realize our ability to serve as a positive influence on our superiors or individuals in higher-ranking positions and leaders to whom we report.

You don't necessarily have to be a business owner or a senior-level executive in order to have a profound and positive impact on an organization. You just need to carry out your divine assignment that God has already given you the grace to accomplish. When you do this, you can't help but to excel in your position. You can't help but to become a force to be reckoned with! And this will get you noticed by your superiors. Now, you may also be thinking, *And this can also lead to a promotion!* This is absolutely possible and probable, but let's take it to a Higher level.

You and your cheerful personality, optimistic attitude, excellent work ethic, powerful testimony, and fervent prayers may get the attention of individuals in leadership positions who may need to be ministered to. This is a prime opportunity for you to *influence up* or positively impact and bless others who are in positions higher than yours within the organizational hierarchy.

Influencing up is not only possible, but it is also extremely powerful. Don't ever believe that you can't positively influence your superiors or that you can't serve as a role model for them. I know this may seem counterintuitive, but stay with me. As one of God's ambassadors, you have the power to inspire your superiors in profound ways that can lead to them strengthening their faith and enhancing their leadership skills and management styles. And if these individuals oversee numerous employees, this can prove to be a tremendous blessing for everyone within their organization and realm of influence. Powerful indeed.

Completing Your Divine Assignment

God will tell you when your divine assignment is over. In Deuteronomy 1:6-8, God told the people of Israel that they had stayed long enough at the mountain and it was time for them to move on. Your "mountain" may be your current job, project, or industry.

Example: The Lord spoke to the prophet Elijah and gave him directions as to where he should go during the drought (1 Kings 17:1-7). God directed Elijah to a brook and told him that he would be fed there because He had commanded the ravens to feed him at that location. The ravens fed him day and night, and Elijah drank from the brook. But after a while, the brook dried up, and it was time for Elijah to follow God's new directions and move on. What brook has dried up for you? Where are you that *used to be* personally and professionally fulfilling?

God will let you know when your brook has dried up because you have successfully completed your assignment and it's time for you to move on. It may be time for you to move on from the team, department, company, or venture and transition to a new phase in your life and business. God has a myriad of ways to let you know when your current assignment is over and it's time for you to transition into a new season. Pay attention to the signs.

One sign is that you might begin to feel the Holy Spirit leading you in a new direction professionally and you may feel a lack of interest and enthusiasm in your current job. Or, you may experience a lack of peace about your position. You might even receive spiritual confirmation and reinforcement that it's time for you to move on, through the Word of God, your dreams, or from other God-fearing individuals. New opportunities may miraculously arise that are perfect for you given your interests, skills, and abilities. Or, God may simply cause your job or position to be eliminated as a way of forcing you to move out of your current assignment and into the new one He has for you. Pray and ask God to reveal His will to you.

As the people of Israel traveled, they would break camp and move whenever God gave them the sign, which, for them, was a pillar of fire by night and a cloud by day (Deuteronomy 1:32-33; Nehemiah 9:19-21; Numbers 9:15-23). When the cloud settled over their tents, they knew God meant for them to stay in their location. And whenever the cloud lifted, they knew God wanted them to break camp and move on. They followed the signs of what God was telling them to do.

Refusing to obey God's directives places you outside of His order, purpose, covering, and anointing. When God gives you a sign and tells you that it's time to move on, *then move*! We know that God operates in seasons, and when your season is done, release it and look to God for the new, exciting one He has in store for you. Don't become stagnate in a job or position that is no longer conducive to your growth, personal mission, and vision. As alluded to in Ezekiel 17:10, it is possible to spiritually die in the same good soil, or environment that used to be enriching for you.

God may be transitioning you to another assignment so that He can move *someone else* into your current position and allow them to grow and mature spiritually and professionally from it. Unfortunately, many of us try to hang on to past seasons in our businesses or cling to old jobs in our careers. Don't become comfortable and complacent in your assignment when God has work for you to do elsewhere, or you will find yourself in position by default versus design.

Are You in Position by Design or Default?

How do you know if your current assignment is by design or default? Let's explore the differences between the two scenarios. When you are in your professional position by design, it means that you are in the position that you are supposed to be in by the divine design of God. It means that through prayer and spiritual discernment, you know without a doubt that you are in His will. Although the job or position may be difficult, you know that it is still divinely ordained by God. You realize that this is where you are to remain planted for this season and that God has told you to stand still for now.

On the contrary, when you are in your professional position *by default*, it means that you are in position by your own fault and defiance to God. It means that you know in your heart that He has given you plenty of signs that "you have stayed at this mountain long enough" (Deuteronomy 1:6, NLT). It means that

He has opened new opportunities for you and even placed the right people in your path to help you, but you still refuse to step out on faith and walk into your new season.

I've found that when it's time for me to move on and transition to a new season, windows of opportunities and blessings just seem to supernaturally open up. Example: After I graduated from Berkeley and was constantly sending my resume to The Coca-Cola Company and conducting many exploratory meetings with their executives, the feedback was always the same: I needed to: 1) gain more sales experience, and 2) get a master's degree. God divinely opened up a window of opportunity at BellSouth Corporation that blessed me to be able to do both. And six years later, after I had spent a season developing my skill sets with BellSouth, God divinely orchestrated the opportunity for me to join The Coca-Cola Company.

In retrospect, I realize that my earlier attempts to get hired by The Coca-Cola Company were futile because I was operating outside of God's will and timing. I needed to learn how to wait on His timing and mature spiritually and professionally before I would be ready to join the company and make positive contributions to it. When He opened the window of opportunity at The Coca-Cola Company, I was at a point where I was ready. I knew that as wonderful as my season at BellSouth had been, it was time to move on. If I had remained in my old position by *default*, I would have been miserable.

In business, I've found that when I am in a position *by design* and operating within God's will and timing, I have a sense of peace and I receive blessings and favor in the forms of professional opportunities, contacts, and financial resources to support me during the process. But when I am in a position *by default* and trying to retain something that is outside of God's will and timing, I don't have a sense of peace, and the situation becomes completely unfulfilling. Now, let's turn our attention to the topic of getting promoted.

Promotion Comes from God

One of the main topics related to management and organization plans is the concept of career tracking and progression. Most people want to get promoted in their careers. I recall a conversation I had one day with one of my colleagues. We were chatting in my office, and she made a comment that proved to be another indication of why I believe *Revelations in Business* is so timely and needed particularly in corporate America.

We were talking about the company's recent reorganization, and I was telling her that even though I had made the decision to transition out of the organization, I thought the organizational changes would strengthen the company and would open up even more career opportunities for her, given her interests. She agreed and said that she was hoping to get a promotion after the re-org because she felt her manager had been holding her back and controlling her destiny for years. I was flabbergasted! No mortal can control your destiny!

Being in the workplace for many years, I've heard horror stories about the tactics that some managers take to try to hold others back or keep good workers from leaving their organizations. I've even been the recipient of some of them myself. But I always felt that God was looking out for me and that He was still in control. I knew that career opportunities come from God not from managers. The Word of God says:

- "Don't put your confidence in powerful people; there is no help for you there" (Psalm 146:3, NLT).

- "Don't put your trust in mere humans. They are as frail as breath. What good are they?" (Isaiah 2:22, NLT).

- "For exaltation *comes* neither from the east, nor from the west, nor from the south. But God *is* the Judge. He puts down one and exalts another" (Psalm 75:6-7, NKJV).

Exaltation, or promotion, comes from God and only God. Remember Who you work for—you are working for God, not your manager (Colossians 3:17). So it is God, not your manager, Who will reward and promote you. Once you have completed your divine assignment and God is ready to move you on to your next opportunity, nothing and no person can stop the will of God (Job 42:2; Proverbs 19:21).

While I believe in being loyal to one's employer, I also believe we should keep our loyalty in the proper perspective. We should be grateful for the professional opportunities that our employers give us, but we should never forget from Whom these opportunities originate—and that is *from God*. Scripture says that "God... raised *us* up together and made *us* sit together in the heavenly *places* in Christ Jesus that in the ages to come He might show the exceeding riches of His grace in *His* kindness toward us in Christ Jesus" (Ephesians 2:4-7, NKJV).

"Joyful are those who have the God of Israel as their helper, whose hope is in the Lord their God" (Psalm 146:5, NLT). Our inheritance, including our position and power or authority, comes from God through our belief in and service to Jesus Christ (Colossians 3:24). God simply utilizes other people as vehicles for giving us favor and blessings in our careers (Proverbs 3:4). Trusting in another person for position and promotion only leads to disappointment and frustration. "Fearing people is a dangerous trap, but trusting the Lord means safety" (Proverbs 29:25, NLT). So be liberated in the fact that your employer or manager does not have the power to control your destiny. You don't have to be concerned with petty office politics, corporate takeovers, reorganizations, and downsizing. God gave you your job, and He is the only One who can take it away.

Preparation for Promotion

You might find yourself in a situation in which you desire to be promoted within your organization and you know that you are within God's will and are sincerely doing your best to live a righteous life, honor your employer and team members, and make significant positive contributions to the business. But you feel that your excellent work has gone without notice because you haven't been promoted.

We know that there are a myriad of factors that can affect our opportunities for professional advancement. A major one is the issue of budgetary constraints especially during times of declining revenue and economic recession. In this case, your promotion may be delayed simply because of the fiscal state of the company and have nothing to do with you or the quality of your work and reputation in the organization. But the majority of promotional scenarios involve three critical factors:

1. The quality of your *work*.

2. The quality of your professional *relationships* with your superiors, coworkers, and constituents (e.g., customers, clients, and suppliers).

3.　How you *rate* against the other candidates vying for the position.

These factors along with the burning desire to advance in our careers, particularly in Western society, get us into the most trouble from a moral, ethical, and spiritual standpoint because it's so easy for us to resort to employing worldly or secular tactics to get promoted. We see them played out in the workplace every day. You know the ploys—unscrupulous behavior, manipulative schemes, disingenuous posturing with superiors, and playing corporate political games.

The Bible teaches us that once we make a commitment to follow God and place our hope and faith in Him, we consequently become redeemed from the useless, aimless, and corruptible traditional ways of living that we inherited from our forefathers (1 Peter 1:18-21). In other words:

> When you commit to pursuing God's divine plan for your life and business, you are no longer dependent on worldly belief systems and conventional methodologies for achieving your goals.

The Bible warns us that a person should not be promoted into a leadership position before they have the maturity and wisdom to be able to function productively in it (1 Timothy 3:6). A word of caution here: If you are attempting to get promoted solely based on your own selfish agenda and cunning tactics without seeking God's will for you, then be careful. God may actually allow you to get the promotion as a means of teaching you a spiritual lesson. But because you didn't seek Him and follow His divine approach and plans for you, He is not obligated to provide you with the grace and anointing you need in order to sustain your new job or position.

When you take this type of approach to career advancement, you're electing to operate outside of God's favor, grace, and mercy. So it will be up to you and your limited resources and human capabilities to maintain your position. You used your own human and worldly tactics to get there; therefore, you will have to use them to stay there. This is a prescription for disaster and a worst-case scenario, because we never want to be without the supernatural power, inexhaustible resources, and sovereign grace, mercy, and favor of almighty God.

Allow Your Work to Speak for Itself and God to Do the Rest

Your line of work is a vehicle for worshipping God. The Bible says that as ambassadors for the Lord, we are to perform good works—not to get promoted but to glorify God (Matthew 5:16; Colossians 3:16-17). And good works that are not done unto the Lord will be burned in fire during judgment day (Jeremiah 1:16; 2 Peter 3:10).

As a Christian business leader, you are called to perform at a level of professional excellence for God in your divine assignment to the extent that the overall quality of your work and contributions are such that you *deserve* to be promoted. Allow your work to speak for itself and God will do the rest.

Once it's the proper time for you to *be* promoted, God will promote you. "Be diligent to present yourself approved to God, a worker who does not need to be ashamed" (2 Timothy 2:15, NKJV). Continue to serve God and draw near to Him (Psalm 73:28; Hebrews 10:22). Humble yourself, and He will exalt you in due time (1 Peter 5:6). God has the power to draw the right people to you, at the right time, to help you achieve what He has preordained. He will provide the professional contacts and connections you need for promotion in His divine timing.

Pre-Promotion Tests

God will often test us before He promotes us. He may ordain certain circumstances and predicaments, such as dealing with difficult clients and coworkers, to serve as growth experiences that will allow us to develop and mature in character. If you constantly find yourself being passed over for promotions, ask God to reveal the reasons to you. And then seek to learn the lessons. He may be testing you. Example: You are not qualified to assume authority over others until you have effectively learned how to submit under the authority of your manager. Examine yourself. Have you genuinely submitted to your manager with a positive attitude?

Once you the pass pre-promotion tests, God will often suddenly and miraculously promote you in a number of ways by, for instance, creating a new position for you, moving your manager into another assignment, transferring you to another company, or relocating you to another geographic area.

God has the power to bless you in ways that are so much better than those of human beings. Continue to walk by faith and not by sight, and "He will lift you up" (James 4:10, NKJV; 2 Corinthians 5:7). Pre-promotion tests and trials always benefit us as well as others because they become a part of our magnificent testimony to others who may find themselves in similar circumstances. In the following section, we'll consider one of the most difficult types of pre-promotion tests: dealing with malicious colleagues.

Dealing with Malicious Colleagues

One of the most common pre-promotion trials involves dealing with malicious individuals. You might find yourself in a situation in which you are being treated unfairly or dealing with colleagues trying to undermine your work or destroy your reputation. Some people, out of fear and insecurity, resort to unethical tactics such as being extremely critical, maliciously attacking the reputation of others, and even sabotaging the work of others. Their goal is to discredit their colleagues in order to raise their alleged credibility and advance their own careers.

If you find yourself on the receiving end of the unscrupulous tactics of others, continue to pray and keep a positive attitude. "Draw near to God and He will draw near to you" (James 4:8, NKJV; 2 Samuel 14:14). Keep glorifying Him by making excellent contributions in the workplace and marketplace. Always respect yourself by telling the truth if you are erroneously accused of something. Use godly confrontation methods if necessary, but, beyond this, just turn the situation over to God.

Don't try to retaliate against your offenders. God is your protector and vindicator (Romans 12:19; Hebrews 10:30; Psalm 37:1-2; 138:7-8; Proverbs 29:26). "Don't say, 'I will get even for this wrong.' Wait for the Lord to handle the matter" (Proverbs 20:22, NLT). Our God is a God of mercy and justice. And Jesus tells us: "Love your enemies! Pray for those who persecute you" (Matthew 5:44, ESV). You and I both know that this is not easy. But wait for God to address the situation. He won't let you down. If you trust Him, He promises to go before you and clear a pathway for resolution (Isaiah 45:2; John 10:4). Jesus says: "I will give you a mouth and wisdom which all your adversaries will not be able to contradict or resist" (Luke 21:15, NKJV). He may expose the deceitful actions of your enemies and bring retribution to them. Or, He may remove you or them from the organization. Whatever the case, He will make it up to you. Just leave the vindication up to Him and watch His marvelous works!

Another reason it's so important to have compassion for our enemies and pray for them is that the Lord says: "Do not touch My anointed ones, and do My prophets no harm" (1 Chronicles 16:22, NKJV; Psalm 105:14-15). As children of God, we are His anointed ones. Our enemies place themselves in grave danger when they mistreat us. We should pray for them just as Jesus did during His time of persecution, saying, "Father forgive them for they do not know what they do" (Luke 23:34, NKJV).

How should we react when the Lord avenges others on our behalf? The Word of God is very clear on this:

> Don't rejoice when your enemies fall; don't be happy when they stumble. For the Lord will be displeased *with you* and will turn his anger away from them.
>
> Proverbs 24:17-18 (NLT)

Never be intimidated by your business associates. When God places you in a divine assignment, you don't have to struggle to keep it. You don't have to worry about your job being jeopardized by corporate restructuring or coworkers trying to attack your reputation or stealing your good ideas and taking credit for them. Just continue making excellent contributions and rest in the fact that your assignment is not over until God says it's over. As Jesus reminds us:

> Do not be afraid of those who kill the body but cannot kill the soul. Rather, be afraid of the One who can destroy

both soul and body in hell (Matthew 10:28, NIV). If God is for you, then who can dare be against you (Romans 8:31)?

Career Success Does Not Equate to Happiness

I feel compelled to include this brief section because we, particularly in Western society, tend be inordinately preoccupied with career advancement. There's nothing wrong with wanting to succeed in our professions, be recognized for our contributions, and compensated fairly for them. But I believe we often subconsciously and mistakenly equate career success with happiness.

We get so caught up in climbing the corporate ladder and ascending in the marketplace to gain more money, power, and respect in an effort to attain joy and happiness. A successful career in and of itself will not make you happy or give you peace. Only the love of God through Christ can give you peace, joy, and happiness (John 14:27).

Real "Added Value"

Regardless of whether you are a manager of others or an individual contributor in the workplace, your organization should somehow be enhanced as a result of having you as a team member. You should always do your best to leave a position or organization better than it was before you assumed or joined it. This is the litmus test to tell if you are adding spiritual value to your commercial organization. This is real "added value."

We don't have to be perfect professionals in order to make commendable contributions to the business arena. Example: David, who was a king over Israel, was ordained by God to lead others, but he was far from being a perfect man. He was an adulterer and murderer (2 Samuel 11:1-27). Yet, God describes David as a man after His own heart (Acts 13:22).

Jacob was a deceiver who stole his brother Esau's birthright. But God still blessed Jacob and designated him as father of the people of Israel. And He went on to use Jacob to accomplish extraordinary feats (Genesis 27:24-27; 35:1-15). God can mold our imperfections in ways that make them perfect in His eyes.

The Bible instructs us to lead sanctified lives, but it is actually God who does the work to sanctify us. We need only to trust Him and refuse to allow the enemy to distract us (Ephesians 4:27). As you gauge your progress in contributing real added value to your organization, consider the following questions:

- Who are you blessing through your business initiatives?

- Whose life is improving because of your leadership?

- How is your organization benefiting because of you?

There are a number of ways in which you can add value to your company. Some of them include doing excellent work; making significant, positive contributions; exhibiting a positive attitude and demeanor; supporting diversity; and coaching, mentoring, and praying for others.

If you are a manager of others, the lives of your team members should in some way be enriched as a result of your leadership and interactions with them. As a leader, don't isolate yourself from your employees. Be accessible to them. Speak positive affirmations into their lives. Encourage, nurture, and develop them. Empower them to make decisions and learn from their mistakes. Do your best to alleviate some of the counterproductive, tangled webs of decision-making bureaucracy that threaten the efficiency and effectiveness of so many companies.

There is so much standardization in business, especially within major corporations, that many employees feel confined when it comes to being proactive and creative. These feelings of confinement and restriction lead to disappointment, boredom, and frustration. And eventually these creative employees end up leaving an organization that may have needed and could have benefited from their new ideas and innovative recommendations.

Add value to your organization by fostering creativity among your employees. Always honor corporate guidelines, rules, and regulations, but be willing to try new approaches, processes, and programs for the benefit of the company. Your ability to appreciate and try new initiatives is often directly related to your appreciation of diversity. Let's further explore the concept of diversity.

Embracing Diversity

Most of us have heard numerous research studies supporting the fact that diversity is good for the bottom line profitability of a company. But embracing diversity also benefits us as individuals because it challenges our belief systems and psychological perspectives. It stimulates growth and maturity—mentally, spiritually, and emotionally.

When I encourage you to embrace diversity, I'm advocating that you embrace fundamental differences among individuals in the broadest sense. I'm encouraging you to be open to diversity of thought, beliefs, gender, age, ethnicity, culture, spirituality, education, intellect, lifestyle, and experience.

Appreciate, pursue, and establish the appropriate diversity initiatives to meet the needs of your organization. Hire people based on talent, capability, efficiency, and ethical standards. As I write this, the media is reporting that for the first time in American history, we're witnessing four distinct generations working side by side in the workplace. We have:

1. *The Traditionalists, Veterans, or Matures* (born 1922-43) who lived through World War II and the Korean War and grew up in an era when most men worked outside of the home and women stayed home and reared children.

2. *The Baby Boomers* (born 1943-60; some say 1946-64) who grew up during a time of economic prosperity while others within their generation were embroiled in the civil rights movement of the time.

3. *Generation X'ers* (born 1960-80; some say 1965-78) many of whom were latchkey kids of dual income families and were significantly impacted by growing divorce rates.

4. *Generation Y* or the *Nexters* or the *Millennials* (born 1979–94) who are the youngest and most difficult to categorize. Most grew up with computers in their homes and tend to be more open to a diverse society.

These four widely diverse groups certainly make for interesting dynamics in the workplace and marketplace and fascinating fodder for organizational behavior professionals and human resource specialists. But it's imperative that we acknowledge, appreciate, and incorporate the precious layers of diversity offered by people within all groups, because we can all certainly learn from one another.

As Christian business leaders, we should not be concerned with establishing a 100-percent Christian workplace and marketplace because this does not allow us the opportunity to serve as effective ambassadors for God and lead others to salvation. Just as Jesus spent time with people of diverse backgrounds, perspectives, and lifestyles, we too are to minister to diverse individuals in word and deed and out of a place of love.

As the founder of AES Corporation, Dennis Bakke acknowledges in *Executive Influence*:[38]

> Most biblical heroes weren't priests or Levites…most weren't social workers or teachers; they labored in secular positions, and the same is true today. The marketplace isn't a bad place; it's the best place for Christians to be.

Another successful leader featured in the book, Donna M. Auguste, founder of Freshwater Software and president and CEO of Leave a Little Room Foundation (LLR), offered the following with regards to celebrating diversity:

> As an African-American woman, I'm used to being in the minority…I'm very comfortable with that…I'm also very passionate about diversity. As a leader, I make it a point to be inclusive…just look at the life of Jesus. What a wonderful example of working with people from diverse backgrounds and situations. Christianity was born because of how He reached out to all kinds of folks without requiring them to change first.[39]

The Bible teaches that in order for us to grow in Christ, we must be diligent in adding to our faith: virtue, knowledge, self-control, perseverance, godliness, brotherly kindness, and love (2 Peter 1:5-7). If you study this list closely, you'll find that it is the prescription for not only growing in Christ but also embracing diversity. And once we begin to understand, appreciate, and incorporate diversity into our initiatives, it is important that we share our insights with others.

A Godly Mentor: Seeking and Serving as One

I love the old adage, "Each one teach one." This epitomizes the spirit of mentoring, or the transferring of knowledge and wisdom. The Bible says that plans often fail because of a lack of counsel, but with the support of wise mentors, our plans have a greater probability of succeeding (Proverbs 11:14; 15:22; 19:27; 20:18). As Luke 14:31 (NLT) aptly points out, "what king would go to war against another king without first sitting down with his counselors to discuss?"

"As iron sharpens iron, so one man sharpens another" (Proverbs 27:17, NASB). Mentors help guide us and keep us sharp, or discerning and astute, in our professional endeavors. So it behooves us to be open to the mentors that God places in our lives and to the wisdom they share (Proverbs 10:21).

Pray for God's guidance in seeking and connecting with godly mentors. A godly mentor is a wise and trusted counselor and teacher who wants God's best to manifest in your life. As you seek to develop a divine management and organization plan and glorify God in your career, it's important that you not only seek out godly mentors for yourself but also serve as a godly mentor to others.

There are many examples of mentor-protégé relationships in the Bible. Moses served as a mentor for Joshua (Exodus 33:11; Deuteronomy 34:9; Numbers 27:18-20). Naomi was a mentor to Ruth (Ruth 1:8-22). Elijah mentored Elisha (1 Kings 19:21; 2 Kings 2:9). Isaiah was a mentor to Hezekiah (2 Kings 20:1-21). Paul was Timothy's mentor (Acts 16:1-5; Philippians 2:19-24). And Mordecai served as a mentor to Esther (Esther 2: 7-11) by being a confidant to her, supporting, advising, and preparing her for greatness. We too have a similar responsibility to those with whom God has entrusted us.

Each of us is an apprentice of God and a protégé of Jesus, so we should also aspire to serve as godly mentors, especially to the next generation of future business leaders. I love the way the Apostle Paul implores, "And you should *imitate me*, just as *I imitate Christ*" (1 Corinthians 11:1, NLT). Seek to have others imitate you in the workplace and marketplace just as you imitate Christ. Paul goes on to say that we are responsible for sharing our godly wisdom, knowledge, and expertise with others so that they, in turn, might also impart them to others (2 Timothy 2:2).

The Word of God advises us to "teach and counsel each other with all the wisdom He gives" (Colossians 3:16, NLT). As Christian business leaders, we are obligated to teach others how to incorporate godly principles into their commercial endeavors. We are called to be the professional role models and coaches for showing others how to conduct business with honor, integrity, and a spirit of excellence and joy. We are to show others how to learn and grow from their mistakes while staying focused on God's plan. Take the time to leverage teachable moments and speak positive affirmations into the lives of others because the Word of God instructs us to "exhort one another daily" (Hebrews 3:13, NKJV).

It's important that I take a moment here to point out the fact that mentoring is often mutually beneficial for both the mentor and for the mentee or protégé. Both individuals have the opportunity to offer unique perspectives and share valuable information and ideas with one another. Example: A mentor who is a senior marketing executive can learn about new consumer trends within younger demographics by mentoring a younger manager. On the contrary, a younger manager can glean tremendous insights about advancing up the corporate hierarchy from a successful, seasoned corporate executive. Let's turn our focus now to a few real-life examples of companies that are industry role models for the divine management and organization plan.

Real-Life Examples of the Divine Management and Organization Plan

· · · · · · · · · · · · · · · · · · · ·

Family Christian Stores

Family Christian Stores, one of America's leading specialty retailers, sells Christian products and church suppliers in over three hundred locations across thirty-seven states. On their corporate website, the leaders of Family Christian Stores® describe their corporate values and God is clearly at the core of them. They state:

> We Believe In...
>
> - God, the Father Almighty, Creator of heaven and earth, in Jesus Christ His Son, and the ministry of the Holy Spirit. We believe in Christ's crucifixion and bodily resurrection, salvation by grace through faith for all people, the fellowship of believers, and life everlasting (John 3:16).
>
> - A Passion for Excellence (Colossians 3:23)
>
> - Modeling Servant Leadership (Matthew 20:26-28)
>
> - Clear and Measurable Accountability (Proverbs 27:17)

- Pursuing New Ideas, with a Willingness to Change (Philippians 3:13-14)

- Building on our Strengths and Investing in People (Romans 12:5-8)

- Teamwork and Building High Performance Teams (Ephesians 4:16)

- Accepting and Learning from Mistakes (Proverbs 3:13)

- Rewarding Results (Proverbs 3:27)

- Having Fun (1 Thessalonians 5:16)

Sony Pictures

In the spirit of creating an employee-friendly, high-performance culture, the senior leaders of Sony Pictures, which produces, markets, and distributes movies and TV shows in over 140 countries, reportedly undertook a study to understand how corporate culture affects employee engagement and energy levels. The *Harvard Business Review*[40] reports that after getting feedback from direct reports, colleagues, friends, and family members, Sony Pictures identified a number of critical issues.

Example: Divisions were fiercely protective of information and, consequently, not collaborating internally. They also uncovered a corporate culture that expected employees to reply to e-mail in the evenings and throughout weekends. The result was that employees felt constantly on call and their inability to separate from work was a source of resentment and energy drain.

To address these issues and others, Sony Pictures instituted training and rituals to promote honesty and better collaboration. Example: They agreed upon an 8:00 a.m. – 8:00 p.m. weekday limit on hours during which employees were expected to respond to e-mails. Outside of these hours, they were free not to respond, and if there was an urgent concern, they agreed that team members would simply call one another.

These are just a few corporate examples that reinforce the fundamental values and principles of a divine management and organization plan. The biblical commandment, "Let this mind be in you which was also in Christ Jesus" (Philippians 2:5, NKJV), refers to you regardless of whether you are a CEO or a newly hired intern. Resolve to make a positive and indelible mark on your organization regardless of your level or position within in it. Accomplish your divine assignment wherever you are in the business world. Finish well and finish strong.

Directives for Executing the Divine Management and Organization Plan

Following are a few suggestions for implementing the divine management and organization plan for your business:

1. Pray for God's guidance and wisdom and allow Him to design the management and organization plan for your business, department, or team. Praise God for divinely connecting you with talented individuals, and consistently pray for everyone in your organization (James 5:16).

2. Be open and flexible. Don't become complacent with the use of standard management and organizational plans and templates. The management model and organization plan that God gives you may be so unique and innovative that others may not have ever seen or heard of them. Allow God to reveal revolutionary plans and programs that

maximize the efficiency and effectiveness of your organization and raise the bar of excellence in the industry (2 Chronicles 6:40; 7:15).

3. Treat your team members well. Encourage your team members to pursue their passion and purpose, and show them how to link them with organizational objectives. Leverage their gifts and talents wisely and compensate them fairly. Create opportunities for formal internship, fellowship, and mentorship programs. You'll find that this will help enhance employee morale and retention. Encourage your team members to develop a career plan for the next three, five, and ten years—even if it does not include staying with your company. Show them that you care about the career path that is right *for them* as individuals (Colossians 4:1).

4. Conduct regular performance reviews so that you are able to get consistent and meaningful input from employees; provide them with formal feedback regarding their progress relative to performance objectives and professional development goals; and identify and address potential issues early in the process. Provide a forum and a process for meaningful discussion and candid feedback. Example: Ask employees to list the top five initiatives that are working, or are successful, as well at the top five that are *not* successful and ask them to provide suggestions for improving them (2 Thessalonians 3:6-7).

5. Take a public stand for the importance of religious freedom. When you find government and public policy initiatives that threaten our religious freedom in the workplace, pray for God's wisdom and guidance as to how He might use you as a vehicle for positive influence and change. And then be obedient. Don't be afraid to take a public stand for God because when you do, He'll protect you (Psalm 94:16; 1 Samuel 2:30; Matthew 10:32).

6. Biblical coaches for the divine management and organization plan include a number of disciples such as Jesus, Mordecai, Joseph, Esther, Nehemiah, Daniel, Ruth, and Naomi. Example: When Peter entered the town of Caesarea and Cornelius fell at his feet in reverence to him, Peter "raised him up, saying, 'get up; I myself am also a man'" (Acts 10:25-26, AMP). Essentially, Peter was telling Cornelius that he was no different, no more special, than him. Remember this as you manage and lead others. Everyone is special and deserves to be respected and appreciated.

7. Praise God for your divine management and organization plan (Nehemiah 9:5)!

In the next chapter, we'll discuss how our spiritual values impact our finances or bottom-line results. But for now, we'll end this chapter with a quote from 1 Peter 5:2 (NLT):

> Care for the flock that God has entrusted to you. Watch over it willingly, not grudgingly—not for what you will get out of it, but because you are eager to serve God.

VII

The Divine Financial Plan

But remember the Lord your God, for it is He who gives you the ability to produce wealth and so confirms His covenant, which He swore to your forefathers, as it is today.

Deuteronomy 8:18 (NIV)

What does profitability mean to you? How can we leverage God's spiritual principles to drive bottom-line profitability? Most of us realize that an accurate, comprehensive financial plan is critical to our business ventures regardless of whether we are seeking outside financing from venture capitalists or financial institutions; financing a business as an entrepreneur; or just tracking departmental expenses within an organization.

The financial section of your business plan includes vital information and data to substantiate that the business is positioned to generate profit and create economic value for shareholders. Documentation including funding sources, income statements, cash-flow projections, balance sheets, budgets, and break-even analyses are typically included in this section of the plan. A solid financial plan allows for continuous assessment of the economic condition of a commercial enterprise.

Most of us are familiar with financial reports such as corporate *annual reports* and *dividend payout statements* as well as with the formal capitalization of companies (i.e., small, mid, large-cap) relative to stock market indices such as S&P Index, NASDAQ, NYSE Index, Dow Jones Industrial Average, Japan's Nikkei 225 Index, Hong Kong's Hang Seng Index, Korea's KOSPI Index, Britain's FTSE-100, France's CAC-40, and Germany's DAX 30.

Interestingly enough, as I write this chapter, every media outlet in the world is reporting the recent upheaval of the American financial system. We are reportedly in the worst recession since the Great Depression of the 1930s. During one historic week, the Dow dropped to some of its lowest points in history; Lehman Brothers, the 158-year-old investment bank, made history with the largest bankruptcy filing ever; Bank of America acquired Merrill Lynch & Co; the U.S. government has stepped in with an emergency loan to keep American International Group, Inc. (AIG), one of the world's largest insurers, from going out of business; and the shock waves continue reverberating throughout international markets.

A few weeks later, media outlets reported the details of the Bernard "Bernie" Madoff scandal in which he, a prominent investment executive, pled guilty to defrauding thousands of investors in what has been called the largest investor fraud ever committed by a single person. Client losses are an estimated $65 billion.

On a recent episode of the *Oprah Winfrey Show*, Oprah and her guest, financial expert, Suze Orman, discussed how the current economic crisis is linked to spirituality. Following are a couple of illuminating comments from the discussion:

We have built an entire economy on lies and deceit and whenever you build something on something that isn't true, it cracks a little it's like building a home or an entire building on a sink hole everything goes falling down and that is exactly what has happened in the United States of America.

—Suze Orman [41]

It's just like the law of cause and effect, it really is more spiritual than financial and it is reflecting the spiritual consciousness...the spiritual consciousness is just being reflected back to us.

—Oprah Winfrey [42]

Indeed, what we are witnessing on Wall Street is not a financial issue. It is a spiritual issue due to lack of morals, integrity, and business ethics.

The "100-100" Rule

As stewards over God's enterprises, it's important that we acknowledge the fact that it is God who gives us the ability to gain wealth (Deuteronomy 8:18). Without Him we can do nothing (John 15:4-5). Even Jesus acknowledges: "I do nothing of Myself; but as My Father taught Me" (John 8:28, NKJV). These scriptures prove the foundation for what I call the "100-100" rule. Undoubtedly, you have heard of the Pareto Principle, also known as the "80-20" rule, which states that for most events, generally 80 percent of the effects come from 20 percent of the causes. This translates in business to mean, for instance, that typically 80 percent of one's business is generated from 20 percent of the clients or customers. Well, the "100-100" rule means 100 percent of our success always comes from God 100 percent of the time.

"Good comes to those who lend money generously and conduct their business fairly. Such people will not be overcome by evil. Those who are righteous will be long remembered. They do not fear bad news; they confidently trust the Lord to care for them" (Psalm 112:5-7, NLT).

The grace, protection, peace, and favor of God are more valuable than money because when we abide in Him, the bounds of financial wealth and success are endless. I once heard a minister admonish that we should love God not just for the *presents* that He gives us, but we should love Him for His *presence*. In other words, we shouldn't love Him just for the *presents* or *material things* that He blesses us with, but we should love Him for His *spiritual existence* or *presence* in our lives and for giving us the power to gain wealth so that we can get the presents!

> Focusing your life solely on making a buck shows a certain poverty of ambition. It asks too little of yourself. Because it's only when you hitch your wagon to something larger than yourself that you realize your true potential.[43]
>
> —President Barack Obama

Three Planning Proverbs for the Divine Financial Plan

As God's ambassadors, we have a fiduciary duty to be fiscally responsible in our commercial endeavors. But how do we accomplish this according to God's standards and guidelines? Once, again, our ultimate business-planning guide, the Bible, provides us with excellent direction in this area. This leads us to our three Planning Proverbs for the divine financial plan, which are as follows:

1. Pursue prosperity instead of profitability.

2. Prosperity follows purpose.

3. Follow God's spiritual economics for financial dominion and prosperity.

Let's start with our first Planning Proverb.

Pursue Prosperity Instead of Profitability

As managers over God's enterprises, we are called to financial stewardship and discipline. We are called to be faithful, prudent, and wise (1 Corinthians 4:2). In business, we often find ourselves focused on the pursuit of profit and wealth creation with our conversations speckled with jargon such as book value, market value, return on investment (ROI), earnings per share (EPS), operating income (OI), net revenue, gross profit, price-earnings (P/E) ratios, and a host of other generally accepted accounting principles (GAAP)—all of which are important to the commercial viability and economic stability of a company.

From a financial planning perspective, few would question the integral linkage between profitability and business growth, but in the spirit of taking our thinking to a Higher level, I believe there is another concept that is more critical to our overall success, and that is the concept of *prosperity*. Let's take a moment to compare and contrast the concepts of *profitability* and *prosperity*.

We know that *profitability* is generally defined as the state or condition of being profitable or yielding a *financial profit*. An enterprise is typically deemed profitable or unprofitable based purely on its financial status and results. In this way, *profitability* is defined based primarily on the parameters of *financial results*.

Prosperity, on the contrary, is generally defined as a prosperous or successful condition or a state of good fortune. The concept of prosperity is broad in scope and includes a number of elements and criteria that may deem an enterprise or individual as being prosperous. Unlike profitability, prosperity is not based primarily on financial parameters.

One way to think of prosperity and profitability, in relation to one another, is that prosperity is an overarching umbrella concept, which includes many different forms of success with profitability being just *one* of them. Unlike profitability, prosperity denotes a broader range of richness and wealth. Prosperity is not just about money. Prosperity is a state of spiritual and material abundance that extends beyond the temporal boundaries of the world. Prosperity transcends beyond the worldly parameters of economics, materialism, and consumerism. Prosperity extends beyond revenue targets, compensation packages, and tax brackets.

The business world values profitability, but God values prosperity. "Trusting in the Lord leads to prosperity" (Proverbs 28:25, NLT). As Christian business leaders, we must detach ourselves from the world's value system and not relegate ourselves to just focusing on profitability. We must raise our value systems to a Higher level by pursuing total *prosperity* instead of just *profitability*. Don't pursue money. Pursue God. Follow His financial plans for your business, and you will prosper (2 Chronicles 26:5). Prosperity should be our primary concern, and profitability should be secondary because profitability is simply *one aspect* of prosperity. The only place where profitability should come before prosperity is in the dictionary.

Types of Prosperity

Prosperity can take on a variety of forms. There is prosperity of love, peace, health, relationships, knowledge, intellect, finances, culture, wisdom, compassion, talent, material items, economic status, business networks, commercial ventures, strategic alliances, talented employees, loyal customers, suppliers, contractors, communities, and a myriad of other examples regardless of our socioeconomic levels.

"The rich and the poor have this in common: the Lord is the maker of them all" (Proverbs 22:2, NKJV). God created the rich and the poor. But God desires for all of us to live abundant and prosperous lives. The Word of God says:

> Beloved, I pray that you may prosper in all things and be in health, just as your soul prospers.
>
> 3 John 1:2 (NKJV)

> And it is a good thing to receive wealth from God and the good health to enjoy it.
>
> Ecclesiastes 5:19 (NLT)

Based on these scriptures, we learn that it is God's will that we prosper not only in financial wealth but also in good health so that we can enjoy the fruits of our labor. I recently read a magazine editorial that was titled, "Your First Wealth is Health."

While our physical health is indeed important, our spiritual health, in the form of salvation from God, is a critical form of prosperity. Every other type of wealth flows from it. While monetary wealth and material abundance are nice to have, they do not satisfy the soul (Ecclesiastes 5:10-11; Psalm 62:10). And they cannot give you the peace and joy that come only from God (Colossians 3:15; John 14:27).

God Ordained for Us to Prosper

"Let the Lord be magnified, Who has pleasure in the prosperity of His servant" (Psalm 35:27, NKJV). God not only ordained for us to prosper, but He also takes pleasure in our prosperity as we fulfill the calling He has on our lives for the advancement of His kingdom through Jesus Christ (Matthew 28:18-20). Ecclesiastes 5: 18-19 (NKJV) tells us:

> It is good and fitting for one to eat and drink, and to enjoy the good of all his labor in which he toils under the sun all the days of his life which God gives him; for it is his heritage. As for every man to whom God has given riches and wealth, and given him power to eat of it, to receive his heritage and rejoice in his labor—this is the gift of God.

God gives us the ability to prosper in our professions and enjoy them. The Bible serves as our guidebook and roadmap for prosperity, and if we follow it, we'll be blessed with prosperity and success (Joshua 1:8).

Throughout the Bible, we're reminded that the Lord desires for us to live prosperous and abundant lives. Example: You can start the business, but it is "God who gives the increase" (1 Corinthians 3:7, NKJV) and makes it prosper. He declares in Jeremiah 29:11 (NIV):

'For I know the plans I have for you,' declares the Lord, 'plans to prosper you and not to harm you, plans to give you hope and a future.'

"The God of heaven Himself will prosper us" (Nehemiah 2:20, NKJV). It is for this reason that He sent His Son Jesus Christ. In John 10:10 (NKJV), Jesus states:

> The thief does not come except to steal, and to kill, and to destroy; I have come that they may have life, and that they may have it more abundantly.

This refers to abundance in every sense of the word—spiritual, mental, emotional, and physical health as well as material goods, finances, and relationships.

Unfortunately, some people still believe that God does not intend for Christians to be financially prosperous. They attempt to support their logic biblically, and one scripture they often reference to support their opinion is Matthew 19:23-24 (NKJV), which states:

> Then Jesus said to His disciples, 'assuredly, I say to you that it is hard for a rich man to enter the kingdom of heaven. And again I say to you, it is easier for a camel to go through the eye of a needle than for a rich man to enter the kingdom of God.'

Those who use these scriptures as rebuttals against the fact God ordained for His children to be financially prosperous fail to continue reading the scriptures immediately following this passage.

If they would proceed in studying Matthew 19:25-26 (NKJV), they would find that:

> *When His disciples heard it, they were greatly astonished, say-*
> *ing, 'who then can be saved?' But Jesus looked at them and said*
> *to them, 'with men this is impossible, but with God all things*
> *are possible.'*

My interpretation of these scriptures is that Jesus is explaining that it's difficult for a rich man to enter the kingdom of heaven, but if he is following God, and not man, then it is indeed possible for him to enter heaven because all things are possible with God. Jesus realized that economic value is an extremely powerful temptation and factor in our lives. He was preparing us for our propensity to become overly focused on financial and material wealth and the danger of placing them over God in priority.

The Bible tells us that the wealth of sinners is stored up for the righteous (Proverbs 13:22). And Jesus reminds us to not worry about what we will eat and what we will wear, but to "seek first the kingdom of God and His righteousness, and all these things shall be added to you (Matthew 6:33, NKJV; Luke 12:31). So clearly, God ordained for us to prosper spiritually, mentally, emotionally, physically, socially, financially, and in *all* aspects of our lives, which includes our commercial business endeavors.

It's important for the world to witness Christian business professionals who are prosperous and operating in integrity. This causes members of our true target audience, particularly unbelievers, to want to know more about us and our accomplishments. And this creates an awesome opportunity for us to fulfill our roles as ambassadors for God by sharing our testimonies with others and bringing them closer to Him.

We know that one of the brand names God gives us is *special* or *peculiar.* He calls us a *peculiar people* (Deuteronomy 26:18, KJV; 1 Peter 2:9, KJV). Your colleagues should see you as being peculiar in a positive way. They should see you as a prosperous, wealthy, blessed person who is committed to Christ. They should see you as one who declares blessings in the name of Jesus and manifests them in business. Your prosperity should inspire others to want to learn more about you and your godly principles for wealth attainment and management. Don't be ashamed of being a "peculiar" person. Rejoice in it because you represent one of God's special, blessed, and prosperous kingdom business leaders!

A Prosperous People

We are a prosperous people who originate from a prosperous lineage—starting with God: "My God shall supply all your need according to His riches in glory by Christ Jesus" (Philippians 4:19, NKJV).

The Bible tells us that Jesus was prosperous:

> For you know the grace of our Lord Jesus Christ, that though He was rich, yet for your sakes He became poor, that you through His poverty might become rich.
>
> 2 Corinthians 8:9 (NKJV)

Following are a few more examples of biblical disciples who manifested the blessings of prosperity by following God's purpose for their lives:

- Abraham: "Abraham was very rich in livestock, in silver, and in gold" (Genesis 13:2, NKJV; Ezekiel 33:24)

- Isaac: "Isaac sowed in that land, and reaped in the same year a hundredfold; and the Lord blessed him. The man began to prosper, and continued prospering until he became very prosperous; for he had possession of flocks and possessions of herds and a great number of servants. So the Philistines envied him" (Genesis 26:12-14, NKJV).

- Jacob: "Thus the man (Jacob) became exceedingly prosperous, and had large flocks, female and male servants, and camels and donkeys" (Genesis 30: 43, NKJV).

- Noah: "So God blessed Noah and His Sons, and said to them: 'Be fruitful and multiply, and fill the earth…every moving thing that lives shall be food for you. I have given you all things, even as the green herbs" (Genesis 9: 1-3, NKJV).

- Mary: "They entered the house and saw the Child with his mother, Mary, and they bowed down and worshiped him. Then they opened their treasure chests and gave him gifts of gold, frankincense, and myrrh" (Matthew 2:11, NLT).

- Zacchaeus: "Now behold, *there was* a man named Zacchaeus who was a chief tax collector, and he was rich" (Luke 19:2, NKJV).

- David: "Now therefore, thus shall you say to My servant David, thus says the Lord of Hosts: 'I took you from the sheepfold, from following the sheep, to be ruler over My people, over Israel'" (2 Samuel 7:8, NKJV).

- Solomon: "King Solomon was greater in riches and wisdom than all the other kings of the earth" (1 Kings 10:23, NIV; 2 Chronicles 9:22).

- Daniel: "So this Daniel prospered in the reign of Darius and in the reign of Cyrus the Persian" (Daniel 6:28, NKJV).

- Job: "After Job had prayed for his friends, the Lord made him prosperous again and gave him twice as much as he had before" (Job 42:10, NIV; Job 1:3; 42:11-12).

- Esther: "Now the king was attracted to Esther more than to any of the other women, and she won his favor and approval more than any of the other virgins. So he set a royal crown on her head and made her queen instead of Vashti" (Esther 2:17, NIV).

- Joseph: "The Lord was with Joseph, and he was a successful man...the Lord made all he did to prosper in his hand" (Genesis 39:2-3, NKJV).

- Lydia: "One of them was Lydia from Thyatira, a merchant of expensive purple cloth, who worshiped God. As she listened to us, the Lord opened her heart, and she accepted what Paul was saying." (Acts 16:14, NLT).

- Boaz: "Now there was a wealthy and influential man in Bethlehem named Boaz, who was a relative of Naomi's husband, Elimelech" (Ruth 2:1, NLT).

- Hezekiah: "Hezekiah was very wealthy and highly honored" (2 Chronicles 32:27, NLT).

While these are a few examples of prosperous people, one could argue that everyone who followed God was prosperous. And this stands true today. You can't help but to prosper when you follow Him!

Are Profitability and Prosperity Mutually Exclusive?

Is it possible to attain profitability without prosperity? Can we be prosperous without being profitable? In other words, are these concepts mutually exclusive in that the occurrence of one precludes the other?

Profitability (i.e., financial success) and prosperity (i.e., holistic spiritual and material affluence) *are not* mutually exclusive. They can coexist. It is possible to have both. And it's possible to have one without the other.

You can be prosperous even when your business isn't profitable. And you can have a booming and profitable business and still not be prosperous. Example: An entrepreneur who is in the red, or losing money with her firm, might still be prosperous in her spiritual life, physical health, and relationships.

On the contrary, an entrepreneur who is profitable or in the black with his company may not have received spiritual salvation and is therefore not prosperous because he's forfeiting the holistically rich and satisfying life that only God can provide. The Word of God declares: "Behold, these are the wicked; and always at ease, they have increased in wealth" (Psalm 73:12, ESV). This scripture confirms that there are ungodly individuals who may be profitable or increasing in financial and material wealth. But they may not be prospering spiritually, emotionally, physically, or in their relationships with others.

Pro-Profitability Does Not Equal Anti-Christianity

Some of us believe that our focus on profitability somehow weakens our Christian values, testimony, and lifestyle. Not true. Pro-profitability does not equate to anti-Christianity. If you are focused on profitability in your business, it doesn't mean that you are operating contrary to Christian values and the Word of

God. Remember, God calls us to be faithful stewards over His businesses and position them for success in the marketplace. He ordained total prosperity for us, and profitability is one aspect of it. Financial success and spiritual salvation can go hand in hand as long as we follow God's principles and commandments.

Where does the notion come from that we can't be genuinely interested in bottom-line profitability and still be spiritual? I believe that it ironically comes from misinterpreted and miscommunicated scriptural references. Example: Most of us have heard the passage: "For the love of money is a root of all *kinds of* evil" (1 Timothy 6:10, NKJV). This scripture is often misquoted as: "Money is the root of all evil." So the implication becomes: If you are a business leader focused on money and profit, then you are focusing on something that's evil and contrary to God, so *surely* you can't be spiritual or a Christian. Unfortunately, this is a common misinterpretation of scripture.

The correct interpretation of 1 Timothy 6:10 is that money in and of itself *is not* a root of evil. It is *the love of* money, or our attitude about it, that is a root of evil. It is our obsession with money and our worshipping and coveting of it that is an origin of all kinds of evil.

The True Cost of Goods (COGS)

The Bible says:

> What good will it be for a man if he gains the whole world, yet forfeits his soul?
>
> Matthew 16:26 (NIV); Mark 8:36; Luke 9:25

> Teach those who are rich in this world not to be proud and not to trust in their money, which is so unreliable. Their trust should be in God, who richly gives us all we need for our enjoyment.
>
> 1 Timothy 6:17 (NLT)

Refuse to worship money and material possessions. Refuse to succumb to profit-deification. To obtain money and luxury goods but lose your soul or salvation in the process is the true spiritual cost of goods (COGS).

The Word of God says we are not to put our hope in financial wealth, which is so uncertain, but we are to put our "hope in God who richly provides us with everything for our enjoyment…take hold of the life that is truly life" (1 Timothy 6: 17-19, NIV). Jesus reminds us to "take heed and beware of covetousness, for one's life does not consist in the abundance of the things he possesses" (Luke 12:15, NKJV). He is warning us to be careful and guard against all kinds of greed because a life is not measured by how much one owns. Our tombstones will be inscribed to reflect our life, loves, and legacy—not our *lifestyles*.

The Word of God says: "Do not wear yourself out to get rich; have the wisdom to show restraint" (Proverbs 23:4, NIV; Psalm 49:16-20). Don't work for the sole purpose of getting rich financially and accumulating material possessions. It's certainly acceptable to want your business to be profitable and to desire some of the finer things in life, but we must keep them in the proper perspective. Remember, money and material possessions are temporary (Proverbs 23:4-5). Make sure your primary focus is on the *eternal* aspects of God, not on the *temporary* trappings of the world (Matthew 7:21-23; 2 Corinthians 4:18).

Do you remember the old saying, "You can't take it with you," which refers to the fact that we can't take material items with us when we die? I believe this adage was derived from God's Word. As 1 Timothy 6:7 (NLT) states: "After all, we brought nothing with us when we came into the world, and we can't take anything with us when we leave it." Naked we came into the world and naked we shall return (Ecclesiastes 5:15). From dust we are taken and to dust we will return (Genesis 3:19).

Becoming so spiritually bankrupt that we begin focusing more on goods than on God is the spiritual law of diminishing returns. As Jesus warns:

> Do not store up treasures on earth, where moth and rust destroy, and where thieves break in and steal. But store up for yourselves treasures in heaven, where moth and rust do not destroy, and where thieves do not break and steal. For where your treasure is, there your heart will be also.
>
> Matthew 6:19-21 (NASB).

The Bible says that we as Christians are not to covet money and material possessions because we cannot serve both God and money (Matthew 6:24; Luke 16:13). "He who trusts in his riches will fall, but the righteous will flourish like foliage" (Proverbs 11:28, NKJV). Our God is a jealous God. He proclaims: "You shall have no other Gods before me" (Exodus 20:3, NKJV; Isaiah 42:8).

Don't be more in love with money than with the *One* who gives you the ability to generate it. Don't get into a position in which you find yourself "praising gods of silver, gold…gods that neither see nor hear nor know anything at all. But you have not honored the God who gives you the breath of life and controls your destiny" (Daniel 5:23, NLT; Romans 1:25).

Financial security is not found in material things like your bank account, investments, real estate, and precious jewels. Financial security is found in God. Whenever you begin to make money your god by worshiping it and coveting material things, you are succumbing to greed and your fleshly nature. When this occurs, you don't have possessions; *your possessions have you.* And this will lead you into a downward spiral of sin, deceit, and destruction (Philippians 3:19; Romans 6:23; 1 Timothy 6:9). And God will find ways to humble you as a means to help you get your priorities in order (Isaiah 2: 9).

Following are five major spiritual costs we endure whenever we focus more on money and material wealth than on God:

1.   Loss of divine protection

   "Don't love money; be satisfied with what you have. For God has said, 'I will never fail you. I will never abandon you'" (Hebrews 13:5, NLT). "What's more, I am with you, and I will protect you wherever you go" (Genesis 28:15, NLT).

2.   Loss of divine provision and prosperity

   God always provides for His children, and His resources are infinite. The Bible makes it clear that God's children "will not be disgraced in hard times; even in famine they will have *more than enough*" (Psalm 37:19, NLT). The Lord tells us that He will give us "a dry path through the sea" (Isaiah 43: 16, NLT) and "rivers in the desert" (Isaiah 43: 19, ESV; 41:18). This means that He will give us abundant and flowing prosperity even in a dry economy and floundering market.

   Example: Recently, the *Atlanta Journal Constitution* reported that Chick-fil-A's system-wide sales were up 12 percent in 2008, a year when many businesses struggled to stay open. Chick-fil-A's president and chief operating officer acknowledged the divine provisioning and protection of God, saying, "I do think that God has blessed our business."[44]

3. Loss of your inheritance

The Bible says that we are "heirs of God and joint-heirs with Christ" (Romans 8:17, NKJV). Jesus implores us to "seek first His kingdom and His righteousness, and all these things will be given to you as well" (Matthew 6:33, NIV; Luke 12:31). He also explains that whatever we give up for Him, we'll "receive a hundredfold, and inherit eternal life" (Matthew 19:29, ESV).

Jesus makes it clear that as diligent followers of God, we are entitled to a rich inheritance in this life and in eternity—which includes the entire kingdom prepared for us since the creation of the world (Mathew 25: 34; 1 Corinthians 6:9). Eternal dividends. He goes on to explain: "In my Father's house are many mansions, if it were not so, I would have told you. I go to prepare a place for you. And if I go and prepare a place for you, I will come again and receive you for Myself; that where I am, there you may be also" (John 14:2-3, NKJV). Focus on being rich, not only in this life but in the afterlife.

4. Loss of personal character enrichment

God is building your personal character for your benefit and His glory. So make sure your financial plans follow His guidelines. When you follow His principles and not purely profit in your business decisions, you'll find yourself growing in knowledge and understanding; strength and wisdom; and the fruit of the spirit, e.g., love, faith, joy, peace, kindness, goodness, faithfulness, gentleness, and self-control (Galatians 5: 22-23)—as well as your bottom-line financial results!

5. Loss of opportunities to bless and witness to others

Money and material goods serve as blessings when we use them within the context of God's principles and for His glory. God is not in the business of building our commercial empires solely for our egotistical desires. The Bible tells us that we are blessed with prosperity so that we may bless others and serve as witnesses for God (Genesis 12:2; 1 Timothy 6: 17-19).

Our success not only benefits us, but more importantly it provides us with countless opportunities to bless others and share our testimonies of how the Lord has blessed us. Remember, your professional and commercial success are not just about you. They're about God's kingdom agenda. Your success also allows you to make an honest living for yourself and support your family. This is critical given the Word of God says that if we do not provide for our relatives, particularly our immediate families, we are worse than an unbeliever (1 Timothy 5:8)!

Your success positions you for offering products and services and providing employment for others. And your success makes it possible for you to help disadvantaged individuals, as the Word of God says: "If you help the poor, you are lending to the Lord—and He will repay you!" (Proverbs 19:17, NLT).

Taking Flesh out of the Financial Equation

In Western society, a common ideology and idiom is to refer to highly accomplished individuals as "self-made" as in: "She's a self-made woman," or, "He's a self-made man." Our egos would have us to believe that our professional success is the result of our own power and a myriad of factors, including everything from our pedigree, talents, and discipline to our education, business acumen, industry contacts, and investment decisions.

As Christians, we must make every effort to take our flesh, in the form of our egos, out of the financial equation. No one is "self-made," neither literally nor figuratively speaking (2 Corinthians 4:7). Not only did God make all of us, but He also divinely ordained and positioned our parents, family members, friends, spouses, ministers, mentors, and colleagues to help develop us into the individuals we are today. In John 15:5 (NKJV), Jesus tells us: "I am the vine, you are the branches. He who abides in Me, and I in him, bears much fruit; for without Me you can do nothing."

You cannot achieve financial independence and overall prosperity apart from God. Who you are and what you have achieved are not by your might and power but *by His Spirit* (Zechariah 4:6; Deuteronomy 8:17). Regardless of our level of success, you and I must always remain humble, because the rewards for maintaining humility and reverencing the Lord are riches, honor, and eternal life (Proverbs 22:4; Romans 12:3).

Our true character and faith are sometimes tested more during times of *prosperity* than poverty or adversity, because prosperity makes it easier for us to take God for granted. But when we're losing major customers and market share or struggling to make payroll and keep the utilities on, we are humbled and driven to pray for deliverance. When our business is growing, our profit margins are increasing, and we're living a comfortable lifestyle, we're more inclined to have a more egotistical and arrogant attitude. We tend to take credit for the success ourselves as opposed to giving God the credit. A dire mistake. Commit to taking flesh out of the financial equation. Now, let's consider how prosperity relates to your purpose.

Prosperity Follows Purpose

· ·

Dollars and Cents Versus Dollars and Sense

Are finances, or the lack thereof, keeping you from focusing on God's purpose for your life and for your business? Are you making business decisions based solely on money or financial factors?

Prosperity has little to do with *dollars* and *cents* and all to do with *dollars* and *sense*. By this, I mean that prosperity in your life is not defined by the amount of money you have but by your sense of who you are in God and your sensibilities to His plan and purpose for your life. When we diligently seek God and His will, He implants within us the thoughts, curiosity, desire, drive, and fortitude to not only succeed but to excel.

Prosperity follows your ability to walk in your divine purpose. Prosperity follows purpose. When you leverage your God-given areas of gifting, calling, and anointing in your profession, you will usually excel in it—and this typically results in overall prosperity, which often includes financial rewards. You can be one of the richest people on earth in terms of financial wealth but be one of the poorest in terms of salvation, spiritual fulfillment, and other forms of prosperity if you fail to pursue your divine purpose, mission, and vision.

We know that in order for our commercial ventures to truly prosper they must emanate from God and align with His divine plan for our life and business. Therefore, your business decisions should be based on the will of God, not on money. When you follow God's will, you automatically open yourself up for Him to bless you with financial wealth and overall prosperity!

One of my favorite books is *Do What You Love, The Money Will Follow: Discovering Your Right Livelihood* by Dr. Marsha Sinetar. The premise of this book resonates with me, because I believe that what we love and have a passion for doing is inextricably connected to our divine purpose, mission, and overall prosperity. The Bible tells us that if we delight ourselves in the Lord, then we will be "like trees planted along the riverbank, bearing fruit each season. Their leaves never wither, and they prosper in all they do" (Psalm 1:2-3, NLT).

Jesus tells us to just "ask, and it will be given to you; seek and you will find; knock, and it will be opened to you. For everyone who asks receives, and he who seeks finds, and to him who knocks it will be opened" (Matthew 7:7-8, ESV). So don't be overly concerned with the economy, interest rates, capital gains taxes, stock fluctuations, and whether or not we're in a bull or a bear market. Don't focus on economic deficit, inflation, recessions, or depressions. Don't obsess over the ongoing dynamics of the commercial arena such as corporate earnings, initial public offerings (IPOs), leveraged buyouts (LBOs), hostile takeovers, and labor costs. And don't become preoccupied with your assets, liabilities, or even your own personal net worth.

Yes, these are all important factors in financial planning for our personal lives and commercial ventures. But when we fail to keep them in the *proper perspective*, they can become overwhelming because most are outside of our span of control. Yet, even though we can't control them, God has still given us dominion over *all things* (Psalm 8:6).

Jesus said that when we are faithful over a few things, He will make us ruler over many things (Matthew 25:23) so "do not despise these small beginnings, for the Lord rejoices to see the work begin" (Zechariah 4:10, NLT). From a commercial business perspective, this means: Be faithful over the small business, and He'll make you a ruler over a larger one. Be faithful over the department, and He'll make you a ruler over a division. Be faithful over a division, and He'll make you ruler over an entire company. Once you get in alignment with His purpose for you, then *prosperity*, in every aspect of the word, will follow.

Your Personal Net Worth in God

In order to live purposefully and prosperously, it's important for us to know our personal net worth in God. At some point in life, you may have calculated your personal net worth, or the difference between your assets and liabilities. But have you taken the time to consider your personal net worth in God? What are your assets and liabilities relative to your relationship with Him and your pursuit of His plan for your life and business?

If you are making progress in achieving your divine purpose, mission, and vision and have positive, tangible results to show for your efforts, then you are accumulating some spiritual assets. On the contrary, if you're not pursuing God's plan for your life and are surrounding yourself with negative, unmotivated people, then you have some serious spiritual liabilities you need to address.

We all have spiritual assets and liabilities, but the goal is to have more assets than liabilities. God justly rewards us for this. The Bible tells us that if we obey and serve Him, we'll spend our days in prosperity (Job 36:11; 2 Chronicles 26:4-5; Proverbs 10:4; 21:5) for "the blessing of the Lord makes *one* rich" (Proverbs 10:22, NKJV). It behooves us to tap into God's inexhaustible resources for prosperity in general and financial rewards in particular.

Your financial rewards will *magnify* as soon as you begin to *manifest* His principles. Your money will become effective when you do. By this, I mean that when you begin to apply godly principles to your life, put them into practice with your business, and become an effective living epistle for God and His kingdom agenda, your financial resources will increase.

When you are willing to deny yourself and give up *everything* to focus on fulfilling God's purpose and plan for your life and business, He promises to reward you *many times over* for your obedience (Luke 9:23; 18:29-30; Mark 12:41-44). And He promises to give you everything you need for your journey as reinforced in 2 Corinthians 9:8 (ESV):

> And God is able to make all grace abound to you, so that in all things at all times, having all that you need, you will abound in every good work.

When you follow God, He will increase and maintain your personal net worth. The key is to focus on a Higher purpose than profit. A wonderful example of this is relayed by Cathie Black in her book *Basic Black*, in which she describes the presentation she and her team gave to Oprah Winfrey on the idea of publishing her (Oprah's) own magazine. Unlike most business pitches, which are typically all about the numbers or the expected financial returns, Cathie states that:

> The beauty of pitching Oprah Winfrey on her own terms—with message rather than money, and with personal impact rather than profit—was that it was also a sound business strategy... First and foremost, you have to

offer a compelling and differentiated product to readers. The rest will follow.[43]

God's Return on Investment (ROI)

God has invested astonishing gifts and talents in all of us and He expects a return on His investment. The Bible tells the story about the parable of talents in Matthew 25:15-30. Jesus relays the story of a master who entrusted and invested talents, or money, with some of his servants according to their individual abilities. To one, the master gave five talents of money. To another, he gave two talents, and to another, he gave one talent. Then, the master left them and went away on a journey.

While their master was away, the servant who had received five talents went at once and traded or invested his money and gained five more. Similarly, the servant who had been given two talents also invested his money and gained two more. But the servant who received one talent went and dug a hole and hid his money.

After the master returned from his journey, he visited the servants to settle accounts with them. The servant with five talents announced: "'Master, ...you have entrusted me with five talents. See, I have gained five more'" (Matthew 25:20, NIV). The master replied to him, "Well done good and faithful servant! You have been faithful with a few things; I will put you in charge of many things. Come and share your master's happiness" (Matthew 25:21, NIV).

The man who was given two talents also reported: "Master, ... you entrusted me with two talents; see I have gained two more" (Matthew 25:22, NIV). Again, the master responded: "Well done good and faithful servant! You have been faithful with a few things; I will put you in charge of many things. Come and share your master's happiness" (Matthew 25:23, NIV).

But the servant who had received only one talent announced: "Master…I was afraid and went out and hid your talent in the ground, see here is what belongs to you'" (Matthew 25:25, NIV). The servant's master replied:

> You wicked, lazy servant! You should have put my money on deposit with the bankers, so that when I returned I would have received it back with interest…take the talent from him and give it to the one who has ten talents.
>
> Matthew 25:26-28 (NIV)

The key takeaway of this parable for us as Christian business leaders is twofold:

1. God expects for us to earn a return on the investment of talents and resources He gives us.

2. God will bless us with even more talents and resources once we prove to Him that we can efficiently and effectively manage the ones He has already given us.

The Word of God says that we reap what we sow (2 Corinthians 9:6; Galatians 6:7). And oftentimes, we reap more than we sow. Example: Isaac sowed in the land and received a hundredfold blessing from the Lord during the same year (Genesis 26:12)! This is one of many examples of believers who received a hundredfold return on their investment. For more examples, take a look at Matthew 13:1-9; 19:29; Mark 10:30; and Luke 8:8.

Why is it possible for us to reap so much more than what we sow when we follow the Word of God? The answer to this question is illuminated for us in Isaiah 55:11. God makes it clear that His Word shall:

- Not return to Him void.

- Accomplish what He pleases.

- Prosper in the thing for which He sent it.

What are you sowing in your business ventures for God? What are you reaping? Commit to giving God the Highest return on His everlasting investment in you. Scripture says: "To those who use well what they are given, even more will be given, and they will have an abundance; but from those who do nothing, even what little they have will be taken away" (Matthew 25:29, NLT).

So multiply your gifts, diversify your financial investments, invest in the spiritual enrichment of others, and put your money where your heart is by refusing to invest in businesses that operate contrary to godly principles.

Follow God's Spiritual Economics for Financial Dominion and Prosperity

The way to achieve financial dominion and prosperity is by allowing God to serve as the ultimate Chief Financial Officer (CFO) of your life and business and by following His spiritual economics. God's spiritual economics are sometimes referred to as "kingdom economics." But what's the difference between conventional economics and spiritual economics? The difference lies in your mentality.

Conventional economics is based on a *scarcity mentality* as it seeks to understand behavior that, given scarcity of means, arises to achieve certain ends. God's spiritual economics, on the contrary, is based on an *abundance mentality* as God makes it clear that He sent His Son Jesus so that we might have abundant lives (John 10:10). And Jesus makes it clear that it is our Father's pleasure to give us the entire kingdom (Luke 12:32).

"The kingdom of God is not a matter of what we eat or drink, but of living a life of goodness and peace and joy in the Holy Spirit" (Romans 14:17, NLT). In order for us to achieve financial dominion and prosperity in business, you and I must incorporate and follow God's principles of spiritual economics. This requires that we make the commitment to begin cultivating "good ground" or a rich and fertile foundation for our commercial initiatives as Jesus declares:

> But he who received seed on the good ground is he who hears the Word and understands it, who indeed bears fruit and produces; some a hundredfold, some sixty, some thirty.
>
> Matthew 13:23 (NKJV)

When the financial plan for your business is based on godly principles, your business will often flourish to a level of success that is beyond one you could ever fathom. This is because "the blessing of the Lord makes one rich" (Proverbs 10:22, NKJV). The favor, mercy, and grace of God are worth more money than you can ever imagine because they are the blessings of God that allow us to generate wealth and prosper. As Jesus observes: "Yes, a person is a fool to store up earthly wealth but not have a rich relationship with God" (Luke 12:21, NLT).

The world economy has no impact whatsoever on God's spiritual economy. Commercial market fluctuations have no bearing on His spiritual economics. The principles of spiritual economics are based on the never-ending abundance and all-sufficiency of God Almighty. The Bible says that "those who trust in the Lord will lack no good thing" (Psalm 34:10, NLT; 37:16-19). There is no lack in God. There's no concept of "not enough" or "being broke" or "down on your luck." God doesn't operate in the realm of luck and insufficient funds. There is *abundance* in God.

The classic Bible story of Jesus feeding a crowd of five thousand with only five loaves of bread and two fish is an example of spiritual economics at work (Matthew 14:13-21; 15:32-39). Another example involves the story of the prophet Elijah who came across a widow in the city of Zarephath (1 Kings 17:8-16).

When Elijah asked the widow for some bread to eat, she replied that she didn't have as much as a biscuit to give him! She told him that all she had was a handful of flour in a jar and a little oil. She explained to Elijah that this was all she had to feed herself and her son and that they planned to eat their last meal together and die because they had no more food.

Elijah told the widow not to worry and to go and do as she had planned, but first make a small biscuit for him, bring it to him, and afterward go and make some biscuits for herself and her son. Elijah explained: "This is the word of the God of Israel: 'The jar of flour will not run out and the bottle of oil will not become empty before God sends rain on the land and ends this drought'" (1 Kings 17:14, MSG). The widow did as she was instructed, and Elijah was right. God miraculously multiplied the flour and oil, and she and her household ate for many days.

You may be wondering, *What do these ancient miracles mean for me and my business now? How can spiritual economics help me with my revenue goals today?* The key point in sharing these miracles of spiritual economics is to show you that as God's child, the world economy doesn't control your supply. When you are obedient to God, He will bless you even during the most difficult of times (Malachi 3:12). He will allow your business to grow during an economic recession. He will allow you to prosper during a national depression.

When times are tough and the economy is weak, God is still strong (Job 9:19; Isaiah 40:26; Joel 2:11; 2 Corinthians 12:7-10). Over the years, as a single women I have been blessed to own and live in six beautiful homes—five of which I built as new constructions. Here's an example of God's spiritual economics at work in real estate: During one of the most challenging economic periods in American history, and with the housing market declining and home foreclosures at an all time high, the Lord blessed me to:

- Sell a half-million dollar house in Atlanta, Georgia, in the fall of 2008 when the market was hitting new lows daily.

- Build another beautiful house in Atlanta in 2008.

- Sell the second house at a profit in 2010 when the economy was still weak and He had opened a door for me to relocate to Dallas, Texas.

- Build another gorgeous home in North Dallas.

God connected me with anointed real estate agents, gave me favor with buyers, and the Holy Spirit led me through the negotiation process with buyers and builders as I pursued His plans for me. I know firsthand what God can do in the most turbulent of times! He performs miracles for me. And He will for you too if you just trust in Him.

People will wonder how you and your business are prospering during such tumultuous times. Herein lies another opportunity for you to leverage this marketing pull-strategy for sharing your testimony for God with these members of your true target audience. *Use it!*

Following are six principles and practical ways you can begin to apply spiritual economics to your business today:

1. Practice wise governance and stewardship.

    As Christian business professionals, we are called to practice wise governance and stewardship in managing God's financial resources and commercial enterprises. God calls us to practice financial prudence in our commercial endeavors. If we are not able to give account of faithful stewardship, He will not allow us to continue to serve as one of His stewards. As Jesus commands: "Give an account of your stewardship, for you can no longer be steward" (Luke 16:2, NKJV).

    God despises dishonesty, and this includes dishonesty in the workplace and marketplace. Scripture tells us:

    > The Lord detests lying lips, but he delights in those who tell the truth.
    >
    > Proverbs 12:22, NLT

    > The Lord detests the use of dishonest scales, but he delights in accurate weights.
    >
    > Proverbs 11:1, NLT; 16:11

The Bible teaches against lying and stealing from God and from others (Exodus 20:15; Leviticus 19:11,13; Deuteronomy 5:19; Ephesians 4:28; Psalm 62:10; Luke 3:13). In business, this includes lying and stealing in every sense, including indiscretions of commission and omission—from corporate embezzlement, insider trading, money laundering, Ponzi schemes, misuse of expense accounts to stock option back-dating and suppressing unfavorable financial data and only reporting data that positions your company favorably.

All of your financial transactions, investments, and statements should be beyond reproach. Make sure that your financial investments and reports are accurate, moral, ethical, and legal. Major corporations in the U.S., for instance, must comply with Generally Accepted Accounting Principles (GAAP) and the Sarbanes-Oxley Act of 2002 to ensure that budgetary statements and corporate earnings reports meet accounting standards and federal guidelines.

If you've made financial mistakes or accounting errors in your business, confess them to God. Be honest with those in authority over you and take measures to correct the situation. The Word of God tells us that God "frustrates the plans of the wicked" (Psalm 146:9, NLT) and that: "*People who conceal their sins will not prosper, but if they confess and turn from them, they will receive mercy*" (Proverbs 28:13, NLT).

2. Practice prosperity planning versus financial planning.

Your primary motive for developing a divine, comprehensive financial plan should be to honor and glorify God through faithful stewardship of the resources He has entrusted to you. Now, you may be wondering, *Shouldn't my primary motive be to create shareowner value?* Yes, indeed, you should be concerned with creating value for your shareholders. But this should not be your *primary* motive. I know this isn't what we've been taught in business school and in the workplace, but stay with me. Here's the main point: shareowner value or profitability is just one of the many forms of prosperity you receive as a result of following God's divine plan for your business.

Take your financial plan to a Higher level. The secular world calls it *financial planning* with a focus on bottom-line profitability. But for us, it's really prosperity planning with a focus on holistic and generational prosperity, which also includes profitability.

When you commit to godly principles of prosperity planning, not only will you produce shareowner value, but you will generate *so much more*. You'll find that your business will often prosper in industry favor; record-breaking earnings; strong stock performance; market growth; wise leadership; honest, talented, and inspired employees; delighted, loyal, and long-standing customers; reliable suppliers; outstanding corporate reputation; commercial longevity; and the list goes on. This is true shareholder value!

3.   Be mindful of wasted capital.

> In the house of the righteous there is much treasure, but in the revenue of the wicked is trouble.

> Proverbs 15:6 (NKJV)

Over the past few years, we've heard countless reports of corporate corruption, fraud, and financial misdeeds from major corporations such as Enron, WorldCom, Arthur Andersen, Tyco, and Adelphia Communications—many of which have gone out of business. They are examples of wasted capital. They are examples of the ways in which some business leaders have wasted their spiritual, intellectual, and moral capital, which could have been funneled for a greater good.

What makes some business professionals waste their capital by engaging in unethical management? I believe one core reason is that they never make a sincere commitment to God, and to themselves, that they will honor Him and adhere to His standards and guidelines in business. Consequently, they govern themselves accordingly by honoring their own selfish desires, adhering to their own standards, and following their own guidelines in business.

Many business leaders become lured into corrupt practices by others, but the Word of God warns us: "Like a partridge that hatches eggs she has not laid, so are those who get their wealth by unjust means. At midlife they will lose their riches; in the end, they will become poor old fools" (Jeremiah 17:11, NLT; Amos 3:10).

"If sinners entice you, do not consent...do not walk in the way with them, keep your foot from their path; for their feet run to evil" (Proverbs 1:10 -19, NASB). And wealth gained by ill-gotten or unjust means:

- Will not be blessed (Proverbs 20:21).

- Is of no value (Proverbs 10:2).

- Takes away the lives of those who get it (Proverbs 1:19).

The Word of God tells us in Isaiah 33:15-16 (NLT):

> Those who are honest and fair, who refuse to profit by fraud, who stay far away from bribes, who refuse to listen to those who plot murder, who shut their eyes to all enticement to do wrong— these are the ones who will dwell on high. The rocks of the mountains will be their fortress. Food will be supplied to them, and they will have water in abundance.

The book of Acts offers a stunning example of how God views financial misdeeds and wasted capital. The situation involves believers who agreed to sell their land and share all the proceeds with the church (Acts 5:1-11). One married couple, Ananias and Sapphira, agreed with the plan. But unlike the others, they decided to keep some of the proceeds for themselves as opposed to donating all of them to the church. They lied and claimed that they had given the whole amount to the church. The Apostle Peter admonished them, saying, "You have not lied to men, but to God" (Acts 5:4, NASB). And they died because of their dishonesty.

4. Be mindful of taxes and debt.

We know that taxes and debt are common aspects of running a company. As faithful stewards, we are to pay our taxes (Matthew 22:17-21) and manage our debt (Proverbs 22:7; Deuteronomy 15: 1-11). God tells us to guard against the temptation to go into unnecessary, excessive debt, particularly since He has declared us, as His children, to be lenders and not borrowers (Deuteronomy 28:44; James 1:12).

We should always repay our creditors (Psalm 37:21). Remember, we are living testimonies for God, and our true target audience is always watching us to see how our prosperity principles and practices differ from those of unbelievers. God knows what we need even before we ask Him (Matthew 6:8). If you're having trouble honoring your creditors, pray and ask God for wisdom and guidance. He will protect and support you by giving you favor with your creditors as well as ideas, strategies, and resources for paying your debt. While it is sometimes necessary, bankruptcy should not be a predominant option for us if we are following God's plan. If you find yourself considering this course, pray and make sure that you are being led by God.

In the book of 2 Kings, there's a story of a widow who came to the prophet Elijah for help. Her creditors were pressuring her and threatening to collect the debt by taking her two sons as slaves if she didn't settle her debt (2 Kings 4:1-7). The widow had only one jar of oil in the house. Elijah advised her to go to her neighbors and borrow as many empty jars as she could get and take them back home and fill them with oil. The widow did as she was told, and God caused the widow's oil to increase. And it miraculously flowed freely until the last jar was filled. Elijah then advised her to: "Go, sell the oil and pay your debt, and you and your sons live on the rest" (2 kings 4:7, NASB).

God used Elijah as a prophet, or counselor, to give the widow financial advice. God also gave her favor with her neighbors, or constituents. And He supplied her with enough oil to not only sell to pay off her debt but also generate enough income for her and her family to live on! God divinely provided the right resources at the right time for her. And He will do it for you. Just ask.

5.   Practice tithing.

As Christians, we know that God commands us to tithe (Leviticus 23:9-14; 27:30-34; Deuteronomy 12:6; 26:12). And we also realize that we are to honor the Lord with our wealth and all of our financial increases, or first fruits and income (Proverbs 3:9; Ezekiel 44:30; Romans 11:16). Tithing is not just an Old Testament law that the Pharisees followed. Jesus says:

> "For I say to you, that unless your righteousness exceeds the righteousness of the scribes and Pharisees, you will by no means enter the kingdom of heaven" (Matthew 5:20, ESV; 23:23). It is still God's plan for us to tithe (Hebrews 7:4-5).

The principle and practice of tithing teaches us to make God a priority. They remind us that we are simply stewards over the commercial enterprises and financial resources that He has ordained for us to manage. Scripture warns us that when we fail to obey God's principles of tithes and offerings, we actually "rob God" and "are cursed with a curse" (Malachi 3:8-9, NASB). According to the Word of God, your tithe should be:

- A minimum of *10 percent* (Leviticus 27:30-32; Numbers 18:26; Nehemiah 10:38; Hebrews 7:2).

- On all of your financial increase or income (Deuteronomy 14:22).

God designed tithing to be proportionate to one's overall income (1 Corinthians 16:2; 2 Corinthians 8:11). So proportion-wise everyone is giving the same amount. Not equal gifts, but equal sacrifices. In God's eyes, the 10 percent is an equal blessing of obedience regardless of whether your business grosses $100, $1,000, $100,000, $1 million, or $1 billion.

We are commanded to tithe on *all* financial increases. So for instance, this includes not only salary and traditional compensation but also stock options, sales bonuses, relocation cash outs, and dividend payouts and total assets like home equity and investment portfolio income. Keep in mind that the minimum tithe of 10 percent *does not* include benevolent offerings of time and money. These are given over and above your tithe.

Now you may be wondering, *Should I tithe on my gross or net income? Should I tithe based on the gross profit of my business as opposed to the net profit after taxes and other withholdings and allowances have been taken out?* Scripture says we are to tithe on "all the increase" (Deuteronomy 14:22, NKJV). So I believe we are to tithe based on gross earnings. And if you happen to be a sole proprietor, then you are to tithe from the gross amount of income that you as a business owner make.

You might also be wondering, *What is the benefit of tithing?* God makes this clear in the following scripture when He says:

> Bring all the tithes into the storehouse so there will be enough food in my Temple. If you do, says the Lord of Heaven's Armies, I will open the windows of heaven for you. I will pour out a blessing so great you won't have enough room to take it in! Try it! Put me to the test!
>
> Malachi 3:10 (NLT)

When we obey God's principles of tithing, He blesses us in ways we can't even begin to fathom (Luke 6:38)!

In Malachi 3:10, God also confirms that tithes are to be brought into the "storehouse," which is a building of worship such as a temple or church. Monetary donations to charities are given over and above tithes. The Bible goes on, in Galatians 6:6, to encourage us, as believers, to contribute to the support of our churches, pastors, and other individuals who minister the Word of God into our lives.

Imagine if every company in America automatically gave a minimum of 10 percent of its gross earnings in tithes and offerings to churches and other charitable organizations. We would not have the astounding levels of poverty that we have today.

One additional note on tithing: I have heard many people express concerns about tithing to a church with a presiding pastor. The gist of their apprehension always seems to center on: *What if the pastor misappropriates the funds?* If this is a concern of yours, then pray and do your research and make sure that the minister, church, and any other charitable organization are indeed reputable. But always obey God's commandments and honor His principles. Don't let your preoccupation with people's potential disobedience to cause *you* to be disobedient to God and miss out on *your* blessings!

DR. K. SHELETTE STEWART

If the church leaders are being dishonest with the use of tithes and offerings, rest assured, the Lord will handle them. God tells us that vengeance is His (Romans 12:19; Hebrews 10:30). "Disgrace comes to those who try to deceive others" (Psalm 25:3, NLT); "misdeeds done in the dark will be brought to light" (Job 12:22); and "wealth gained by dishonesty will be diminished" (Proverbs 13:11, NKJV).

If you know *for a fact* that the church leadership is mismanaging funds, pray and follow the promptings of the Holy Spirit regarding what God desires for you to do in the situation. If you are actually a member of the church in question, you might consider joining another congregation that operates in integrity unless you believe God has placed you there on divine assignment to raise the standards of their leadership and management.

One example, commonly offered by individuals who seem to distrust the intentions of church leaders, is that of prosperous ministers or preachers of the Word of God. For some reason, many of us readily accept independently wealthy CEOs, athletes, musicians, and actors, but find wealthy ministers unacceptable.

We know that God ordained prosperity and that He sent His only Son so that we might have life and have it *more abundantly* (John 10:10). Therefore, all of God's ministers and ambassadors on earth should be prosperous. And we know that financial wealth is one form of prosperity. For those who ask: "Why should ministers have luxury vehicles and private jets?" My response is: "Why *shouldn't* ministers have luxury vehicles and private jets?" The Bible says: "The wealth of the sinner is stored up for the righteous" (Proverbs 13:22, NKJV). We are children of the Most High God! If ministers are humbly and righteously following the will of God, preaching His Word, and serving others as He ordained, then it's up to God as to how He chooses to bless them.

6. Be mindful of reverse-tithing.

Connecting Your Business Plan with God's Purpose and Plan for Your Life

376

After we tithe the first 10 percent, the Lord watches to see how effectively we manage the remaining 90 percent. He's checking to see if we're using our financial wealth and prosperity for honorable, kingdom-building purposes.

When you honor the Lord with your business and finances, He will continue to give you "plenty" (Proverbs 3:10). And when you demonstrate to God that you are faithful in managing minimal resources, He will give you authority over even more (Luke 19:17). When you surrender to His will in your professional endeavors, it's not unusual for you to find yourself wading in the blessings of abundant prosperity to the point that you can begin operating within the realm of reverse-tithing, which is when you're in a position to tithe 90 percent of your income and live off the remaining 10 percent!

I first heard about the concept of reverse tithing when I saw a televised interview that featured Rick Warren, the author of the fascinating book, *The Purpose Driven Life: What on Earth am I Here For?* In the interview, he commented that, as a result of the significant royalties from his book and other intellectual properties, he and his family are now in a position to practice reverse-tithing by tithing 90 percent of their income and living comfortably off the remaining 10 percent. He and his wife continue to lead other kingdom-building initiatives such as healthcare and leadership programs in Africa. Now this is an example of following God's spiritual economics for financial dominion and prosperity.

In order for us to successfully apply God's spiritual economics for financial dominion and prosperity, it's imperative that we have the right attitude and mind-set. We'll explore this topic in the next section.

In the Red versus in the Black Mind-Set

Jesus explains: "I tell you the truth, the Son can do nothing by himself. He does only what he sees the Father doing. Whatever the Father does, the Son also does" (John 5:19, NLT). Jesus has the right mind-set. He knows where His power comes from: God. This same power is available to us today. It allows us to live prosperous lives and set new levels of success in the commercial arena. But we have to have the right mind-set and attitude. We must possess what I call an "in the black" or blessed mind-set as opposed to an "in the red" or cursed one. Following are examples of both:

In the Red / Cursed Mindset	In the Black / Blessed Mindset
Live to be wealthy: In order to be wealthy, I must save my money and invest well.	Give to be wealthy and prosperous: In order to be wealthy, I must give of my money, time, and talents and invest in others. In order to get, I must give. (2 Corinthians 9:7; Acts 20:35; Proverbs 11:24-25; Proverbs 22:9; 1 Timothy 6: 17-19)
I will pay my employees the least amount possible.	I will compensate my employees fairly. (Deuteronomy 24: 14 – 15; Leviticus 19:13)
I will shift jobs to less developed countries so I can reduce costs. It doesn't matter as long as stockholders are pleased and I can get a promotion out of it.	I will pray for God's wisdom and counsel in weighing all the "costs" (e.g., spiritual, financial, human, domestic, and international) of shifting jobs to less developed countries. (Job 15:8) I will wait on God's divine guidance because I want God to be pleased with my decision. (Psalm 40:13; Galatians 1:10; James 5:7-8; Isaiah 61:3)
My competitors are more wealthy than I am—and they are atheists!	I will not worry about my competitors and their unbelief. I will pray for their salvation (Matthew 7:21-23) because Jesus says: "But anyone who hears my teaching and doesn't obey it is foolish, like a person who builds a house on sand" (Matthew 7:26). "As for me and my house, we will serve the Lord" (Joshua 24:15).

Real-Life Examples of the Divine Financial Plan

Following are a few real-life examples of successful executives and companies practicing God's spiritual economics in business:

American Family Life Insurance Company (Aflac)

American Family Life Insurance Company (Aflac) chairman and CEO, Daniel P. Amos, announced that he's giving up the $13 million severance package he would receive were he to leave the company. As one of the longest-serving CEOs at an American publicly traded company, and with nineteen years as chief executive, Mr. Amos isn't necessarily in danger of being fired. But as reported in the *Atlanta Journal Constitution*, Mr. Amos observes:

> I thought that clause in my contract went against that pay-for-performance policy…today everyone is so nervous I think the only thing that matters is trust and integrity, and that's important to shareholders. [45]

While I'm not privy to all the details involved in this particular case, I do believe that it is an exceptional example of placing principle before profit.

1st Christian Realty, Inc.

Angela C. Griffin, the owner of 1st Christian Realty, Inc. based in Atlanta, Georgia, conveys their mission statement in local magazine advertisements as follows:

> Here at 1st Christian Realty, Inc. we pledge to put GOD
> first. Buy or Sell a home through our company and we will
> donate the first 10% of our commission to your church.

The leaders of 1st Christian Realty not only promise to put God first in their business, but they also add credence to their promise by honoring and practicing the biblical principles of tithing the first 10 percent of their income (Hebrews 7:2; Leviticus 27:32; Numbers 18:26; Nehemiah 10:38).

Berryman & Henigar Enterprises

Reinforcing the principles of tithing, the former chairman and CEO of Berryman & Henigar Enterprises states in Executive Influence: "We give ten percent of our pre-tax profits to Christian ministries."

Hobby Lobby

God commands: "Keep my Sabbath days of rest, and show reverence toward my sanctuary. I am the Lord" (Leviticus 19:30). The leaders of Hobby Lobby honor the Sabbath, or the day of rest ordained by God, by closing all of their stores on Sundays.

Their corporate website relays their statement of purpose, which includes the following commitment: "Providing a return on the owners' investment, sharing the Lord's blessings with our employees, and investing in our community."

Sunrise Assisted Living

In the spirit of promoting prosperity in the form of healthy employees, Sunrise Assisted Living, one of America's largest eldercare providers, reportedly gives their employees $500 a year that may only be spent for wellness purposes such as attending spiritual retreats, joining exercise programs, and completing courses on nutritional guidance or how to quit smoking. Ultimately, this benefits the organization's bottom line, because healthier employees equate to improved productivity and reduced health care costs for employers.

Hearst Magazines

Another example of promoting health and prosperity among employees as well as clients involves Hearst Magazines. The president of Hearst Magazines, Cathie Black, describes in her book *Basic Black* how she and her team instituted Mind, Body, Soul. This program includes a relaxing three-day getaway at a resort with motivational speakers, music, and presentations for some of their female employees and clients.

This event is not only personally rejuvenating for participants, but it's also a wise business investment because it offers a wonderful setting for cultivating meaningful and productive relationships with their clients, which has led to new business opportunities for the company.

Sony Pictures

Sony Pictures recently instituted a number of programs to support their employees. Example: The company subsidizes healthy meals for employees at a new on-site restaurant, has built a new fitness center including consultation from a dietician, and offers employees paid time off each month to volunteer for nonprofits. Sony Pictures senior executive, Amy Pascal states:

There's no question that this investment we've made in our employees has energized and motivated them and helped us stay strong in the midst of very tough times.[46]

Chick-fil-A

The ownership and management of Chick-fil-A make their Christian beliefs and lifestyle evident in company policy, which dictates that all of their restaurants will be closed on Sunday, one of the busiest sales days of the week, in honor of the Sabbath. In the section on their corporate website titled "Why We Are Closed on Sunday," they share the following:

> Our founder, Truett Cathy, made the decision to close on Sundays in 1946 when he opened his first restaurant in Hapeville, Georgia. He has often shared that his decision was as much practical and spiritual. He believes that all franchised Chick-fil-A Operators and Restaurant employees should have an opportunity to rest, spend time with family and friends, and worship if they choose to do so. That's why all Chick-fil-A Restaurants are closed on Sundays. It's part of our recipe for success.

Chick-fil-A's honor of godly principles has translated to bottom-line benefits for the company. Their annual sales and profit figures are often significantly higher than their competitors who are open on Sunday. Moral of the story: Take a stand for God and He will take a stand for you. The Lord makes this clear when He says: "Those who honor Me I will honor, and those who despise Me shall be lightly esteemed" (1 Samuel 2:30, NKJV; Matthew 10:32).

Directives for Executing the Divine Financial Plan

Following are four suggestions for practical ways of implementing the divine financial plan for your business:

1. Develop a prosperity plan instead of a financial plan.

    Pray for God's guidance in transforming your financial plan into a prosperity plan. Include strategies and tactics for gaining not only prosperity of financial wealth but also prosperity in terms of wise leadership and board members; healthy, knowledgeable, and compassionate employees; loyal customers and clients; reputable suppliers; and divinely ordained strategic alliances and business opportunities (Deuteronomy 30:9-10).

    Institute lunchtime prayer groups and prosperity forums for employees on topics such as spirituality, purpose, prosperity planning, and health and wellness. Invest in the generational prosperity of your employees by offering academic and need-based college scholarships and grants for their children.

2. Seek professional advice for your prosperity plan if you need support.

    Pray for guidance in being divinely connected with wise and godly counselors (Proverbs 4:5; 21:20).

3. Biblical prosperity coaches include a number of disciples such as Jesus, Esther, David, and Joseph (Zechariah 8:12).

4. Praise God for giving you the power to gain financial wealth and prosperity. As you continue to prosper in life and business, remember to humble yourself and always give all the glory to the Lord. "Let him who boasts boast

only in the Lord" (2 Corinthians 10:17, NIV; Deuteronomy 8:18; Psalm 10:5).

In our next and final chapter, we'll explore ways to ensure that we leave a positive and lasting legacy. But for now, I'll end this chapter with a quote from the leaders of Hobby Lobby as stated on their corporate website:

We believe that it is by God's grace and provision that Hobby Lobby has endured. He has been faithful in the past; we trust Him for our future.

VIII

The Divine Exit Plan

> However, I consider my life worth nothing to me, if only
> I may finish the race and complete the task the Lord Jesus
> has given me—the task of testifying to the gospel of God's
> grace.
>
> Acts 20:24 (NIV)

Where do you plan to take your business? What's your exit strategy? What will be your legacy as a business leader? In other words, how are you going out? Some of us start businesses with a goal of maintaining an enterprise that can be operated for years to come and passed on to future generations in the family. Others start companies with the ultimate goal of attaining an IPO (initial public offering), selling the business, and moving on to another exciting venture.

Regardless of the endeavor, it's important to develop a plan for transitioning from one professional opportunity to another—whether it's selling your firm and pursuing another career opportunity, leaving one company to go to another, moving from one job assignment to another, shifting from one industry to another, or just retiring altogether. The section of your business plan in which these strategies are outlined is called the exit plan.

A comprehensive exit plan benefits you as well as your employees, investors, and constituents. It encourages you to give careful consideration to how your business will evolve and grow, and it forces you to establish succession strategies and a timetable for key targets and milestones. Before we proceed with our Planning Proverbs, it's important that we make the distinction between two commonly intertwined concepts: *legacy* and *inheritance*.

Legacy Versus Inheritance

As we continue exploring the divine exit plan, we'll frequently refer to the terms legacy and inheritance. It's important that we distinguish between these two concepts because they're often used interchangeably, but their meanings are quite different.

I like the way John Maxwell compares and contrasts the concepts of *legacy* and *inheritance* in *The Maxwell Leadership Bible*. He states that anyone can leave an inheritance. An *inheritance* is something, such as money or material possessions, you leave *for* your family or loved ones that may bring *temporary* happiness but fades as it is spent or used. On the contrary, he defines a *legacy* as something that you leave *in* your family, such as spiritual values, that *permanently* transforms them and lives on long after you die.

You must realize that the legacy of your business and your legacy as an individual are inextricably connected. You may already have an exit strategy for your business, or you might not have given much thought to one—let alone considered its importance within a *spiritual context*. Don't worry. Now is your opportunity to transcend beyond conventional perspectives of simply having an "exit plan" or "exit strategy" to actually establishing a divine exit plan for your life's work that honors God regardless of whether you are exiting and moving on to another position, department, company, industry, retirement, or to ultimately be with the Lord.

Three Planning Proverbs for the Divine Exit Plan

Our three Planning Proverbs for the divine exit plan are as follows:

1. Your donation is more important than your duration.

2. Don't just go, but grow to the next level.

3. Your history is actually His story.

Let's proceed to our first Planning Proverb:

Your Donation Is More Important Than Your Duration

The late Christian Holocaust survivor, Corrie ten Boom, observed that the measure of a life is not its duration, but its donation. It is your contribution, or donation, to the world that is most important, not the length of time, or the duration, in which it takes you to make it. Never underestimate your ability as an individual to make a significant and meaningful contribution to the world.

As Christians, we are called to manifest God's glory on the earth so that His will is done "on earth as it is in heaven" (Matthew 6:10; Luke 11:2). We are chosen by God for the High calling of priestly work (1 Peter 2:9) and called to radically transform the world. For those of us who are planted in the business arena, the commercial marketplace is one of our target domains.

God is not only concerned about you getting into heaven, but He's also concerned about you getting heaven into the business world. As Christian business leaders, we are to bring heaven to the earth in general and to the business world in particular. We are called to positively affect the commercial marketplace for the sake of God's kingdom agenda. God expects us to bloom and produce fruit wherever we are planted. So we must commit to doing our fair share of the required work by making meaningful contributions or "donations" in the workplace and marketplace in order to expand the body of Christ (Ephesians 4:16).

You and I know that we are all on earth for a finite period of time. Take a moment to ask yourself the following questions:

- How am I using my time?

- How does my line of business enable me to leave a positive donation or a lasting contribution to the world?

- What am I doing now to enhance the quality of life for others after I have moved on to my next divine assignment?

As an individual, you are either storing up blessings of mercy or curses of inequity (Deuteronomy 11:26; 30:19). Check yourself. Make sure you are focused on the former of the two.

Business World Changers

As business professionals, we often think about the challenging and changing business environment we face, but we seldom think about how we should be challenging and changing the business environment we face in profound ways. Commit to challenging and changing the business world. Don't let the business world change you in a negative way. Apply your biblically based convictions to the commercial arena and become a true business world changer.

Don't just seek to be successful in your profession just to benefit yourself or your family. Seek to benefit and be significant to future generations for the glory and kingdom of God. God told Abraham: "I will bless you and make your name great; and you shall be a blessing" (Genesis 12:2, NIV).

God's plan wasn't just to bless Abraham as an individual, but it was to bless him so that he could also be a blessing to others. Likewise, our blessings are not just for us and our families; they are also for others—our employers, managers, coworkers, employees, customers, clients, suppliers, and other associates.

Jesus said that those of us who are blessed and favored by God will inherit the kingdom prepared for us from the foundation of the world (Matthew 25:34), "for it is God who works in you to will and to act according to His good purpose" (Philippians 2:13, NIV). But the unrighteous and wrongdoers will not inherit nor have any share in the kingdom of God (1 Corinthians 6:9).

Don't Just Go, but Grow to the Next Level

In Western society, we always seem to be in a rush to go to the next level or to get promoted or gain more status, fame, or fortune. Going to the next level is not necessarily a negative as long as we are also growing to the next level of excellence in the process and as part of God's plan and purpose for our lives and businesses. Don't just go, but grow to the next level.

Connecting Your Business Plan with God's Purpose and Plan for Your Life

We've all heard the saying that someone has "arrived" or reached a certain pinnacle of success. But the truth is that we never really ever "arrive." As Christians, we're always on a constant dynamic and progressive journey as God completes His sovereign work in us. He is always working in our lives and businesses. We should always be growing in Him and keep growing until our last breath (1 Peter 2:2; 2 Peter 3:18). In order for our organizations to grow, we must grow as individuals. As the former chairman of the ServiceMaster Company, C. William Pollard, states in *The Soul of the Firm*: "If growth is to sustain itself, the people of the firm must also grow."

"The Station"

"The Station" is a poignant essay by the late Robert J. Hastings. The premise of this provocative piece of work is that as adults we rush through life with this idyllic vision of a final destination or station. The notion is that that on a certain day or at a certain hour, we'll pull into the station, and once we get there, all of our dreams will come true and all the pieces of our lives will fit together perfectly like a completed jigsaw puzzle. But until then, we continue to rush through life in eager search of our utopian station.

"When we reach the station that will be it!" we cry. The station of "When I buy a new 450SL Mercedes-Benz…!" "When I put the last kid through college…" "When I have paid off the mortgage…" "When I get a promotion…" "When I sell the business…" "When I retire…" "…*then* I shall live happily ever after." But as Mr. Hastings, so eloquently points out, "sooner or later, we must realize there is no station, no one place to arrive at once and for all. The true joy of life is the trip. The station is only a dream. It constantly outdistances us."

I share Mr. Hastings' commentary to make the point that we should not be in a rush to arrive at a particular station in life or at a certain milestone in the commercial arena. Don't rush God. Enjoy the present and enjoy the journey. As Mr. Hastings observed: "'Relish the moment' is a good motto, especially when coupled with Psalm 118:24 (NLT): This is the day the Lord has made. We will rejoice and be glad in it.'"

Grow with the Process

As a child, I remember hearing the lyrics of an old spiritual hymn that said, "I'll believe I'll run on and see what the end will be." It's important to keep growing in life and in business, but you shouldn't run on without God and try to rush the process. And you certainly can't see what the end will be by staying stagnate or complacent and refusing to be obedient to God after He has shown you that it is time to exit one season and transition to another.

Don't try to rush the process. And don't try to slow it. *Grow with the process.* And don't be afraid to *grow on* to the next milestone in your divine exit plan. Example: It may be time for your business to expand internationally, be sold, increase the number of employees, merge with another company, or just chart a new strategic course.

God's timing for our commercial growth, like His timing for every aspect of our lives, is always perfect. When going from one business venture to another, ideally, you should *grow into it.* The Lord knows exactly when you are ready for a new season (Ecclesiastes 3:1). As you mature and make positive contributions where you are planted in the business world, He will often move you into a new season of professional growth and commercial opportunity.

The Bible tells us: "He who began a good work in you will carry it on to completion until the day of Christ Jesus" (Philippians 1:6, NIV). We are never really done with God's work. As the title of Nell Mohney's book implores: *Don't Put a Period Where God Put a Comma.* So "keep on growing in knowledge and understanding" (Philippians 1:9, NLT). Keep growing personally and professionally, and be open to exiting one season and transitioning into the new, exciting, rich, and rewarding one He has for you.

Divine Reinvention

None of us are perfect. Some of the principles in this book may have brought attention to opportunities in your life for personal and professional growth and improvement. As Norman Vincent Peale said, just "ask the God who made you to keep remaking you." This is divine reinvention.

Perhaps you've been dishonest in some of your business dealings, mistreated your employees, executed questionable marketing strategies, or just refused to embrace your God-given mission and vision. The most important thing you can do is pray, confess your sins, repent to God, and ask for His forgiveness. When we do this, God says: "I will forgive their wickedness, and I will never again remember their sins" (Jeremiah 31:34, NLT; Psalm 103:12). Not only does God remove and forgive our sins, but He also *forgets* them! Do likewise and forgive yourself and others. And do your best to resolve any outstanding issues you might have with others.

Maybe you find yourself on the other end of the spectrum where, instead of committing the offense, you might actually be the one who has been offended, hurt, used, or abused. Perhaps you have been taken advantage of financially in some of your business dealings, maligned in the media, served with a lawsuit, mistreated by your employer or colleagues, or dismissed from your job. The most important thing you can do is pray and ask God to heal and restore you—mentally, spiritually, emotionally, physically, and perhaps even financially.

Jesus said:

> Come to me, all of you who are weary and carry heavy burdens, and I will give you rest.
>
> Matthew 11:28 (NLT)

> So after you have suffered a little while, He will restore, support, and strengthen you, and He will place you on a firm foundation.
>
> (1 Peter 5:10 NLT; Job 33:26; Psalm 30:2)

> Then the Lord your God will restore your fortunes. He will have mercy on you...
>
> Deuteronomy 30:3 (NLT)

> The Lord says, "I will give you back what you lost..."
>
> Joel 2:25 (NLT)

God is always working in your life and in your business. When you are exiting one season, there is always another one awaiting you. The Lord tells us that the glory of our latter place will be greater than the former "'and in this place I will give peace,' says the Lord of hosts" (Haggai 2:9, NKJV). God takes us from glory to

DR. K. SHELETTE STEWART

glory, strength to strength (Psalm 84:7). The best is always yet to come. Embrace your new season and grow on!

Your History Is Actually His Story

I recall some of the lyrics of an old gospel song that said: "Let the work I've done speak for me." What will your work say about you after you are gone? It's important to note here that when I reference "after you are gone," I'm referring to the time after you have moved on or exited from your current assignment in business to your next one as well as when you ultimately go to be with the Lord. We know that God is always transitioning us from one season and guiding us into another. Sometimes the move is temporary, and sometimes it's for an eternity.

Your history is actually His story. What I mean by this is that God is designing the patterns of your life into a magnificent kaleidoscope that will tell the story of your life and business in ways that glorify Him and minister to others long after you are gone. All that has happened in your life and transpired with your business are a part of God's divine purpose and plan. They are a part of *your history*, which also make them a part of *His story* or account and testimony to others of His sovereign work in your life.

How Do You Live Your Dash?

A few years ago someone shared a wonderful poem with me titled "How Do You Live Your DASH?" The author is unknown, but I was so moved by the premise of the poem that I've shared it with many people over the years. The poem refers to the dash that appears between the date of birth and date of death on a tombstone. The dash represents all the time a person spent alive on earth. What really matters is how we live our dash, not how much we own—the houses, cars, and cash.

Consider the following comment from the Apostle Paul: "And I trust that my life will bring honor to Christ, whether I live or die" (Philippians 1:20, NLT). Now, think about your own life. What will your dash stand for? What will your epitaph say? Anne Frank observed: "How wonderful it is that nobody need wait a single moment before starting to improve the world." How will you improve the world? What will be your excellent contribution to the business world?

Leaving a Spiritual Legacy in the Commercial Arena

Make sure your pursuit of professional success reflects your spiritual obedience to God and not just your own egocentric desires. We're not in business just to make money, be happy, and die. Make your business and ultimately your life count. Let them serve as blessings to generations of people who come after you so that they too may know God and walk in purpose. Vow to leave a spiritual legacy in the commercial arena.

The Bible says that David served God's purpose for his generation and died (Acts 13:36; 2 Samuel 5:4). How are you using your God-given abilities and talents to serve your generation? In what ways are you storing up blessings for future generations? As God's sons and daughters, we must be committed to leaving positive testimonies and life-enhancing legacies and:

> Telling the generation to come the praises of the Lord, and His strength and His wonderful works that He has done...that the generation to come might know them,

the children who would be born, that they may arise and declare them to their children, that they may set their hope in God, and not forget the works of God, but keep His commandments.

Psalm 78:4-7 (NKJV)

The greatest legacy of all is the knowledge of God (Philippians 3:8; Psalm 78:1-8; 3 John 1:4). The Bible says that a wise man leaves an inheritance for his children's children, or his grand-children (Proverbs 13:22). Let's go deeper. Think beyond your grandchildren to your children's children's children—your great grandchildren. What are you sowing now to pass on to them? What will be your legacy?

Let's go even deeper. I challenge you to think beyond your own family lineage and bloodline. Just as the Bible tells us that one of the greatest gifts we can give God is a future generation of children who know Him, one of the greatest gifts that we as Christian business leaders can give God is a generation of future business leaders who know Him and who understand the importance of connecting their business plans with God's purpose and plan for their lives.

Give some thought to the following questions:

- What legacy are you leaving in the business world?

- How will future business leaders be blessed as a result of your life? What do you vow to pass down to the business leaders who have yet to be born?

- When your life is over, what will your true target audience say about you? Did they see or experience the Christ in you?

Part of being a business-world changer and a legacy builder for God's kingdom purposes involves an understanding that where you are today affects tomorrow, not only for you and your family, but also for your current business associates and the future generation of leaders who follow you. This is the level of consciousness to which we must rise.

Give serious thought to some of the ways that you can leave more than just an inheritance of material and financial wealth. Seek to bear the eternal fruit of spiritual prosperity. Impart and pass on to others a rich heritage and strong legacy of godly values, spiritual lifestyle principles, and an honorable attitude and approach to business that extends far beyond traditional mental models, cultural barriers, social paradigms, corporate protocols, and religious practices. It is our responsibility to tell each generation about God's faithfulness (Isaiah 38:19). None of us can afford to be apathetic or complacent. We still have so much work to do.

Personal and Global Significance

Connecting our business plans with God's purpose and plan for our lives has both personal and global significance. Personally, we maximize our fulfillment and professional success in business by following God's principles and commandments. Globally, we support the prospering of the business community at large by helping to thwart one of Satan's main goals: to control the world by controlling the global marketplace.

When you educate others on how to incorporate godly principles into their business plans and practices, you are significantly raising their level of spiritual awareness and potential for success. You are showing them how to build their businesses on the solid foundation of the Word of God and equipping them with

wisdom to share with others. So indirectly you are actually blessing *multitudes* of current and future business leaders! Example:
When you lead a colleague to salvation, that person will often
lead others to Christ, and those individuals will in turn lead others to salvation. So by leading one person to Christ, you have the
potential to indirectly lead legions of people into the salvation of
God through Christ.

When you build your business on the rock of God's Word, the
gates of hell will not prevail against it (Matthew 16:18). "Now
unto Him who is able to keep you from stumbling," (Jude 1:24)
and your commercial ventures from faltering, "be glory and maj-
esty, dominion and power, both now and forever" (Jude 1:25).

The Real Prize

You know that we struggle against satanic forces in life and in
business, but do you know what the struggle is for? It's for your
life. "For the wages of sin is death, but the gift of God is eternal
life in Christ Jesus our Lord" (Romans 6:23, NKJV; 2 Corinthians
5:8). The Apostle Paul sums this up for us in his counsel to the
Corinthians. During their struggles, he encourages them by
drawing an analogy between runners who are training for a competition and those of us who are believers of God. Paul explains:

> Do you not know that in a race all the runners run, but
> only one gets the prize? Run in such a way as to get the
> prize. Everyone who competes in the games goes into
> strict training. They do it to get a crown that will not last;
> but we do it to get a crown that will last forever.
>
> 1 Corinthians 9:24-25 (NIV)

Paul reminds us that the runners in competition undergo strict training to win a prize that will not last, or that is temporary. But we believers, on the contrary, should run and press on toward the prize that will last forever. The real prize for us is the crown that will last forever: *eternal salvation*. In today's dynamic global marketplace, it's easy to become preoccupied with short-term, material, and temporal prizes as opposed to the ultimate eternal one of spiritual salvation and citizenship in heaven (Philippians 3:20-21).

The Bible tells us that there is no condemnation for those who belong to Christ Jesus, and because we belong to him, the power of the life-giving Spirit has freed us from the power of sin that leads to death (Romans 8:1-2). Jesus says:

> If anyone is ashamed of me and my words in this adulterous and sinful generation, the Son of Man will be ashamed of him when he comes into his Father's glory with the holy angels.
>
> Mark 8:38 (NASB)

He also declares that the unrighteous "will go away into everlasting punishment, but the righteous into eternal life" (Matthew 25:46, NKJV).

"How do you know what your life will be like tomorrow? Your life is like the morning fog—it's here a little while, then it's gone" (James 4:14, NLT). We need to lead a righteous lifestyle during our short time on earth because eternity is an infinitely long time!

In the end, we will be judged according to our works, or what we have and have not done. The Bible says that each of us must work out, or show the results of, our own salvation (Philippians 2:12; Psalm 62:12; Romans 14:10). God confirms this for us in Ezekiel 18:30 (NLT):

'Therefore, I will judge each of you, O people of Israel, according to your actions,' says the Sovereign Lord. 'Repent, and turn from your sins. Don't let them destroy you!'

Jesus tells us:

> I am coming soon! My reward is with me, and I will give to everyone according to what he has done.
>
> Revelation 22:12 (NIV)

This is also reinforced in the following passage:

> Therefore we make it our aim, whether present or absent, to be well pleasing to Him. For we must all appear before the judgment seat of Christ, that each one may receive what is due him for the things done while in the body, whether good or bad.
>
> 2 Corinthians 5:9-10 (NKJV)

Stay focused on the real prize. Commit to leaving a legacy that has eternal significance. Be a legend—one adorned with the crown that lasts forever. One who lives in eternity with Him. Make your mark on the business world and make it a positive and lasting one for God's glory. Leverage the profound spiritual gifts God has placed in you to bless others long after you have moved on. These are the gifts that truly keep on giving long after you are gone. This is the type of legacy building that needs to be pursued for God's kingdom purposes. If not you, then who? If not now, then when? You are the business world leader you've been waiting for.

Real-Life Examples of the Divine Exit Plan

The former CEO of the $12 billion AES Corporation, Dennis Bakke states:

> A corporation's goal should not be to make money or create jobs, or be an instrument of the state. From my understanding, the purpose should be to use what it has been given to make the world a better place.[47]

In his comment, Bakke eludes to the key focal question that serves as a litmus test for the divine exit plan for individuals and corporations: How did we glorify God and make the world a better place in the process?

In 2003, when I was in the final stages of completing my doctoral program, my dissertation committee chairman, Dr. Eldon Bernstein, encouraged me along the process by telling me that if I did a great job on my dissertation, he would introduce me to the Pulitzer Prize-winning scholar and economic historian who is widely credited with founding the discipline of business history, the legendary Dr. Alfred D. Chandler Jr. I was thrilled!

Born in Guyencourt, Delaware, on September 15, 1918, Dr. Alfred DuPont Chandler, Jr., was the great-grandson of Henry Varnum Poor, a founder of Standard & Poor's Corporation. While he was not a blood relative of the DuPonts who founded DuPont Chemical, his middle name reflects longstanding connections with this prominent family as his paternal great-grandmother was actually raised by the DuPonts after her parents died of yellow fever when she was a child.

Dr. Chandler was raised in the Episcopal Church with a strong belief in God. Later named "America's preeminent business historian" by *Fortune Magazine*, Dr. Chandler is best known for establishing business history as an independent and valid field of study. Over his long and legendary career, Dr. Chandler chronicled and analyzed businesses around the world and produced a vast amount of books and articles stemming from his research.

So with anticipation of meeting this living legend, I boarded a flight to Boston one sunny morning in June. Dr. Bernstein picked me up from the airport. And we soon arrived at Dr. Chandler's home, which is within walking distance from Harvard University where he graduated magna cum laude and later served on the faculty of the Harvard Business School for many years, maintaining an office as Professor of Business History Emeritus.

We were blessed to spend the afternoon with Dr. Chandler and his lovely wife, Fay Martin Chandler, who is an accomplished artist and founder of The Art Connection, an organization that facilitates the donation of works between artists and nonprofits. We toured the Chandlers' beautiful high-rise apartment, had lunch in their dining room, and later retired to their living room, where we chatted for a couple of hours about their family and his extraordinary life and career.

In a humble and nondescript manner, Dr. Chandler showed me his Pulitzer Prize and Bancroft Award, both of which he won along with the prestigious Newcomen Award for his groundbreaking book, *The Visible Hand: The Managerial Revolution in American Business*, which is commonly referred to as one of the twentieth century's best business history books. He graciously autographed my personal copy of *The Visible Hand* for me. We took photos to commemorate the occasion and later said our good-byes. I will never forget that day.

Dr. Chandler passed away four years later. When I think about him, I think about a life that was well lived. A life propelled by divine mission and vision, a career centered on a passion for intellectual rigor, research and teaching that exemplified service and excellence, and a profession that spawned contributions that enhanced society in general and the fields of academia and business in particular.

Although Dr. Chandler had connections with renowned industry pioneers and business leaders, he did not rest on his laurels of familial heritage. He still maintained his academic pursuits, which allowed him to revolutionize the writing of business history and leave a legacy of thought leadership and intellectual contributions that will continue to edify others for years to come. A divine exit indeed.

While we may have a tendency to think that such an extraordinary legacy is out of our reach, we must always remember that it is not. All things are possible with God (Matthew 19:26; Mark 9:23; 10:27). Every day that we are alive is a privilege and an opportunity to lay the foundation for a magnificent and enduring legacy. And we have an obligation to do so for God.

After You Exit, He Will Live

H. J. Heinz Company, J.C. Penney, Ford Motor Company, Chrysler Corporation, Levi Strauss & Company, Walt Disney, Hasbro, and J.W. Marriott are just a few examples of successful companies with names and reputations that are inextricably connected to the names and reputation of their founders. Can you guess which one of these corporate founders was a missionary at the age of nineteen? The Answer: J. W. Marriott.

As a Christian business leader, your name and reputation are directly connected to your business, or professional work, and ultimately they are inextricably connected to your Founder, God. Remember, you are a living testimony for Him. Jesus tells us: "Heaven and earth will pass away, but My words will by no means pass away" (Matthew 24:35, NKJV; Mark 13:31; Luke 21:33). After you exit, He will live. After you exit and move on to your next season, your testimony for God lingers with others who are left behind. And this residual testimony can be as weak or as strong as you make it.

After You Exit, You Will Live

The Apostle Paul said according to the Amplified Bible: "For me to live is Christ [His life in me], and to die is gain [the gain of the glory of eternity]" (Philippians 1:21, AMP). As believers, we know that at the end of this life, we will be reunited with Christ and our loved ones who were believers who have already passed away. So even after you are absent from your body, you will still be present with the Lord. After you exit, you will live. I like the way one executive captures the concept of life after death in the book *Believers in Business*: "This is just the practice. The real game is played in the hereafter."[48]

"Physical training is good, but training for godliness is much better, promising benefits in this life and in the life to come" (1 Timothy 4:8, NLT). Jesus died so that we could have eternal life. Because of the death of Jesus on the cross and His resurrection, physical death is neither the end of our story nor the final exit plan. Jesus tells us:

This world is fading away, along with everything that people crave. But anyone who does what pleases God will live forever.

1 John 2:17 (NLT); Mark 8:35

Most assuredly, I say to you, he who hears My word and believes in Him who sent Me has everlasting life, and shall not come into judgment, but has passed from death into life.

John 5:24 (NKJV)

I am the resurrection and the life. He who believes in me will live even though he dies; and whoever lives and believes in me will never die.

John 11:25-26 (NIV)

Because I live, you will live also.

John 14:19 (NKJV)

Exiting in Style

Jesus tells us that the "gospel of the kingdom will be preached in the whole world as a testimony to all nations, and then the end will come" (Matthew 24:14, NIV). "'As surely as I live,' says the Lord, 'every knee will bend to me, and every tongue will confess and give praise to God'" (Romans 14:11, NLT; Isaiah 45:23).

In the end, how are you going out? Do you plan to exit with style? When I mention the phrase "exiting with style," I'm referring to the process of transitioning from this temporal world into eternity in a manner that epitomizes God's commandments and principles. A way that conforms to *His style.*

Jesus reminds us: "Where I am going, you cannot follow now, but you will follow later" (John 13:36, NIV). No one knows the day or hour when Christ will return—not the angels in heaven and not even Christ Himself. Only God knows the exact time (Matthew 24:36-44). So we must stay alert and make certain that we are ready for His return and in a position to live with Him forever (Mark 13:32-33; 1 Thessalonians 4:16-17).

How you exit this world is up to you. Either you will have fulfilled your divine purpose, mission, and vision or not. In the book *Ruth Bell Graham: Celebrating the Extraordinary Life,* the late Ruth Bell Graham, wife of the Reverend Billy Graham, offers her perspective on the topic: "Pray the fragrance of His presence may through you grow doubly sweet, till your years on earth are ended and the portrait is complete."[49]

Through us, God "diffuses the fragrance of His knowledge in every place. For we are to God the fragrance of Christ among those who are being saved and among those who are perishing" (2 Corinthians 2:14-15, NKJV). I challenge you to make sure your fragrance is sweet and your portrait is complete. In the end, each of us must give an account of our lives to God (Romans 14:12; 2 Corinthians 5:9-11). I believe most of us want to be in a position to exit with peace, grace, and no regrets so that "when He appears, we may have confidence and not be ashamed before Him at His coming" (1 John 2:28, NKJV).

The Bible says that on judgment day:

> Each one's work will become clear...because it will be revealed by fire; and the fire will test each one's work, of what sort it is. If anyone's work which he has built on *it* endures, he will receive a reward.
>
> 1 Corinthians 3:13-14 (NKJV)

Make sure that your work in life and in business is based on the blueprint of God's Word. This is the only way for your work to pass the test of the fire.

Your ultimate legacy will be what God says about your life and business. In the end, we all want to see His face, and experience the glory of heaven and the river with the water of life (Revelation 22:1-5). Like Jesus, we want to be able to honestly say to God: "I have glorified You on the earth. I have finished the work which You have given Me to do" (John 17:4). Like Paul, we want to be able to say: "I have fought the good fight. I have finished the race, I have kept the faith" (2 Timothy 4:7, NKJV). And ultimately we want to hear God declare: "Well done, my good and faithful servant" (Matthew 25:21,23, NLT).

I've heard it said many times that the Word of God does two things: it comforts the afflicted and afflicts the comfortable. In order for you, as a Christian business leader, to exit in God's divine style, you must have the courage, fortitude, and conviction to plan, manage, and execute your business based on God's everlasting principles. After reading this book, you now have tremendous insights on how to accomplish this. You and I can no longer claim ignorance. We now know the truth, and it will set us free (John 8:32).

Oliver Wendell Holmes once said: "One's mind, once stretched by a new idea, never regains its original dimensions." The Bible tells us:

> *It would have been better for them not to have known the way of righteousness, than to have known it and then to turn their backs on the sacred command that was passed on to them.*

> 2 Peter 2:21 (NIV)

Illuminating this point further, the Word of God says:

> Therefore to him who knows to do good and does not do it, to him it is a sin.
>
> James 4:17 (NKJV)

> Woe to that man who betrays the Son of Man! It would be better for him if he had not been born.
>
> Mark 14:21 (NIV)

God gives us grace in the areas in which we lack knowledge. But once we gain knowledge, we are responsible for abiding by it. We can't knowingly disobey God and expect Him to bless our lives and businesses.

As God's ambassadors in the marketplace, it's time for us to rise and set a new standard of excellence in the commercial arena. It's time for us to focus on leaving a legacy that is holy, righteous, sacred, and eternal. The only way to accomplish this is by connecting our business plans with God's purpose and plan for our lives. And this is the only way to truly maximize your personal fulfillment, professional success, and overall significance.

You can never lose by connecting your business plan with God's purpose and plan for your life. Recently, God revealed to me the overarching philosophy and approach that He desires for us to take as His ambassadors:

1. Do business until He comes (Luke 19:13).

2. Do it with excellence (Philippians 1:10-11).

3. Then "be still and know that I am God" (Psalm 46:10).

4. And know that God causes all things to work together for the good of those who love Him and are called according to His purpose (Romans 8:28).

I pray that *Revelations in Business* has enhanced your knowledge, awakened your sensibilities, increased your awareness, and heightened your perspective to the point that you now see your business as not just a way of making money but as a ministry for His Highest purpose. Commit to achieving your individual purpose and spiritual goals in cadence with your professional objectives and business imperatives. As Christian business leaders, our goal should not just be to connect our business plans with God's purpose and plan for our lives, but our ultimate vision should be a world in which not doing so is considered unthinkable. This is divine revelation in business.

Directives for Executing the Divine Exit Plan

Following are five suggestions for implementing the divine exit plan for your business:

1. Pray for God's wisdom and guidance regarding what the divine exit plan should be for your commercial venture. Always ask Him to reveal the timing during which you should transition from one professional opportunity to another (Luke 12:2; Matthew 2:12).

2. Begin with the end in mind. Ask for spiritual discernment from God regarding what He ordains for your legacy to be as an individual and what He ordains for the legacy of your business as an entity. Once He reveals the areas in which He desires for you to focus, begin establishing

the appropriate goals, objectives, strategies, and tactics to facilitate each legacy (Ecclesiastes 3:11; Ephesians 5:10). Begin with the end in mind and work toward it.

3. Develop a succession plan for your business. Regardless of whether you are simply moving from one team to another within the same company or retiring from the helm of a multi-billion dollar corporation, it's critical that you have a comprehensive succession strategy and plan in place. This will help ensure that the right people are groomed to assume appropriate positions and responsibilities and that they have all of the necessary fundamental data and information to succeed after you have transitioned out of your divine assignment (John 1:15).

4. Coaches for the divine exit plan include the lives of many disciples such as Jesus, Mary (the mother of Jesus), Abraham, Job (book of Job), Ruth (book of Ruth), Esther (book of Esther), and Paul (Genesis 28:15).

5. Praise God for the blessing and journey of entering and exiting various seasons in life and in business. As you continue to prosper, always give God the glory for the honor and privilege to serve as His vessel. We don't always know the plan, but we know The Planner. May all of your exits and entrances be according to God's divine purpose and plan (Ezekiel 42:11).

I pray that you will continue to be blessed in life and in business. We'll end this last chapter with a couple of quotes for us to keep in mind:

> Don't worry about what you do not understand. Worry about what you do understand in the Bible but do not live by.[50]

> —Corrie ten Boom

But anyone who hears my teaching and doesn't obey it is foolish, like a person who builds a house on sand.

—Jesus Christ
Matthew 7:26 (NLT)

Amen.

Afterword

Born poor. That was what they said about him. They said he'd never amount to anything. After all, he was born poor by society's standards. But he was blessed with loving and supportive parents who were determined that he would be educated and have a better life than they had. He loved working with his hands, but his father thought it best for him to pursue a career in teaching. His father had a plan.

Black ice. That was what the police report indicated as the cause of her parents' death that day in December. Black asphalt covered by a thin sheet of ice caused her father to lose control of the vehicle as it went plunging down the embankment. As an only child, she immediately knew that she could no longer rely on the proverbial parental safety net. She would have to make it on her own. Her goal was to finish college even if it meant working three jobs at a time to pay her tuition. She had a plan.

Years later, after graduating from college, she earned an academic scholarship to a prestigious graduate business school. By this time, he had achieved his father's dream of becoming a teacher and was serving as a professor and advisor for her as she progressed through grad school.

As a student of his, she came to look at him as not only a mentor but also as the father figure she lost on that tragic winter day long ago. As she prepared to graduate from business school and looked forward to starting her own business, she often called on him for advice.

She was thrilled and excited, yet fearful and nervous, about her upcoming entrepreneurial venture. As they reviewed her business plan, she often wondered if she could really succeed out there on her own in the real world. As always, he was able to eradicate her fears by telling her to not be afraid, simply saying, "I am with you always, even unto the end of the world, for I am Jesus Christ, son of the living God."

—Dr. K. Shelette Stewart

About the Author

Business people don't plan to fail; they simply fail to follow God's plan.

Dr. K. Shelette Stewart

Dr. K. Shelette Stewart has over twenty years of leadership experience in strategic business planning, marketing, and national account sales with Fortune 500 companies including The Coca-Cola Company, BellSouth Corporation, and Hostess Brands. She holds a bachelor's degree in Psychology, a master's in International Affairs & Development, and a Doctorate in Business Administration. She has conducted empirical studies and published articles on the topic of the relationship between strategic planning and growth in small businesses.

Shelette is the Associate Director of Business Development for Executive Education at the Southern Methodist University Cox School of Business. She is also principal and founder of Stewart Consulting, LLC, a leadership development and business-consulting firm based in North Dallas, Texas, serving both corporate and nonprofit clients. The mission of Stewart Consulting is take business to the Highest level by helping business leaders connect their business plans with their purpose so that they excel personally and professionally and drive performance, productivity, and bottom-line profitability for their organizations.

Shelette is a professional speaker and author of the book *Revelations in Business: Connecting Your Business Plans with God's Purpose and Plan for Your Life.* Her empirical research has been published in the *Journal of the American Academy of Business* and she also created the content and curriculum for the *Revelations in Business* workshop for business leaders. Since resigning from a leadership position with The Coca-Cola Company to pursue God's plan for her life, Shelette has become a living testament for the principles of *Revelations in Business.*

A former board member of the Warren Holyfield Boys & Girls Club, Morehouse School of Medicine—School of Public Health Visiting Committee, and recipient of The 2003 YWCA of Greater Atlanta and The Coca-Cola Company Salute to Women of Achievement Award, Shelette resides in North Texas. She is available for keynote presentations, seminars, workshops, general consulting, and coaching sessions nationally and internationally.

To schedule an engagement or learn more ways to maximize your personal fulfillment and professional success in business, visit www.revelationsinbusiness.com or www.stewartconsultingLLC.org for more insights.

List of Reference Materials

Abrams, Rhonda. *The Successful Business Plan: Secrets and Strategies Fourth Edition*. Palo Alto, CA: The Planning Shop, 2003.

American Marketing Association (www.marketingpower.com).

Ash, Mary Kay. *Mary Kay*. New York, NY: Harper & Row Publishers, 1987.

Atlanta Journal Constitution (January 30, 2009); "Chick-fil-A 'Blessed' with Increased Sales" by Joe Guy Collier.

Atlanta Journal Constitution (November 14, 2009); "Chick-fil-A on Verge of Milestone" by Bob Keefe.

Atlanta Journal Constitution (November 15, 2008); "No 'Parachute' for top Aflac executive" by Peralte C. Paul.

Benioff, Marc & Carlye Adler. *The Business of Changing the World: Twenty Great Leaders on Strategic Corporate Philanthropy*. New York, NY: McGraw-Hill, 2007.

Bernard, A.R. *Happiness is:…Simple Steps to a Life of Joy.* New York, NY: Simon & Schuster, 2010.

Black, Cathie. *Basic Black: The Essential Guide for Getting Ahead at Work (and in Life.* New York, NY: Crown Publishing, 2007.

Blanchard, Ken & Phil Hodges. *The Servant Leader: Transforming Your Heart, Head, Hands, & Habits.* Nashville, TN: Thomas Nelson Publishers, 2003.

Briner, Bob. *The Management Methods of Jesus: Ancient Wisdom for Modern Business.* Nashville, TN: Thomas Nelson Publishers, 1996.

Burkett, Larry. *Business By The Book: The Complete Guide of Biblical Principles for the Workplace.* Nashville, TN: Thomas Nelson Publishers, 1998.

Businessweek.com. *http://www.businessweek.com:/1999/99* ("Religion in the Workplace: The Growing Presence of Spirituality in Corporate America," by Michelle Conlin, cover story article; November 1, 1999).

Businessweek.com. http://www.businessweek.com/1999/99_50/b3659121.htm ("AES's Dennis Bakke: A Reluctant Capitalist: The CEO on putting social service over profits -- and on management lessons from Mother Teresa," by Lorraine Woellert, December 13, 1999).

Butterworth, Eric. *Spiritual Economics: The Principles and Process of True Prosperity.* Unity Village, MO: Unity Books, 1998.

Covey Leadership Center (www.franklincovey.com).

Covey, Stephen R. *The Seven Habits of Highly Effective People.* New York, NY: Free Press, 2004.

Covey, Stephen R. *Principle-Centered Leadership.* New York, NY: Fireside, 1990.

Crane, Christopher A. & Mike Hamel. *Executive Influence: Impacting Your Workplace for Christ.* Colorado Springs, CO: Navpress, 2003.

Drucker, Peter. *The Effective Executive: The Definitive Guide to Getting the Right Things Done.* New York, NY: HarperCollins Publishers, 2006.

Goldwasser, Thomas. *Family Pride: Profiles of Five of America's Best-Run Family Businesses.* New York, NY: Dodd, Mead & Company, 1986.

Greenleaf Center for Servant Leadership (http://www.greenleaf. org/whatissl/index.html).

Griffith, Stephen. *Ruth Bell Graham: Celebrating the Extraordinary Life.* Nashville, TN: Thomas Nelson Publishers, 2007.

Harvard Business Review (http://hbr.org/2010/06/the-productivity-paradox-how-sony-pictures-gets-more-out-of-people-by-demanding-less/ar/1).

Hillman, Os. *The 9 to 5 Window: How Faith Can Transform the Workplace.* Ventura, CA: Regal Books, 2005.

Krause, Jennifer. *The Answer: Making Sense Out of Life One Question at a Time.* New York, NY: Perigee Books, 2007.

Maxwell, John C. *The Maxwell Leadership Bible*. Nashville, TN: Thomas Nelson Publishers, 2002.

Meyer, Joyce. *How to Succeed at Being Yourself: Finding the Confidence to Fulfill Your Destiny*. Tulsa, OK: Harrison House, Inc., 1999.

Meyer, Paul J. *Unlocking Your Legacy: 25 Keys for Success*. Chicago, IL: Moody Press, 2002.

Mitroff Ian I. & Elizabeth A. Denton. *A Spiritual Audit of Corporate America*. San Francisco, CA: Jossey-Bass, 1999.

Mohney, Nell W. *Don't Put a Period Where God Put a Comma: Self Esteem for Christians*. Nashville, TN: Dimensions for Living, 2006.

Nash, Laura. *Believers in Business: Resolving the Tensions between Christian Faith, Business Ethics, Competition and our definition of Success*. Nashville, TN: Thomas Nelson, Inc., 1994.

Nash, Laura & Scotty McLennan. *Church on Sunday, Work on Monday: The Challenge of Fusing Christian Values with Business Life*. San Francisco, CA: Jossey-Bass, 2001.

New International Version Bible. Colorado Springs, CO: International Bible Society, 1984.

New Living Translation Bible. Wheaton, IL: Tyndale House Publishers, 1996.

New King James Version Bible. Nashville, TN: Thomas Nelson, 1994.

O: The Oprah Magazine (December 2008; p. 238-239, 280).

Paul, Peter J. & James H. Donnelly. *Marketing Management Knowledge and Skills.* Chicago, IL: Richard D. Irwin, Inc., 1995.

Pollard, C. William. *The Soul of the Firm.* Grand Rapids, MI: Zondervan, 1996.

Quotes.com (Michelangelo quote: http://www.brainyquote. com/quotes/quotes/m/michelange108779.html)

Sinetar, Marsha. *Do What You Love, The Money will Follow: Discovering Your Right Livelihood.* New York, NY: Dell Publishing, 1987.

Smith, Nancy R. *Workplace Spirituality: A Complete Guide for Business Leaders.* Peabody, Mass: Axial Age Publishing, 2006.

Stanley, Charles F. *Living the Extraordinary Life: Nine Principles to Discover It.* Nashville, TN: Thomas Nelson, Inc., 2005.

Stanley, Charles. *Success God's Way: Achieving True Contentment and Purpose.* Nashville, TN: Thomas Nelson, Inc., 2000.

Stanley, Charles. *Walking Wisely: Real Guidance for Life's Journey.* Nashville, TN: Thomas Nelson, Inc., 2002.

Stewart, K. Shelette. *Formal Business Planning and Small Business Success: A Survey of Small Businesses with an International Focus.* Cambridge, MA: Journal of American Academy of Business, 2002 (p. 42-26).

Stewart, K. Shelette. *Formal Business Planning and Small Businesses: A Survey of Small Businesses with an International Focus in Atlanta* (master's thesis). 1995.

The Amplified Bible. Grand Rapids: Zondervan, 1965.

The Art Newspaper.com – International Edition (2002). "David Rockefeller on Art" by Cristina Carillo de Albornoz.

The Conference Board (http://www.conference-board.org/aboutus/about.cfm).

The King James Version Bible. Nashville, TN: Thomas Nelson, 1989.

The Message Bible. Colorado Springs, CO: Navpress, 2002.

The New American Standard Bible. Anaheim, CA: Foundation Press, 1973.

The American Customer Satisfaction Index (www.theacsi.org; February 19, 2008 press release).

The Foundation Center (foundationcenter.org/gainknowledge/research/pdf/keyfacts_corp_2007.pdf; accessed June 24, 2007).

Theology Today (October 2003; article by Craig R. Hovey of Fuller Theological Seminary).

The Quotations Page. (Retrieved January 30, 2005, from http://www.quotationspage.com/quotes/Helen_Keller/ html).

The Oprah Winfrey Show (September 23, 2008 episode featuring Suze Orman).

The Three –In-One Concise Bible Reference Companion. Nashville, TN: Thomas Nelson Publishers, 1982.

Warren, Rick. *The Purpose Driven Life: What On Earth Am I Here For?* Grand Rapids, MI: Zondervan, 2002.

Weinstein, Art. *Defining Your Market: Winning Strategies for High-Tech, Industrial, and Service Firms.* Binghamton, NY: The Haworth Press, Inc., 1998.

Wendy's Corporation (www.Wendys.com).

Williamson, Marianne. *A Return to Love.* New York, NY: HarperCollins Publishers, 1992.

World Book Dictionary. Chicago, IL: Thorndike and Barnhart, 1978.

U.S. Small Business Administration (www.sba.gov).

Society for Human Resource Management (www.shrm.org).

Yahoo.com (http://biz.yahoo.com/rb/080922/financial_aig_willumstad.html; AIG's ex-CEO refuses $22 million severance payout; accessed Monday September 22, 2008).

Endnotes

1. Harvard Business School Bulletin: "Spirit at Work: The Search for Deeper Meaning in the Workplace," (April 1999).

2. Laura Nash and Scotty McLennan, *Church on Sunday, Work on Monday: The Fusing of Christian Values with Business Life* (San Francisco: Jossey-Bass, 2001).

3. Ibid. (135).

4. Ibid. (Endorsement Page).

5. Ibid. (2).

6. Martha Lagace, Harvard Business School Working Knowledge for Business Leaders: "Can Religion and Business Learn from each Other? (November 12, 2001).

7. Laura L. Nash, *Believers in Business: Resolving the Tensions between Christian Faith, Business Ethic, Competition, and Our Definitions of Success* (Nashville: Thomas Nelson Publishers, 1994), 5.

8. Christopher A. Crane and Mike Hamel, *Executive Influence: Impacting Your Workplace for Christ* (Colorado Springs: Navpress, 2003), 98.

9. Michelle Conlin, "Religion in the Workplace: The Growing Presence of Spirituality in Corporate America," *Businessweek. com. http://www.businessweek.com:/1999/99* (November 1, 1999).

10. The Atlanta Journal Constitution (May 11, 2008).

11. The Soul of The Firm (p.50).

12. Business Week (December 13, 1999).

13. Marc Benioff and Caryle Andler, *The Business of Changing the World: Twenty Great Leaders on Strategic Corporate Philanthropy* (New York: McGraw-Hill, 2007), 43.

14. Executive Influence (p. 146).

15. Marianne Williamson, *A Return to Love* (New York: Harper Collins, 1992). 190-191.

16. Dr. Ian Mitroff, *A Spiritual Audit of Corporate America* (San Francisco: Jossey-Bass, 1999), 51.

17. The Business of Changing the World (2007).

18. *Church on Sunday, Work on Monday* (Foreword).

19. Stephen R. Covey, *The Seven Habits of Highly Effective People* (New York: Simon & Schuster, 1989), 22.

20. Executive Influence (p. 67).

21. Executive Influence (p.95).

22. Executive Influence (p. 45).

23. Los Angeles Times (April 25, 2010).

24. Executive Influence (p. 146).

25. Cristina Carillo de Albornoz, "David Rockefeller on Art" *The Art Newspaper.com – International Edition* (2002).

26. Church on Sunday, Work on Monday (back cover).

27. A Spiritual Audit of Corporate America (p. xiv).

28. "Religion in the Workplace: The Growing Presence of Spirituality in Corporate America." *Businessweek.com. http://www.businessweek.com:/1999/99*

29. Executive Influence (p. 64).

30. Executive Influence (p. 146).

31. C. William Pollard, *The Soul of the Firm* (Grand Rapids: Zondervan Publishing House, 1996), 54.

32. The Soul of the Firm (p. 54).

33. Ken Blanchard and Phil Hodges, *The Servant Leader* (Nashville: Thomas Nelson, Inc., 2003), 55.

34. Peter Drucker, *The Effective Executive: The Definitive Guide to Getting the Right Things Done* (New York: Harper Collins, 2006), 85.

35. In Touch Magazine – First Baptist Atlanta: "Dan Cathy: Leading the Next Generation at Chick-fil-A" (January 2008).

36. Bob Keefe, "Chick-fil-A on Verge of Milestone," *Atlanta Journal Constitution* (November 14, 2009).

37. Cathie Black, *Basic Black: The Essential Guide for Getting Ahead at Work (and in Life)*, (New York: Crown Business, 2007), 101.

38. Executive Influence (p.95).

39. Executive Influence (p.73).

40. Harvard Business Review (June 2010).

41. The Oprah Winfrey Show (September 23, 2008 episode).

42. The Oprah Winfrey Show (September 23, 2008 episode).

43. President Barack Obama to Knox College, Commencement Address, June 4, 2005.

44. Joe Guy Collier, "Chick-fil-A 'Blessed' with Increased Sales" *Atlanta Journal Constitution* (January 30, 2009)

45. Peralte C. Paul, "No 'Parachute' for top Aflac executive" *Atlanta Journal Constitution* (November 15, 2008).

46. Harvard Business Review, June 1, 2010; Dallas Morning News, June 20, 2010.

47. Executive Influence (p. 93).

48. Laura L. Nash, *Believers in Business: Resolving the tensions between Christian faith, business ethics, competition and our definitions of success* (Nashville: Thomas Nelson Publishers, 1994), 175.

49. Stephen Griffith, *Ruth Bell Graham: Celebrating the Extraordinary Life* (Nashville: Thomas Nelson Publishers, 2007), 36.

50. A.R. Bernard, *Happiness is: ...Simple Steps to a Life of Joy* (New York: Simon & Schuster, 2010), 19.

listen|imagine|view|experience

AUDIO BOOK DOWNLOAD INCLUDED WITH THIS BOOK!

In your hands you hold a complete digital entertainment package. In addition to the paper version, you receive a free download of the audio version of this book. Simply use the code listed below when visiting our website. Once downloaded to your computer, you can listen to the book through your computer's speakers, burn it to an audio CD or save the file to your portable music device (such as Apple's popular iPod) and listen on the go!

How to get your free audio book digital download:

1. Visit www.tatepublishing.com and click on the elLIVE logo on the home page.
2. Enter the following coupon code:
    fb64-dd77-2dd5-41ec-4847-9c68-47b9-7c29
3. Download the audio book from your elLIVE digital locker and begin enjoying your new digital entertainment package today!